"Creator, Great Spirit, our F
forever reaching out to us.
thread in Laurence's journo
mode of communion, finding our most sacred insights and understandings
of spirit and truth in Laurence's unique eternal journey."
   -- **Rev. Dr. Linda Lucero Nishikawa, Founder and President, Sacred First Nations for Peace**

"Having the courage to show such an intimate relationship is such a beautiful aspect of our dear brother Laurence. It is an example of how we can delve deeper with our own personal relationship with our Heavenly Parent."
   -- **Denthew Learey, Regional Vice President, Family Federation and President of YSP**

"Laurence Baer is one of the most sincere believers I know who also puts true family values into practice. This book peers into his honest relationship with God and his explorations in the vast sea of spirit world."
   -- **Miilhan Stephens, Pastor, Manhattan Family Church**

"The authentic expression of sincere heart for God is palpable in each journal entry. The loving expression of God's reply to each journal entry is revolutionary. A true dialogue that touches the heart and makes the voice of God audible."
   -- **Laura Herbers van Zutphen**

"Laurence Baer exhibits thrilling new possibilities in our human relationship to God; we as beloved children relating to our attentive, emotional, enthusiastic, and appreciative Heavenly Parent. How wonderful to share in the unfolding of this precious relationship, which is the potential heritage of each of us."
   -- **Kristina M. Seher, Head of School Emerita, The Principled Academy**

"An uplifting day-to-day account of Laurence's relationship with God, whom he sees as his loving Parent -- both Mother and Father. Not only does Laurence talk intimately to God, but God talks back; and we get to eavesdrop! It may be 'normal' that God would consistently provide words of inspiration to Laurence, but Laurence's reciprocating encouragement of God is a real surprise, a refreshing example of a contemporary filial son's spirituality."
   -- **Dan Fefferman**

"Laurence's book reveals the life-giving richness of personal give and take action with Heavenly Parent and Heavenly Mother. He is an example of taking personal responsibility for the guidance received, and sharing it with humility."
　-- **Dr. Tyler Hendricks, President Emeritus, HJ International Graduate School for Peace and Public Leadership**

"A fascinating, insightful, and remarkable reading for our troubled times, in which many people have lost sight of true spirituality and a personal, living relationship with God. Laurence Baer takes us on his exciting personal journey of discovering the divine within and reconnecting with our Creator in a profound and real way, filled with love and emotion. A book whose time has come!"
　-- **Dr. Angelika Selle, Former President, Women's Federation for World Peace USA**

"Laurence Baer's gift to the rest of us is his uncommon authenticity as a human being. Whatever else is going on in your life, this book will speak to the part of you nobody else knows. It will comfort your heart and give you hope."
　-- **Larry Moffitt, author of *Searching for SanViejo: Notes to my Younger Self***

"I would encourage anyone who is seeking a personal and heart-felt relationship with God to read Laurence's journal, "Taking God Seriously". It offers something we all need - a personal, genuine, and honest relationship with our Heavenly Parent God."
　-- **Rev. Andrew Compton**

"This is an amazing and heartfelt revealing of Laurence's journey for peace and love. I believe there's much here that is relatable and universal for each of us."
　-- **William P. Selig, DMin, BCC, Hospital Chaplain**

"Only one percent receiving the testimony of the Holy Spirit was not enough 2000 years ago, in the time of Jesus. Likewise, without at least 30 – 40percent of this generation accomplishing this much of Jacob's Course (1st Blessing victory – intimate communication with God)... we can hardly fulfill the Hope of God's Calling us: Towards international/int-"racial" Trinity -Family Oneness with God, and the consummation of Human history (Isaiah 11:9)"

-- **Carlton Johnson Harvard '79 Social Anthropology/Comparative Religion**

"Many of us will only recognize and call out to our Heavenly Parent if the plane we're on suddenly encounters turbulent weather. Here is a man whose daily journaling reveals his desperate desire is to know God's plan to help heal the turbulence of this world."

-- **Jim Howell, President, Washington Times National Weekly, retired**

"Laurence Baer's journaling provides detailed insight into the daily consciousness of a religious person in dialogue with God (Heavenly Parent). It provides an example of the value and impact of written prayer and meditation."

-- **Gordon Anderson, Ph.D., Philosophy of Religion**

TAKING GOD SERIOUSLY

Volume 1 of the series: PARTNERING WITH GOD

By Laurence Baer

With a Forward by Dr. Achille Acolatse

Copyright © 2024

All rights reserved. Except for use in reviews, no part of this book may be reproduced, translated into a foreign language, stored in a retrieval system, or transmitted in any form or by any means, electronic, mechanical or otherwise, without the prior written consent of the author. Published by the author on Amazon.

ACKNOWLEDGEMENTS

I consider myself blessed and graced beyond my wildest imagination. I believe that this grace, or something similar, is available to every man, woman, and child fortunate enough to be alive right now, during this Golden Moment in history, while Dr. Hak Ja Han Moon, God's Only Begotten Daughter is still alive as well.

The list of those to whom I am indebted is literally endless. I will try to list the most prominent, and ask the forgiveness of anyone and everyone whom I omitted. But I am deeply grateful to all who have helped and guided me in my life, and all who have forgiven my mistakes.

Special gratitude to:

Heavenly Parent, whom I now also relate intimately to as my Heavenly Father and Heavenly Mother, My Teacher, my Mentor, my Coach, my Cheerleader, my Dearest Friend, and my Eternal Partner.

Rev. Sun Myung Moon, True Father, called by Jesus at the age of 15 to inherit His mission and to fulfill the Marriage of the Lamb to establish the True Parents of Mankind, which Jesus was blocked from completing. I first met Rev. Moon in 1974 and pledged my life to him that year, following a brief talk he gave to some 20 of us in the living room of a small house on Dana Street in Oakland, CA. He matched me to my beloved wife, Muriel in 1979, in the Ballroom of the New Yorker Hotel. He, together with Dr. Hak Ja Han Moon, presided over our Marriage Blessing in 1982 at Madison Square Gardens, adopting us into God's lineage. He gave me my mission, and in many ways my destiny.

Dr. Hak Ja Han Moon, True Mother, like Jesus, born as the first coming of God's true child, God's Only Begotten Daughter. I first met her in 1976, when I went to speak with Mrs. Onni Durst in her home. Dr. Moon, then 33, shocked me with her brilliance and beauty. I will never forget that encounter.

Here is a photograph of our couple receiving the Blessing at Madison Square Gardens. Thanks to Muriel's brother, Philippe, for this historic photo.

Thanks to our siblings David, Janet, Philippe, Michel, and Stefen and their families. Thanks to our children, Gamaliel, Jehiel, Danniel, Andrew, and Joelle, and their families and in-law families.

Thanks to my spiritual Mom, Poppy Richie. We met on Sproul Plaza on Berkeley Campus at her witnessing table, where we played guitars together and sang "You Are My Sunshine". Poppy stood by that table day after day after day, through sun and rain, where she met so many of God's lost children. She was stabbed by a disturbed man, recovered, and continued witnessing. Without that incredible dedication, I might well have missed finding God.

Thanks to my spiritual teachers, mentors, best friends, and Grandparents, Dr. and Mrs. Durst who guided me from spiritual infancy and quickly entrusted me with far greater responsibilities than I deserved, and immediately forgave me whenever I made mistakes. I love both of them so profoundly.

Thanks to all the pioneers and current leadership of this historic movement to fulfill God's dream on Earth. I am especially grateful to Dr. Gi Seong Lee global director of the Cheon Shim Wons, Dr. Ki Hoon Kim who is the American director, and Pres. Demian Dunkley who has tirelessly helped bring our American Movement into much closer resonance with True Mother's heart.

Thanks to our spiritual children and their families, especially Ken Whitmore, Linda Lindstrom, George Detlefsen, Tony LaHogue, Carlton Johnson, Bob Honeycutt, Sam Harley, and Ken Tassey, each of whom connected to True

Parents through Muriel or myself well more than 40 years ago and received the Blessing.

Thanks to all the brothers and sisters in our movement, and I have known more than I can count, who have lived incredibly noble lives of sacrifice and love, seeking to end God's suffering and mankind's suffering, and to build God's Kingdom on Earth. Many have gone on to other callings. I deeply appreciate their sacrifices and I believe God will never forget them.

Thanks to those saints in the spiritual realm who have guided and protected me and my family, including Jesus, whom I called upon to guide my life one Sunday service while at boarding school. Thanks to Hyo Jin Nim and Heung Jin Nim, True Parents' two eldest sons, both ascended, and for Dae Mo Nim, Dr. Hak Ja Han Moon's mother, who has played a profound and intimate role in my and my family's development.

Thanks to Deganawida and Jigonhsasee, through whom Jesus worked powerfully to guide the providence in America, and who have been helping me significantly to grow in my awareness, passion, and desire to bring victory in America.

Thanks to Dr. Linda Lucero Nishikawa, who, at True Parents personal request as their official emissary to 1st Nations, has been straddling both the Spiritual and Earthly realms for 40 years desperately trying to help America to get our buttons on right.

Thanks to Chaitanya and Vishnupriya who are working with me and my dear friend David in efforts to restore the creation and lay the foundation for Heaven's economy.

Thanks to Rabbi Gamaliel, who together with our maternal grandmothers, is Abely serving as one of the three co-chairs of our Ancestral Committees. Thanks to Dr. George and Pat Detlefsen, now both ascended, who are guiding our ancestral committees. George especially, has been a wise, loving, and at times, very funny guide, who will be my dear friend forever.

Thanks to all our ancestors who through their faith, their service, and their sacrifice, paid the price for Muriel me to receive God's grace. Muriel and I are both profoundly indebted to our respective parents, Richard and Babette Baer, and Pierre and Colette Petrik.

Thanks to the countless numbers of angels who responded to our request and are working actively and powerfully with our ancestral committees.

Thanks to Dianne and Eva-Maria who have both offered healing and guidance and precious spiritual insights
Thanks to Ernest, who supported me so sincerely since 1992, first as my assistant, and then as my spiritual leader, but always as my dear friend, and for Dr. Achille, who, even in just a few years, has become the leader to whom I feel most closely connected in heart, because of his own incredible heart and faith.

Thanks to Randy Francis who has quietly supported and guided much of my public work since we moved to the DMV region in 1988.

Thanks to Tyler, Angelika, Alain and the others who have generously served as sounding boards, mentors, and guides on this journey, and to Osmarina, a fellow journaler who has been such a bright light for our Morning Devotions.

Thanks to the leadership and staff of our Las Vegas Cheon Shim Won who took such personal and loving care of me during my retreat there.

Thanks to all those who generously endorsed this book. Their names appear under their endorsements.
Big thanks to Dietmar. You are amazing.

Thanks to Ron and Connie for starting me on the path of journaling.

Thanks again to Carlton for your incredible intercessory prayers and tireless friendship.

Thanks to Jim and Linda our dearest friends and companions since the days of RBA 40 years ago.

Thanks for Dr. Yong who inspired me through his Morning Devotions and embraced my ministry to offer vitality elements, and for David and Kathy and the faithful group who participate in our weekly zoom meetings.

Thanks to Stefan for your editorial help and AI insights. Thanks to NanJoo for your design and formatting help. Thanks to Richard for your web help.

Thanks to John and Denny who have become family to me.

Thanks to Jacques, my business partner and brother.

Thanks to all my music collaborators and friends, including but not limited to Otmar, Dan, Frank, Mehrdad, Richard, Justin, Loren, Mark, Art, Daryl, Will, Angela, Sunhwa, Chris, Hannah, Diane, Joshua, Oji, Peter, and all the others.

Thanks to our yoga friends and our tai chi friends.

I will stop here. It is an arbitrary place to stop, because the list is endless. I pray for God's blessings on each and every one.
Gratefully,
Laurence Baer

Note:

I have added a glossary of terms at the end of this book, as some of the words used within the Unification Movement may be unfamiliar.

FORWARD

When Laurence approached me and asked me to write the Forward for this book, my immediate response was, "Sure, I'll do anything for you." It was spontaneous and heartfelt, based on my relationship with Laurence. I am a religious leader. I serve as the Senior Pastor for the Family Federation for World Peace and Unification of America's Southeast Region, which includes nine states including the District of Columbia and Puerto Rico

Having taken the time to immerse myself in the writing of this Forward, which for me is a great honor, I have come to recognize that it is no simply task. "Taking God Seriously" is a groundbreaking, and I believe historic work – a profound and deeply moving extended dialogue between our Heavenly Parent and an individual. Each entry has two sides. First Laurence writes a message from his heart to God. And then, God responds. Based on this Forward, it is my sincere hope and wish that you will be able to give your sincere consideration and attention to Laurence's message and that it will inspire you to do the same.

Laurence, in his Introduction, shares his reasons for launching this dialogue, which took seven years from when the idea was first set before him, until he united with that idea and wrote his first entry on July 13, 2022. He was seeking to deepen his personal relationship and communication with God, and through this, to grow spiritually. Our Movement's Founders, Rev. Sun Myung Moon and Dr. Hak Ja Han Moon have both shared deeply about God from their own personal and intimate communications with Him. And based on those communications, Rev. Moon wrote the Divine Principle and numerous related texts which explain deeply and penetratingly about God's nature and the history of God's providence. Also, in many of Rev. Moon's speeches, he shares intimately about God's heart and hopes and dreams, such as in his wonderful book "Twelve Talks" published in 1973.

I know Laurence to be a man of highest integrity, deep faith, and a very broad, inquisitive, and penetrating intellect. I first got to know Laurence in 2019, when I was serving as the Senior Pastor for our Washington, DC Church. Dr. Hak Ja Han Moon had announced that each couple in our movement should endeavor to share the Marriage Blessing with 430 additional couples, expanding the scope of the grace which could be brought to the world.

Laurence's response was unique. Based on the work he had initiated twenty-one years earlier, Laurence returned to BWI Airport, and established a Marriage Blessing table there quickly completing his goal and helping many other couples to fulfill theirs. But he didn't stop there. Realizing that just offering the Blessing was only the start, Laurence organized a monthly educational program at the Washington Times Building, which he funded himself. Laurence and his wife Muriel were among the very first Cheon Bo Victor couples in America.

Only later did I come to learn more about Laurence's background and history within our movement.
He joined 50 years ago at the age of 21 in Oakland, California, and spent much of his career in the movement working very closely with Dr. and Mrs. Durst on special missions of one kind or another. He did not have a high public profile. For 7 years he developed and managed businesses for the Oakland Church, launching building service companies in Los Angeles, Houston, and New York. Many who worked under him went on to take significant responsibilities in the Movement.

Laurence worked for two years on President Durst's senior staff, and then in 1983, he was assigned by Dr. Durst to organize a global conference in Geneva, Switzerland under the chairmanship of Hon. Robert B. Anderson, President Eisenhower's former Treasury Secretary and Eisenhower's first choice to run for President in 1960 rather than Nixon. The weeklong conference included 70 top global political and financial leaders and concluded with a decision to launch the Global Economic Action Institute under the leadership of Dr. Durst and Secretary Anderson. Laurence was selected as the sole staff member working directly with Anderson to create and develop that organization, where he served for 10 years as Executive Assistant to the three Chairmen.

In 1997 Laurence was serving as the Laurel, Maryland Community leader when the providence authorizing members to share the Marriage Blessing first began. At that time, following a deep prayer, he was inspired to meet with the Manager of BWI Airport who assigned to him the only table in the airport designated for outside organizations. Laurence trained and assisted 40 families to fulfill their Blessing goals. Among those families were the Salonens and the Leones. Shortly after that, Neil Salonen hired Laurence to serve as his personal Executive Assistant for Blessing 97 at RFK Stadium and continuing on for 4 years.

Also, during that time, the conditions were set for our members to begin Ancestral Liberations and Blessings centering on the activities of our training center in CheongPyeong, South Korea. Laurence and Muriel took seriously Rev. Moon's guidance that we must educate and direct our ancestors in the spiritual world following their Blessing.

In late 2020, Dr. Chung Sik Yong was appointed as the Family Federation Continental Leader for North America, and almost immediately began a daily national zoom call for prayer and study which he dubbed "Morning Devotion". In addition to doing his extended prayers every morning, Laurence also set a condition to faithfully attend Morning Devotion every day from its beginnings in 2020 until 2027 to support Dr. Yong. He pledged to invest his utmost each morning. He regularly shared his inspirations in the chat and also began offering his music videos. Those became very popular and for the first time many in our Movement got to know Laurence.

Laurence is a dedicated man for God's Providence. He has a sincere heart to comfort God's heart by enthusiastically sharing his knowledge of the Divine Principle with the world. Laurence is spiritual and has spent lot of time meditating and seeking insights from God. I encourage you to read this book to learn more about him and his relationship with God.

May God Bless and Guide each of you, your families, and your endeavors.

Dr. Achille Acolatse, Senior Pastor
Family Federation For World Peace and Unification, SR2, USA

May, 29, 2024

INTRODUCTION

"As this is the time in which Heavenly Parent, who is intangible and invisible, can work in substantial way with True Parents on earth, you should be able to experience, feel, and act on your own initiative without True Parents teaching you at every stage. This is life in the kingdom of heaven on earth. Rather than with your own thinking, you must know how to lead for the sake of world peace through attending God"

Dr. Hak Ja Han Moon – conveyed by Dr. Yong-cheon Song, International President of FFWPU 5/28/23

I grew up in Niagara Falls, New York into a family of doctors. My grandfather and father were both doctors, as are my brother and sister. Looking back, it was a very idyllic environment with incredible natural beauty. As children, we would spend all day, many days, playing on the boulders at the bottom of the gorge which embraced the Niagara River in the nearly 5 mile stretch between the falls and the base of the escarpment in Lewiston, New York.

When I was 14, I entered Loomis, a boarding prep-school in Windsor, CT, where I graduated in 1970. Here is a picture of me, my senior year, rock climbing and rappelling at the Shawangunks, just west of Poughkeepsie, New York.

After graduating, I spent two years at Rutgers as an art and music major, before discovering that neither focus had sufficient claim on my heart to motivate me to seriously invest.

After a little time off I finally decided that I wanted to better understand parapsychology, and after reading about a number of different Universities, I chose UC Berkeley. I transferred there and changed my major to physics, while also taking a course in neuropsychology. That was in schoolyear 73-74. During that year, on three occasions, I bumped into members of the Unification Church, founded by Rev. Sun Myung Moon and his wife, Dr. Hak Ja Han Moon, affectionately known as True Parents. Each encounter corresponded to one of the speaking tours Rev. Moon held in the East Bay area. On the third occasion, I decided to go ahead and attend an evening program. I immediately felt that I had found my home. And after listening to a few talks, I realized that someone had already figured out what parapsychology was all about, and that I probably shouldn't spend the next 6 years reinventing that wheel. But most importantly, I deeply felt that I had found a community where I could realize my own potential. That was extraordinarily liberating and empowering.

For my first 7 years, once I got settled, I ran our church's carpet cleaning business. First, as the sales manager of our company in the Bay Area. But then I started subsidiary companies in three separate locations: Los Angeles, Houston, and finally New York City. It was great management training, both on the business side and also on the people side.

In 1982 I went to work in the President's office at our US Headquarters. That same year, my wife and I participated in the Marriage Blessing of 2075 couples at Madison Square Gardens.
In 1983, I was tasked to help organize a global conference in Geneva, Switzerland, chaired by Eisenhower's former Secretary of the Treasury, Robert B. Anderson. We brought together some 70 finance and banking leaders from around the world to consider solutions to the global debt crisis.

Here is one of the break out discussions from that conference: L-R: Myself; Jelle Zijlstra, former Prime Minister of Holland; Alfredo Machado G, former President, Central Bank of Venezuela, Bernard Asher, General Manager, HSBC; and Duck Woo Nam, former Prime Minister of Korea.

Here is a photo of Secretary Anderson and myself in the early years of the GEAI.

After a week of very stimulating talks and discussion groups, it was decided that the assembled group should continue working together through a new organization which we called "The Global Economic Action Institute." I was asked to serve as the sole staff member to Chairman Anderson, and retained the title of "Executive Assistant to the Chairman" for all three of the institute's chairmen over 10 years. When Anderson stepped down in 1987, he was replaced by former Senator and Presidential Candidate Eugene McCarthy for two years, and then by former Prime Minister Sir Robert Muldoon of New Zealand.

The GEAI grew to include some 14 Chapters in countries around the world, and hosted two very well-attended monthly breakfasts, one in New York and one in DC. We held significant conferences and meetings around the world, and I clocked far more miles in airplanes that I would recommend for a lifetime.

After the GEAI folded in 1992, I worked in the private sector, with the exception of a four-year period between 1997 and 2001 when I was hired to serve as the Executive Assistant to Neil Salonen, a former President of our Church in America and then, the Secretary General of the Family Federation for World Peace. I served as the Director of the Family Federation office for Washington, DC during that time, and I helped organize Blessings 1997, 1998, 1999, and 2000 working collaboratively with Dr. Tom Walsh, under the direction of Neil Salonen. I also served as the Director of our Maryland Church for three years.

Between 1983 and 1994 we had four sons, and then a daughter. They grew up in our church community and each became extremely successful in his/her own field. I stayed actively involved in church programs and campaigns, and participated in our church band in Maryland.

In the late 1990s, our movement began a new type of Marriage Blessing - one which extended that sacrament to couples in the spiritual realm. My wife and I participated in this effort. As conditions were successfully set by Rev. and Mrs. Moon, this grace was able to expand to more and more generations of our ancestors. In 2012, the way was opened up to liberate and bless up to 210 generations. In December of that year, we held a celebration at our home for some 1600 couples of our ancestors whom we had blessed.

At that time, I had the inspiration to organize them into committees. We appointed three co-chairmen to oversee the committees, and we wrote up clear assignments for each committee. A dear friend of ours, George Detlefsen, PhD, a prominent physicist who died in 2005, had participated along with us in 1982 at the Madison Square Gardens Marriage Blessing. Since none of our ancestors had ever known Rev. or Mrs. Moon personally, I prayed and asked Dr. George to serve as a senior advisor to those committees. I diligently updated each committee's assignments 2-3 times per year, and I prayed for them daily.

For my first 40 years in our movement, I never had what I would consider direct communication with God. I prayed regularly and consistently, and sometimes I would have strong intuitions that turned out to be accurate. I could see God working regularly in situations around me, and on a few occasions, I felt God's spirit and was moved to tears. But even though I was originally interested in parapsychology, I honestly never had what I would consider "communication" with any spiritual beings, people or angels, nor did I have any actual conversation with God. Nor had I ever had any visions.

The closest I came to some kind of spiritual communication would be when I was writing songs. On occasion, I would hear a melody, or sometimes, part of a lyric would come to me.

In 2015 that began to change. A friend of mine had had a good experience attending a seminar by Ron Pappalardo, an Associate Pastor in the Spiritualist Church, who was introducing people to various exercises to learn to communicate with God. My wife and I drove from Columbia Maryland to Columbus Ohio for a weekend workshop August 1 – 2 of that year. For two days, Ron guided us through numerous exercises, and meditations to try and communicate with God, or to at least become more in touch with our own spiritual senses. I found it quite frustrating. All around me, many of the participants were having legitimate and inspiring experiences. In my case, much to my own disappointment, nothing seemed to have any effect on me. However, at the end of the workshop, he tried one final exercise, which he called "journaling". It simply involved meditating for a bit, and then writing a sincere note from my heart to God. Once we finished that, we were then to begin writing a note back to ourselves from God. Ron instructed, "Just write whatever comes into your heart". Here is my first journal with God, dated 8/2/15. I transcribed God's "voice" in bold italics:

> Dear Heavenly Parent.
> Thank you for this seminar. It has made our connection so much more intimate, even though I still feel like I'm swimming through a pool of molasses and in a stupor trying to connect to you consciously. I'm sorry for being so thick.
> What Ron just said about connecting with his own children, I am continually shocked by the resentment and sense of threatenedness that come back at me from my children...
> I feel like I am completely unaware of the ways in which I threaten and hurt them. At this point they are all married, so in that sense I should certainly chill and just sit back and celebrate them and support them. Are you confident to take responsibility to reach out to the next generation without pressure and guidance from me to my children?
> I understand that you have been working through history longing for three generations to be connected to you. So, I would hate to fail you somehow and let this opportunity slip away because of my own lack of discipline to train our children successfully. On the other hand, it would be so much more joyful, just to love them and endorse them and let them live their own lives with confidence that they have received all that I can teach them and knowing that you will work with them and even more so with their children to guide them going forward.

I have done my best to organize our spirit world to support them and their families too. Did I do it effectively or are there ways I could improve? Is it enough? I would sure relish some feedback and guidance. Let's be a team, with active give and take on the strategy level. In the time I have left on Earth, I could sure get a lot more done for you and the providence if we could develop that active give and take.
I'll stop here and listen.

My dear son, thank you for all your efforts and hard work. You sure have grown over the years, and now, as a grandfather, you are beginning to understand my heart more. Each person has their own course. There is only so much you can guide them. However, if you love them unconditionally, the time may come when they will ask you for guidance. When that happens, then they can receive it more. People like to discover things for themselves. No one likes to be pushed. When you give something to someone who is longing for it, it is not a push, it is a gift. You are quenching a thirst. That is the exact opposite. That is why I wait until people long for me. To reach out to someone before then is counterproductive. And even then it is important to be measured on how much you give. If you keep giving after an appetite is satiated, it quickly can turn to pushing.
Focus on unconditional love. Celebrate your amazing children. Ask them how you can support them in their dreams. Love them with my love. Let's do this together.

Wow. That's a paradigm shift! Please help me hold onto it in the moment.

Please continue journaling. I will welcome the opportunity to dialogue with you in this way. Let's do great things together.

When I showed Ron what I had written, he was very excited. He said "this is clearly in a different voice. I believe this is actually God speaking to you."

I thought about it for a few days, and finally decided, "No, I'm not going to play games and pretend I'm actually talking to God." And I filed it away.

Then a few weeks later, on August 28, 2015, I turned 63. That morning, just as I had been doing for nearly 2 decades, I prayed for well over an hour before breakfast. Only this morning was different. The moment I completed my prayer, I suddenly had a remarkable vision.

My life flashed before my eyes. It was divided into three 21-year courses. Each of those was divided into three 7-year courses. I was clearly shown the meaning and purpose of each of those 7-year courses. And then this vision focused in on the years 1994 – 1997, and I heard a voice explain, "These were the most difficult three years in your life. That was because they were the first three years of your third 21-year course, and you had to set a foundation. After that, you could receive great blessings. And that is exactly what Rev. and Mrs. Moon had to go through after Rev. Moon died."

It was stunning. It was very powerful. It was definitely not my imagination.

In fact, for three years beginning in 1994, our family truly struggled financially. The company I had started failed, and we were broke. However, 1997 was the first year in which members in our church were authorized to offer the marriage blessing to neighbors, friends, and family. I was the community leader in Laurel, Maryland at the time, and I prayed for guidance on how to help the couples in my community to respond to this new opportunity. I got the inspiration to meet with the Manager of BWI Airport in Baltimore, and he graciously received me at the top of the tower there. I explained that I wanted to set up a table in the airport to offer marriage rededication ceremonies. To my great surprise, he agreed. He gave me the only table in his airport which was set aside for outside groups.

Each couple was given the goal to bless 185 couples. We quickly completed ours, there in the airport, and I helped some 40 other couples to also achieve their goals. One of those couples was the Salonens, and I was soon hired as Neil's Executive Assistant for the next four years. You could say I had a "Joseph experience", going from the dungeon to the Prime Minister.

I did not process that "63rd birthday" revelation with much maturity. Of course, I felt very loved by God. I felt very special. But I didn't think about it any more deeply. Clearly this was a birthday present from God, recognizing and honoring my three 21-year courses on this earth. What more could there be to it? I asked a few friends, "Did you ever receive a revelation from God?" When they replied, "no", I smiled back, "well actually, I did", trying not to sound too proud of myself, although of course I was so very proud.

Three years later, in 2018, I started having a very strong desire to hear some kind of a report from Dr. George and our ancestral committees. I had been praying for them for 6 years. I had been asking for help from my ancestors, especially regarding several projects that I wanted to launch for the sake of peace and prosperity in the world.

In addition, by 2018, on the foundations of the sacrifice of Dr. Hak Ja Han Moon and our global movement, the providence of ancestral blessings had been expanded to 430 generations, and our couple had been able to complete those ceremonies. And so, our committees had grown. But now, in 2018, as had been the case 21 years earlier in 1997, couples were being asked once again to share this marriage blessing with family, friends, and neighbors. This time with a goal of achieving 430 couples.

Finally, on Sept 15, 2018, we had our first reading with Dr. George and our Ancestors, with the help of a dear friend who is an extremely gifted medium and who has trained and refined her skills for decades. During that reading, George explained that all the resources I needed for my projects would be forthcoming, but I would never find them if I didn't complete our goal of blessing 430 couples.

That was a surprise, and also a confrontation. I had felt that having helped 40 couples in 1997, I probably didn't need to do any more such blessings. Here's a relevant excerpt he shared:

> "We're being led by the Holy Spirit in the flesh. And we don't need to understand what she's saying. We don't need understanding why she's saying it. It's like we're little kids in kindergarten and if our mother says you cannot go out without your shoes! 'But I want to go barefoot' - You have to put your shoes on. 'Why?' Because I say so. So sometimes we just have to do what we're told - even if we don't understand it. By and by, we'll understand later on because a mother has access to information that we do not and sometimes she goes through certain gyrations that to us look like 'what is this all about?'
>
> But she actually does know what she's doing, even if we don't. We don't need to understand it. It's OK.
>
> I just saw you with this little stainless-steel tray - a nice little edge on it. I think you can buy them at the Dollar Tree – with the holy wine - like you're at a cocktail party serving people. But with the little cups. There is a number somehow doing that 430. It will help us. It's not just for those people it's for us too. It will help us move through to another dimension, to another level."

Based on that guidance, our family completed our full goal of 430 couples in a few months, and soon after we completed 43 couples who qualified as full members. We were among the first couples in America to register as Cheon Bo Victors, which we did at the first induction ceremony held in Korea on October 10, 2020.

Between September 15, 2018 and August 16, 2021, we had a total of 6 readings with Dr. George and our Committees, with the help of my friend, the medium. The content of those readings is profound and historic. But I will publish them in a separate book. However, on September 30, 2021, on the occasion of our 7th scheduled reading, something unexpected happened.

The medium prayed to begin the session and then said:

> "Well, this is interesting. I'm being told to go home. The first thing I heard is 'what are you doing here?'
>
> I have a brief message: 'Just take care of your own business. Just do what you've been doing and let the Holy Spirit guide you. When you get inspired, God is speaking to you. When you go through a third party, there's always something lost in the translation. So, center your heart and let God guide you directly. Don't be dependent on a relation. Know, be still, and know that I am God. And I speak directly to you. And you will get the information that you need on a need-to-know basis.'
> And I'm being shoed away, like with a broom. Like that cat who's come in and doesn't belong in the house. I'm being told, 'go home and do your homework'. I see you rolling up your sleeves, and like a child, sitting down to finish your homework.
> And it just hung up on me."

I laughed and said, "Have they ever hung up on you before?" She said, "No, never."

Then she spoke again:

> "Somebody else is giving me a little extra here ...
> I see that you have work that you need to complete. You need to turn it in. And it's time to graduate to the next level. And I feel that exactly what that is will be revealed to you directly. You need to trust more that God is guiding you. And you don't need a third party."

That was September 30, 2021. It took me until July 13, 2022, before I reached the point where I could, in faith and confidence, begin a sincere and trusting dialogue with God. That time period was 286 days. 40 weeks and 6 days. The gestation period of a human baby. Kind of a rebirth.

Shortly after I began my journaling, I gained a deep sense of how incredibly vulnerable Heavenly Mother's heart truly is. I realized, to my great shock and distress, that my first journal message, at that weekend workshop with Ron

Pappalardo, was the fruit of 63 years of her tears, longing for this prodigal son to return home. She had to be so careful and measured, so as not to chase me away. She could not reveal how much her heart was in stress, hoping that I wouldn't run away. She finished that message casually, with:

> *"Please continue journaling. I will welcome the opportunity to dialogue with you in this way. Let's do great things together."*

But as I shared above, I didn't continue. I left her hanging. Her long-lost child, finally home for 1 day, then gone. I imagine that she almost went crazy, each day, hoping for me to write another message, and each day being so hurt when I didn't.

After 26 days, she felt she had to do something. On the occasion of my 63rd birthday, she gave me an incredible and very personal vision. In that vision, she explained that just as I had to go through a 3-year foundational course at the beginning of my 3rd 21 years, so too, True Parents had to do the same thing when Rev. Moon ascended. It was only later, when I was reading Dr. Hak Ja Han Moon's memoir, *Mother of Peace,* that I realized the significance of that day. To commemorate the 3-year period of devotion that Dr. Moon dedicated for her husband following his ascension, she determined to launch the SunHak Peace Prize. The first SunHak Peace prizes were awarded on the evening of August 28, 2015, in Korea, in real time while I was praying in Maryland and when I received that revelation.

Heavenly Mother gave me that amazing vision, out of desperation, to encourage me to trust her and to continue journaling. But I was so thick and immature, I didn't think at all about God's heart. In a totally self-centered and juvenile response I became obsessed with the fact that "I" received a real revelation from God.

Finally, in 2021, after Muriel and I had been inducted into the Cheon Bo Won, we stood in a position where God could now directly intervene in our lives. In our theology, we call this the "Direct Dominion". Finally, at that point, in her instructions to me during our 7th and final reading with Dr. George, Heavenly Mother gave me very direct guidance and instructions.

> *"So, center your heart and let God guide you directly. Don't be dependent on a relation. Know, be still, and know that I am God. And I speak directly to you."*

Still, even after that guidance, it took me an entire 40-week period to reach the point in my heart, where I could actually begin **TAKING GOD SERIOUSLY**.

Eleven days after I started journaling in earnest, it hit me, just how much I had hurt Heavenly Mother's beautiful heart, by turning my back on Her. On July 24, 2022, I sincerely apologized for taking so long to respond. Heavenly Mother just brushed it aside and said:

> ***"Don't worry about what you missed by not beginning your journaling earlier. I was dropping a seed. It had to germinate."***

God is Amazing.

JOURNALING

7/13/22 *I Have Been Waiting For You To Feel Comfortable And I Am So Glad That You Have Now Determined To Write Me Daily. I Will Be There For Us.*

Dearest Heavenly Father & Mother,
I am really excited to begin our new more intimate relationship. Thank you for the beautiful and remarkable ways in which you are sharing your heart and your sensitivities with Ron and Connie and with Carlton. I'm sincerely sorry that I lacked confidence that you could speak to me like that, or in some similar way unique to our relationship. I really hope that through these journalings we can develop an exciting skin touch relationship of heart, and that my heart can develop and grow to resonate more fully with yours.
I hope that I can experience your love more deeply and express that love more intentionally and more spontaneously in all my relationships. I hope I can more effectively prioritize my time and energies, so that I can maximize my impact for you and for True Mother, and for the providence. I hope I can more effectively discern which individuals and which projects are worthy of my investment, so that I can accomplish the most benefit for you and True Mother at this time. I'll stop here in this first greeting. Thank you from the depths of my heart for this privilege to journal with you in this way.
Love eternally,
Laurence

Dear Laurence,
I too am excited about this chance to journal with you. I have been waiting for you to feel comfortable and I am so glad that you have now determined to write me daily. I will be there for us. You are someone I have been working with and raising up for your entire life, and I want to work with you on so many levels. But first, let's get to know each other more heartistically.
Please let me know what you are feeling. Then we can move on to the external. I promise we will get to all of it and much, much, more. This will be exciting. I'll be waiting for you each day.
I love you very much.
Heavenly Parent

7/14/22 *The Holy Spirit Never Had A Single Child. True Mother Had 14, And On That Foundation Has Adopted 8 Billion.*

Dearest Heavenly Parents,

I hope it's OK for me to address you as "Parents", even though I understand that you are the unified harmonized being of Father and Mother. But through the testimonies of Ron and others on his zoom calls, and through Father's sharing about Heavenly Mother, I have come to recognize that there is a whole half (perhaps the deeper half?) of your heart and nature that I don't know, and I desperately want to know. I suddenly realized today that the providence you are prosecuting in America is absolutely necessary. In spite of all your efforts, America as a fallen nation, has become more and more corrupted by Satan in these last days. Everything needed to be separated into Cain & Abel camps, and Cain needed to attempt to establish its "bizarro" version of the Heavenly Kingdom first, before Abel could rise up and embrace Cain with love fulfilling the foundation of substance.

But given the timeline of True Mother's providence, it all needed to happen in light speed. The spirit of division swept across America so powerfully. Political polarization, with Cain's side lying to attack Abel's side just as Satan lied to Eve, and just as communism lied to dominate democracy. But we also became polarized in our movement, and we became polarized in our nation over vaccines, and even within our own families. All of these schisms must now be healed with parental true love. There is so little time. Thank you for your mighty works. You are truly a God and Parents of infinite love.

I am so grateful to True Father for working so powerfully and urgently to restore and transform the Spirit World. This returning resurrection is the golden moment for hundreds of billions of spirit men to support True Mother and receive the vitality elements necessary to become divine spirits. Surely with your infinite love and forgiveness, once you are completely liberated and empowered in your full sovereignty, it doesn't need to take massive lengths of time to restore those in hell, right? Surely with the concerted love and compassion and investment of restored mankind, it can happen very quickly, right? It's not fair for you to have to continue to wait for thousands more years before you can realize your full original ideal.

I'll stop here. I love you very much and I desperately long for a deep and vibrant exchange between us through these journal dialogues. Please write through me now.

Love,
Laurence

Dear Laurence,
I love you too, very profoundly. Yes, because of True Mother's heart and conditions and incredible efforts, and because of True Father's amazing efforts in the Spirit World, everything is speeding up to light speed. You will see more and more amazing things happening in the days and weeks ahead. Each day is like a century – hold on tight and don't hold back. This is the rollercoaster of all of history!

I am igniting the fire of True Parents' love in America. The Pentecost was powerful, based on the love of the Holy Spirit; but True Mother's love is the substantial perfection of that love. The Holy Spirit never had a single child. True Mother had 14, and on that foundation has adopted 8 billion. It is an entirely unprecedented expression of my Mother's heart. Thank you for your love for True Mother. Through True Mother, you can come to know and experience my heart, my Mother's heart, so much more deeply. I love America so much.
Love Eternally,
Heavenly Parent

7/15/22 There Is So Much That I Want To Manifest, And So Few People I Can Work Through To Accomplish It At This Time. Please Teach Others.

Dearest Heavenly Parent,
I am so exhilarated with your energy & love through our collaboration! Yesterday I felt a strong sense that I should find and prepare birthing candles for Jay and Lisa, and I texted Jay to advise me of Lisa's progress. Within a few hours he texted me that they were already at the hospital! I feel such a connection of heart with you and through you to the universe. Thank you! And then Eli was born en caul – how amazing was that (1 in 80,000)! I felt that it was an amazing grace from you and angelic protection.
Life in partnership with you is remarkable and exciting!
Eternally,
Laurence

My Dear Son and Partner,
It is even more exciting for me! There is so much that I want to manifest, and so few people I can work through to accomplish it at this time. Please teach others. Yes, CheongPyeong is an example of what I was able to manifest through Dae Mo Nim. We need to build the Bering Strait Tunnel and Railroad and much more. Please be faithful to your devotions and conditions, they are exemplary and make it much easier for me to work through and with you.
And congratulations on your beautiful new grandson!
Love,
Heavenly Parent

7/16/22 The Greater The Struggle, The Sweeter The Victories And The More Precious The Memories.

Dearest Heavenly Parent,
I really appreciated the opportunity to attend Kevin's memorial service yesterday. It was very uplifting. My appreciation for Kevin, and for his amazing relationship with you, and his love for his family, for Jesus, for America, for True Parents, has grown tremendously. I am sorry I didn't try harder to get to know him and his family while he was alive. But thank you for such a precious brother.

I was encouraged by the connection of heart bridging so many divided groups at that event. We need to heal True Parents' family. I was amazed by how many people you could touch through one man, and touched by the idea of creating unforgettable memories in the hearts of other people.

Thank you for the opportunity to love and care for Micah and Joelle this week. Please help me to deeply touch their hearts.

Love,
Laurence

Dearest Laurence,
Yes, unforgettable memories are an expression of my heart. They are eternal. True Parents most valued their common victories. Those were victories to accomplish my dream. The greater the struggle, the sweeter the victories and the more precious the memories. Every challenge is an opportunity for a blessing – like you wrote in one of your first songs, "Build your home on love". I like that one.

I'm looking forward to collaborating with so many of my children like I did with Kevin, like I did with Jesus, like I have done with True Parents, and with you. The greater the challenge the sweeter. Creating the universe was all consuming and completely draining, but the exhaustion was sweet. You had a taste of it after cleaning carpets for an entire weekend with no rest, and then going in the ocean – in Santa Monica or in Galveston. So sweet. You don't even feel like resting. That kind of effort to manifest love. I'm really up for that! Are you game?

Love,
Heavenly Parent

7/17/22 *I Promise To Share Remarkable Things With You Through These Exchanges. But Most Importantly, I Am Interested In Sharing My Heart With You. I Am Hugging You!*

Dear Heavenly Parent,
I'm so profoundly grateful to be so embraced and blessed by you. Today over dinner, Gamaliel, NanYoung, Micah, and Joelle were taking the initiative together with Danniel who emailed, to plan our next family reunion. I didn't

have to initiate anything. I feel that you are blessing our family so profoundly. Eli is a beautiful new grandson, and Joelle is doing so well managing her pregnancy, research, and marriage.

Today I witnessed to Justin and he was totally open, receptive and inspired. Thank you!

I was struck by how serious Dr. Yong was this morning conveying Father's words from 1961 about the times we are entering now. He said there would be 7 years of challenges and trials and hardships and that we need to be ready.

Please know, Heavenly Parent, that I will never leave you unto death. I will not lose faith, or turn from you ever. I love you passionately, and I owe everything to you.

I pray that our family can stay united centering on you for now, but over time, we can center on True Parents and your lineage. It surprised me to realize how divided our own family has become over politics, news, and vaccines. If anything, I hope these years of challenges can bring us much, much closer to you and True Parents. I hope it can shorten the time of your suffering dramatically. I really want to get to know you so much more intimately, and to work with you hand in hand. Thank you for all you have given me.

Love Eternally,
Laurence

Dear Laurence,
Thank you for your life and death commitment to me based on your sincere love. Thank you for witnessing to Justin tonight. He too is very special. I am sincerely sorry that there must still be much suffering before we reach the Kingdom of Heaven. It can't be avoided. I will be with you every step. Together we can shorten that time for many.

If you remain grateful as you are now, and as True Father was in even much more dire circumstances, you will eternally cherish this suffering as perhaps your greatest blessing. I will not be indebted to you, even though I will always feel indebted. I love you also more than words can express. I am so grateful that you decided to journal with me. I promise to share remarkable things with you through these exchanges. But most importantly, I am interested in sharing my heart with you. I am hugging you!

Love,
Heavenly Parent

7/18/22 Stay Focused, Stay Deeply Connected With Me In Heart And We Can Slice Through This Period Of Tribulation And Lay The Foundation For Heaven Together.

Dearest Heavenly Parent,
Thank you for showering your love every day! Today I was deeply inspired by the breakthrough with Tom regarding GiveNet. I hope I can be properly sensitive to all the relevant nuances as I approach True Mother's throne at this time in history.
I meant what I said Heavenly Parent, despite whatever happens during this time. I will not lose my gratitude towards you, nor my absolute faith, obedience, and love towards you. I will follow the example and path that True Father set, to achieve your liberation in the shortest possible time. I feel that you have given me almost unlimited possibilities to creatively initiate. I want to utilize those opportunities wisely to achieve the best possible results for you. I would deeply appreciate your guidance so that I can optimize my impact, and so that I don't miss any really important opportunities.
I love you eternally!
Laurence

Dearest Laurence,
Thank you for your love, your loyalty, and your commitment. I will work closely with you. I instructed you to offer GiveNet to True Mother when you received your first grid healing through Dianne. You are doing well with that project.
I am inspired about your interview with Dietmar. Let's see what kind of impact that can make.
Stay focused, stay deeply connected with me in heart and we can slice through this period of tribulation and lay the foundation for Heaven together.
Love Eternally,
Heavenly Parent

7/19/22 *Yes, You Can Call On My Support For Healing When You Pray. There Is Tremendous Support Available.*

Dearest Heavenly Parent,
I am so grateful for all your grace and blessings. Yesterday when Joelle was coming down with covid in Annapolis, everything was so clear, and I felt tremendous spiritual support. Micah was able to mobilize and recovered quickly with the acidill, ginger, and peppermint tea. Joelle was able to safely return home and then went through the worst of the infection yesterday without the need to visit a hospital, and today her temperature was gone. I feel that you powerfully accepted my prayer for her healing. Thank you!!!
Thank you for helping me establish a channel for offering GiveNet! And of all the people, through Henri. I repent that I have always felt such a wall between Henri and myself. I hope that this project will afford me the

opportunity to restore my past arrogance and establish a relationship of respect and love as his younger brother.

And Heavenly Parent, I am grateful for Dietmar's reaffirmation to do our interview, even though it is postponed yet again due to covid. Please accept my 2-meal fast today on top of all the other fasts I've done to prepare for this interview. Please pour your heart and your voice and your spirit through this interview when it does happen, and then please mobilize the entire spirit world to make this interview go totally viral, and testify to True Parents and especially True Mother in front of all mankind. I am so grateful!!!
Eternally,
Laurence

Dear Laurence,
I am so inspired to work together. Yes, you can call on my support for healing when you pray. There is tremendous support available. And I am really inspired by your work with David. David's team has embraced the vision of working with True Mother. You have fulfilled the guidance I gave you through Dianne and through True Father to offer this project to True Mother. It will dramatically contribute to the transformation of Africa into Heavenly Africa. It will touch millions and millions of my precious children and connect them to True Parents and me through the Blessing.
And regarding your interview with Dietmar, that will happen and will be the beginning of a platform I have been preparing to reach the whole world about True Mother's role as Christ on the Earth at this time. I gave you the song about Tamar 2 decades ago. Kevin gave you the culmination of his life's work through "Realizing Jesus". It will have a powerful and significant impact, just you wait and see!
Love,
Heavenly Parent

7/20/22 *There Are Manifold Possibilities That Already Exist In The Realm Of Idea, But Need To Find A Home In A Physical Person's Heart And Mind In Order To Be Realized. But Then There Are Infinite Possibilities That Are Waiting To Be Conceived By You, My Children, Who Have Infinite Creative Potential.*

Dear Heavenly Parent,
Good morning! Just walking out of the house to the porch to write to you is profoundly transformational. It is peaceful, and the birds are chirping musically, and I am lifted out of the trivial crises happening in the home to the patient ancient longing of nature for the coming of your Kingdom. We are so close! True Mother is amazing. She is cosmic, reshaping the course of

nations with her absolute conviction and profound love. I so deeply want to help her in ever greater ways. I feel so very blessed and privileged. And at the same time, I can't neglect my own family and tribe which are the necessary and precious foundation on which to stand.
I love you very much. Do you have something you would like to share with me today?
Love Eternally,
Laurence

**My Dear Son,
Thank you. I am so energized working with you. You really have caught True Parents' spirit and heart of responsibility, and that nothing is impossible working with me. That was central to Father's incredible legacy; his conviction that there were unlimited possibilities and that relaxing even a moment meant sacrificing some of those unlimited possibilities. That is actually true. But, of course, there will be others, like you, who pick up those abandoned threads and make them real. There are manifold possibilities that already exist in the realm of idea, but need to find a home in a physical person's heart and mind in order to be realized. But then there are infinite possibilities that are waiting to be conceived by you, my children, who have infinite creative potential. As long as it is rooted in and empowered by true love, each of those infinite possibilities will be beautiful and holy. Isn't this creation remarkable?
Love Eternally,
Heavenly Parent**

7/21/22 *There Is Still Great Healing That Is Needed In The Native American Family. But Yes, They Will Play A Significant Role In The Future.*

Good afternoon Heavenly Parent, it has been hectic and I'm sorry I was not able to finish my prayers in a timely manner and then go directly to journaling earlier than this. Today, reading the 1-hour Divine Principle manual, I was struck by the description of fallen mankind's situation. We have been dominated by Satan.
You made your covenant with the Pilgrim Fathers based on their devastating sacrifices and remarkable faith and dedication that first winter in 1620/21. But I realized today that you were under no illusions about the ability of Satan to invade and corrupt and dominate America. I believe you had great hope for the peaceful and harmonious cooperation between settlers and Native Americans, but again, you had no illusions about what could and in fact did transpire. I expect that the 400 years of atrocities suffered by Native

Americans had a connection to Korea's suffering, through the Mongolian Peoples' link. Is that true? I suspect, like African Americans, that now is a time when Native Americans will be called to play an important role in building your Kingdom. They really do seem to represent your feminine spirit. What is your vision for their role at this time in the providence? I'll stop here. Is there anything you would like to share with me now? I love you eternally,
Laurence

Dear Laurence,
Yes, I made a covenant with the Pilgrim settlers because I am a parent of heart and my heart was deeply moved. I hadn't ever seen a people so filled with Christ's love, and so determined to build my Kingdom. I prepared the path for them, but they ran along that path. You can't imagine how much hope that gave me! Did I anticipate frictions between the settlers and the Native Americans? Yes, but I prepared for a friendly reception, and it didn't have to go the way of war. The Native Americans were not a monolithic culture. But if the success could have been solidified in Plymouth, then who knows! At the time of Jesus' birth, it was not predetermined that Israel would fail. In fact, just the opposite. I invested long and patient care to prepare Israel and in fact the entire world for Jesus' birth. In the end, everyone has their own responsibilities, and even one person, if central enough, can destroy centuries of work. You experienced that yourself with the Global Economic Action Institute.
American governments have systematically sought to destroy Native American culture and heritage. It has been pretty gruesome. I can bless the remnants. They carry with them the fortune of those unjustly mistreated, yes like Korea. Your own spiritual son, Carlton, is one, and I am working with him in a unique and important way. There is still great healing that is needed in the Native American family. But yes, they will play a significant role in the future. I like your Tecumseh video by the way. Native Americans have been great patriots of America.
I deeply appreciate your commitment to our dialogues.
Love Eternally,
Heavenly Parent

7/22/22 You Know That There Have Been Times In The Providence When The Chosen People Have Been Asked To Die For The Will. Some Died Willingly. They Will Be Forever Blessed For Their Love, Loyalty, And Sacrifice. Now Is A Time When Hopefully We Can Build The Kingdom Through Living For The Will.

Good morning Dearest Heavenly Parent.
Thank you for today. I feel extremely embraced in your love. Thank you for True Mother's encouragement that we must let all mankind know of True Parents. There is no longer a need for war, nations, or religions. I want to fulfill my role and responsibilities as an owner of Cheon Il Guk and inspire others to do the same. I want to inspire our family and tribe.
Thank you for the news through Kiyoko that Andy is stabilized. You are a gracious loving parent. Your own son died at a very similar age to Andy's. Also, Kiyoko lost a daughter at the same age. Surely the restoration of the cosmos is far more important than the life or death of any one person and I offer myself and my family up to you in gratitude to use as you see fit. But I am profoundly grateful that you have protected Andy through multiple life and death episodes. He has such a surprisingly beautiful heart and mind. Surely you have some specific and significant plan for him, and I believe he is especially gifted to be someone who loves and mentors children and youths. He said he would love to teach philosophy. Whatever happens, I know you will continue to hold him close to your heart.
I want to shift my focus today to prepare for the Dietmar interview. Especially based on Mother's words this morning, I am really excited to proclaim True Parents through Dietmar's platform. I hope we can develop it into a powerful trumpet to wake up the entire world to True Parents. Thank you so much. You have given me so much more than I could ever have dreamed of. I am eternally yours,
Laurence

Dear Laurence,
Thank you for your beautiful message today. I am deeply touched. You are one of those who has fully awakened and whose heart resonates in joy with True Parents. How inspiring! Please tell all 8 billion people on the Earth about True Parents now. I will surely help you.
Thank you for your sincere heart regarding Andy and even your own life and that of your family members. You know that there have been times in the providence when the chosen people have been asked to die for the will. Some died willingly. They will be forever blessed for their love, loyalty, and sacrifice. Now is a time when hopefully we can build the kingdom through living for the will. I love Andy very much. I accept your sincere offering and I can use that.
Keep working hard at your areas of responsibility. Know that I am working harder – of course because I am your parent. I am proud of you and deeply, deeply grateful.
Love eternally,
Heavenly Parent

7/23/22 *All My Children Have Been In A Coma All These Centuries. No One Could Feel My Heart. But Now You Can. You Can't Begin To Imagine What That Means To Me. Honestly, You Can't. There Are No Words.*

Good morning my dearest Heavenly Parent,
Thank you for enveloping my life in your incredible blessings and grace. I can never repay you. Dr. Yong's message this morning set me onto thinking about just how omnipresent and pervasive sin actually is. We are so immersed in it that we become insensitive in spite of all our efforts. It occurred to me that even Jesus was born with ancestral sin, even though he had no original sin. What an unimaginably massive task you have faced to save this world. How have you maintained your determination and your compassion and your forgiveness for so long?
I apologize for having so little to show. I will try harder and more diligently. Please give me more focus, energy, and skill to use time much more efficiently. I am accused by all the opportunities I let slip away and by all that I fail to accomplish. I'll get better. You've carried this responsibility all alone for far, far, far too long.
Do you have a message for me today? I deeply hope so.
Love eternally,
Laurence

My Dear Laurence,

Thank you for feeling my heart. I am so grateful. All my children have been in a coma all these centuries. No one could feel my heart. But now you can. You can't begin to imagine what that means to me. Honestly, you can't. There are no words. You are saving me. I am so grateful.
This is the feeling I had when Jesus was born. It didn't matter that he had already been betrayed by his physical father. It didn't matter that he received almost none of the royal welcome I tried to prepare for him. The three kings were a window dressing to cover my shame before my son, but they immediately evaporated at the first sign of danger.
Yes, Jesus was not free from sin. He was free from the original sin, but he had to grow and make mistakes and atone for his mistakes. But I loved him so much. I let him know how much I loved him, the way I should have done with Adam and Eve. I wanted their development to be an unfolding of discovery, of surprise, where they could be delighted again and again as they came to realize just who they were, and then who I am. Can you imagine? I held back from pouring my

heart out to Adam and Eve out of love! Out of some misguided dream of a perfect fairy tale.

Don't repeat my mistake. Love your children with all your might. Pour your love over them like Mary poured oil on Jesus. Father determined to love all mankind before loving his own children. No one knows my heart like he does. No one knows my pain like he does. No one knows my regret like he does.

We must and will reclaim every one of my children, but never again put your own children on the alter. If you love me, please, please smother your own children in true love.

Love eternally,
Heavenly Parent

7/24/22 *Don't Worry About What You Missed By Not Beginning Your Journaling Earlier. I Was Dropping A Seed. It Had To Germinate.*

Good Morning Heavenly Parent!
I find to my great joy that I am looking forward with increasing enthusiasm and inspiration to these dialogues each day. Thank you from the bottom of my heart for your precious messages. I am so regretful that I didn't take your first message seriously enough, several years ago, when you asked me to continue journaling at that time. I missed out on so much, but you have been so kindly patient. You are truly my Father and my Mother.

I was struck yesterday in preparing the report for George, by a portion of the message I was given that I had completely forgotten about. It spoke about the history of fossil fuels and how at first mankind failed to recognize their potential, then they harnessed it, and now it needs to phase out. At the time I considered that only as a metaphor. But now I see it was a much more direct message for me relating to wind project you have assigned to me.

I'm sorry I didn't get to my presentation for Dietmar yesterday, but I will today. And if you have a song you would like me to write for Tuesday night, I would deeply welcome that! I love you so very much.

I invite you with all my heart to respond now.
Thank you!
Love Eternally,
Laurence

Dear Laurence,
Good morning, and thank you for your wonderful message this morning. Don't worry about what you missed by not beginning your journaling earlier. I was dropping a seed. It had to germinate. Through your goals and investment into Morning Devotion, you have significantly grown and elevated your heart and spirit. I know that you

can feel that. Now is a great time for us to launch our dialogue through journaling. I am 100% committed.

What you are now spearheading through your wind project will be centrally involved in the restoration of the planet. I heard your thought as I said that: "Why did Father have such little interest in this project when he came to you spiritually during your session with Dianne?" He said to deal with "staff". This is not something that Mother will deal with personally, in contrast to GiveNet. This is an external project. It will externally help restore the planet and it will result in great funds to support the providence. But Mother is working on the most internal level, centered on restoring My children. She did mention that China should irrigate the Gobi Desert. This will enable that request.

I will see if there is a good song to offer you for this month. If not, you will undoubtedly come up with a great one on your own. I am your #1 fan!

Love Eternally,
Heavenly Parent

7/25/22 *We Are All One Family Now. I Am Opening The Gateways For Each Of Their Hearts. It Must Be Done Carefully, Individually. I Can't Lose Even One Of You.*

Dearest Beloved Parents,

I'm so happy to greet you now after a long day. This is a different feeling than greeting you right after morning prayers. I've poured out a lot of energy today and I feel emptied, but very good. It was productive. I had determined to work on my interview for Dietmar but kept putting it off. And mysteriously the interview kept being postponed. Finally, last night I started practicing it and realized to my shock just how sloppy and unfinished the power point really was. I'm so sorry and sincerely ashamed. You deserve my very best. So do True Parents and Jesus. That was not my very best. Only a haphazard first draft. I want to uphold your dignity. I want this interview to go super viral and shake the internet and world.

So today, right after morning devotion, I pledged and then went straight to the power point. That was 7:45 am, and I finished my revision after 4 pm. I still have one page of notes to integrate. Also, I would love to have a better recording of Tamar. In my opinion, it should come from Justin. I put in a call to him. I sincerely hope he is willing and even honored to sing it. Maybe you could put in a good word? I don't feel I have the right to pay for this now until our family finances are settled down. So, I expect it will only happen if he is truly inspired.

During my 1-hour Divine Principle reading, Andy called back. That's the first I heard from him or Jordanne in several days. He seems to be doing well and

is hopefully out of the woods for risk of a dangerous blood clot. Thank you so much for keeping an eye on him. You are so generous and gracious. His main risk now is head trauma. Are there head trauma prevention angels? If so, do you have one to spare?
Interestingly, while I was working on the power point, Gamaliel and his family were building an awesome chicken fence. Today, for the first time, they free-ranged! First eggs coming soon! Gee, Heavenly Parent, with Andy and Jordanne out exploring the Sierras, and Gamaliel and NanYoung creating chicken paradise, this feels like a little sliver of the 3rd Blessing. I'll stop here. I hope you still have a message for me so late in the day. I love you so deeply. Please take me into your heart.
Love Eternally,
Laurence

Dearest Laurence,
Thank you for your great work today on the power point. Yes, the better the quality, the more I have to work with to wake the world up to the reality of True Mother. What you have created is awesome. It is very innovative and I know it will touch a lot of hearts.
I also had a busy and productive day, so connecting with you when we have both poured out our best is very sweet. We can share war stories from the long day, and dream about tomorrow's victories.
A lot of people in the morning devotion community look up to you. Thank you for mentoring them. We are all one family now. I am opening the gateways for each of their hearts. It must be done carefully, individually. I can't lose even one of you. You are more advanced than most. Please feel ownership for that community. You are accurate, there is a spiritual awakening happening centered on that community. It is happening faster than you realize. This journaling is a part of that. Please understand and be mindful of your importance and deepen your shimjeong towards that awakening.
Be at peace. You are so loved.
Eternally,
Heavenly Parent

7/26/22 *To Be A True Co-Creator, You Need To Think Like A Creator. That's Easy For Me, But There Haven't Been So Many Of My Children Who Have Successfully Gotten It.*

Good morning my beloved, glorious Parent.
This morning in my prayer I was thinking about the point which Dr. Yong had raised some time ago about how the virtuous circle of love keeps growing. Only love. That creates eternity. Nuclear explosions, stars, all burn

out eventually, although those time frames are on a much different scale than our normal frame of reference. But love, that's the grand prize! That's the holy grail. You've been searching for that holy grail since before time. I suspect since long before time.

The 7 mottos of Cheon Il Guk citizens begin with thinking and visioning. True Father spent more time thinking than perhaps anything else. How much you must have thought to invent the fundamental laws of the cosmos. How many models did you play out in your incredible mind, before the idea began to take shape? Did it exist before you conceived of it? Did you discover it? I'm guessing you assembled it with perfect balance and design. Eventually – who knows how long – eventually you were ready to pull the trigger. You had the framework that you could believe in, and on which you could begin your quest.

Did the big bang proceed on autopilot? Certainly not completely. You clearly intervened in this solar system to achieve perfect balance to sustain life. But perhaps significantly on autopilot? That would have afforded you more time to plan and then to experiment.

The atomic table is an elegant language of energy configuration with which to paint your masterpiece. DNA is a marvelous language with which to code biological attributes. You tested, experimented, challenged, seeking to find the optimal designs. Very large? Very small? That golden mean. Leave room for future growth as better nutrition is developed!

When the entire thing blew up in front of you, there was never an option. Never a choice. Not even for a moment. Not really. You were absolutely committed from long before the word "bang".

But surely Humpty Dumpty is a metaphor for the fall. All the King's horses, and all the King's men could never restore it. We have had wars for millennia. Only the King Himself, and even then, only through the most exhaustive investment of love and jeongseong. But it is happening. It is truly happening.

You are beyond amazing. Thank you for Jesus. Thank you for True Parents. Thank you for Hyo Jin Nim, Heung Jin Nim, and Dae Mo Nim. Bits of the shell are reforming. The heart and soul are being reconstituted. This time there are already True Parents. No possibility of invasion again. Your miracle – the eternal explosion of true love – will finally happen. That will surely create whole new realities, level after level of greater joy, beauty, heart, miracles. Surely there will be unending manifestations of beauty & reality that even you will have never imagined. It will happen, thanks to you! Hallelujah! I am in awe.

Love eternally,
Laurence

Dearest Laurence,

Wow, you deeply inspire me. How many people in all of history do you think understand in their hearts and minds what you just shared on 3 pages of notebook paper? You have given me an unforgettable memory and experience. This will bind us together eternally. We can experience this explosive, unfolding together – are you game?

Thank you for sharing my message about the Pentecost this morning at Morning Devotion. A lot of the participants perked up, focused, recommitted, and drew closer in heart. That makes it much easier for me. To be a true co-creator, you need to think like a creator. That's easy for me, but there haven't been so many of my children who have successfully gotten it. I deeply appreciate you.

Love eternally,
Heavenly Parent

7/27/22 The Fall Of Adam And Eve Was A Sudden Tsunami. It Was Overwhelming Beyond Words. The Fabric Of Creation Unraveled. The Entire Purpose Of Creation, The Reason For My Creating For Billions Of Years Vanished Before My Eyes. Then It Was Gone.

Dearest most beloved Heavenly Parent,

It's been a busy morning and now afternoon, and I apologize for not journaling with you earlier. This is a holy moment now, the wind is calm, the crickets are chirping in the trees, the chickens are quiet – it is very peaceful here now.

This morning, I had some insights. In my prayer I realized just how close you were to your ideal when it exploded in your face. Just days away, probably less than a year. After anticipating for 14 billion years plus all the time before time. You created Adam and Eve to be so profoundly sensitive to love, to be able to fully receive and reciprocate all your love so powerfully. As much as Lucifer was being overwhelmed by the strength and power of that love, you were feeling that a million times more, and you were intoxicated in anticipation. Then all hell broke loose, literally. I can't begin to imagine your feelings, but I deeply want to. The children born after that were much less attuned to love than Adam and Eve. And after Cain and Abel, they sank far lower. Was that just a natural artefact of their separation from you? I think not. George said that now, every 10 years, you are opening up a new portal and the children born after that are on a higher vibration. I'm guessing that you disabled the love sensitivity of mankind after Adam's family, to limit the strength of our heart bonds to Satan's realm. Thank you. Perhaps similar to antidepressant meds – to tone down the nightmare – tone down everything. And to make it easier for you to extricate us from the tangled web of sin that was imprisoning us. Thank you for all the unknown things you did to save us. Probably most of them we may never know.

I read in the one-hour lecture today that before you could erect your Kingdom, it was providentially necessary that Satan establish his distorted and false version of the Three Blessings so that we could overcome those on the global level and establish your Kingdom. That was why you made America as a microcosm of the world – very different from Israel or Korea – which were very homogenous – even though America is the Second Israel. By overcoming Satan's three false blessings in America, it represents doing so in the entire world. That is reason number two for the world wars. It is similar to the battle of David and Goliath. When David stepped out to fight Goliath, he spiritually took on the mantle of Israel's elder son. A son of hyojeong. By having a symbolic war between those two, you limited the risk of damage to the chosen people – your people. Thank you for giving America the chance to redeem ourselves by putting us in that position. We won't fail you.

I love you so very much. Do you have something to share with me?
Eternally and faithfully yours,
Laurence

Dearest Laurence,
The fall of Adam and Eve was a sudden tsunami. It was overwhelming beyond words. The fabric of creation unraveled. The entire purpose of creation, the reason for my creating for billions of years vanished before my eyes. Then it was gone. The complete loss of your loved ones echoes through the universe. Then it becomes so empty. Total silence. Nothing comes back. My infinite love, poured out in urgent desperation just disappeared into a black hole. Dead silence.
Yes, there are stages of grief. I went through all of them.
First, during the generation between Adam and Eve's fall and the growth of their children. And then with the murder of Abel. The MURDER. That was Satan's official claim over the cosmos. Like the Death Star destroying an entire galaxy.
After that my grief exploded beyond comprehension. I had to come to terms with the immeasurable enormity of the task facing me. I had to concentrate so strenuously to find and receive even the tiniest expression of goodness among mankind just to maintain myself and my sanity. Even just one person who could feel my heart and exhibit kindness or love became so precious.
Creation was effortless. I was inspired in love to give 200%. It was never a burden. But restoration has been torture. Each step takes so much effort. It has been indescribably draining. Like climbing a mountain with 1000 pounds of weights, or trying to run in wet cement.

We are finally back to where we were, and much further. We still need to complete the ideal though. At the time of Adam and Eve, that only required that they receive the Blessing. Now we need to establish Cheon Il Guk as a real nation. We are so close. I will not take any chances this time.
You are correct in your understanding of America's role, very similar to David's. I am with America. As long as there is a core of faith, I will make sure you don't fail. There is and you won't. This is the time.
Finally, finally.
Thank you. Thank you.
Eternally yours,
Heavenly Parent.

7/28/22 *We Are In The Kingdom Building Business Now. You Wanted More Responsibility? You Have It. Unlimited. Create Something Holy Out Of The Ruins Of This Old World. I'll Be Your Absolutely Faithful Wing Man. This Is Going To Be Thrilling.*

Good morning Dearest Heavenly Parent,
I hope you are feeling inspired today. I realize that your inspiration could only be a net inspiration, the residual of the balance between your pain and your hope. I'm so sorry. I am feeling the hope perhaps because my sensitivity is so dull, I haven't felt much of anything, but now I feel great hope and energy. Thank you!
Dr. Yong shared Father's description of two types of members this morning, Intellectual and Spiritual. Intellectuals are developing inwardly and spiritual people are developing outwardly learning how to engage with the world. Throughout history you have been able to find a few good spiritual people who could be absolutely obedient, and they became your levers to move reality. They didn't understand very much. You couldn't really describe them as co-creators, or as children in that sense, but rather, as faithful servants of heart – who could feel and be inspired by your love and spirit. Interestingly, the Kabbalah did reveal your truth in important ways. It was behind the scenes, but through Rabbi Gamaliel the Kabbalah providence attempted to intervene in Jesus's providence, albeit unsuccessfully.
Jesus was surely the first perfected union of the intellectual and spiritual. He did transform reality. He was the first real co-creator with you. I'm sure he was intimately aware of the Kabbalah.
Father came as the perfection of the union between intellectual and spiritual, the perfection of your ideal of co-creator. Thank you for True Parents.
In my life I felt that I was clearly an intellectual, and that my spiritual sensitivities have been very underdeveloped. I feel that this was very intentional on your part, to protect me as you raised me up for a very

significant external mission. Thank you for that protection. My life has been extremely guided and protected.

Interestingly you appointed 4 spirits to guide our ancestral committees: 2 men who were perhaps the foremost intellectuals, Rabbi Gamaliel, the Kabbalah Master Holy Man; and Dr. George, a cutting-edge computer scientist who practiced practical aestheticism. The other two, our two maternal grandmothers endured quietly during WW2 while their children suffered and underwent great dangers. They both developed deep mother's hearts as the providence for the mission of True Parents was laid.

I deeply appreciate the protection through my period of indirect dominion – although as a result I felt distant from you and unfulfilled, and very externally motivated. Thank you for guiding me to fulfill Cheon Bo, after which you began to accelerate the process of helping me upgrade my heart and spirit. I feel that my life is now coming into balance and that I can now stand as a true co-creator with you. I am so profoundly blessed. Eternally thank you!

I hope you have something to share with me today.

Love eternally,
Laurence

Dear Laurence,
Thank you for your thoughtful understanding. Those who can be absolutely united with me, one in heart AND have matured both intellectually and spiritually are the substantial embodiments of the ideal world at this time of the building of the Heavenly Kingdom. As the Principle states, science and religion have been on separate tracks to resolve human ignorance since the Fall, but must be united in the last days. How will that happen? In individuals. You are microcosms of the cosmos. Institutions are comprised of individuals. An institution can't combine religion and science if the individuals of that institution can't do so within themselves. Those who can truly do it, as citizens of Cheon Il Guk are the real pioneers of the Kingdom of Heaven. There are some now, but many more coming.

But intellect is not just science, it includes economics which becomes the basis for politics. We are in the Kingdom building business now. You wanted more responsibility? You have it. Unlimited. Create something holy out of the ruins of this old world.

I'll be your absolutely faithful wing man. This is going to be thrilling.
Love eternally,
Heavenly Parent

7/29/22 You Have No Idea How Precious Your Grandchildren Are, But I Do. Thank You For This Opportunity To Spend Time With Them.

Dearest Heavenly Parent,
This has been a long day trying to love and support my family. I'm so happy to be able to spend this time with you tonight and exhale. Even as I want to give even more to you, I can see how important it is to me and to you that I fully invest in my family as well. You have repeatedly mentioned that as has Dr. Yong – family is my front line. I want to build heaven and expand heaven. But never at the expense of my relationship with you. That would be an oxymoron. I am so deeply grateful for each precious member of our family. You have blessed us beyond measure.
And thank you for speaking through Muriel tonight regarding the issue with my CPAP. I'm so happy to be able to have restful sleep this weekend.
I love you eternally. Would you like to share something tonight?
Laurence

Dearest Laurence,
Thank you for your efforts today. This is an important weekend for your family. Leave it up to me, I'm significantly involved. You have no idea how precious your grandchildren are, but I do. Thank you for this opportunity to spend time with them.
Please have a deeply joyful and heartistic weekend. Please inspire the people.
Love eternally,
Heavenly Parent

7/30/22 *You Have Been Working For Over 21 Years To Manifest Hyojeong Culture Through Your Songs. It Has Made A Significant Impact In The Universe And Now You Are In A Great Position To Share Your Understanding And Multiply It And Inspire Others.*

Dearest Heavenly Parent,
Thank you for this rich and full day. When I offered my presentation today, I learned and understood so much as you spoke through me. It touched many people's hearts.
Also, thank you for providing new special friendships for Gianna and Abram. That completely transformed their hearts. So precious.
And finally, thank you for the chance to sing tonight. I felt your heart as I sang and I believe it moved others as well. I want to work hard to deepen my relationship with you every day. Thank you.
I hope you have something to share with me tonight.
I love you eternally,
Laurence

Dearest Laurence,
Thank you for sharing your heart today at Camp Shehaqua in so many ways. You made a big difference in the spirit of the weekend. Others will get inspired to give more too. You have been working for over 21 years to manifest Hyojeong Culture through your songs. It has made a significant impact in the universe and now you are in a great position to share your understanding and multiply it and inspire others.
It grows. Thank you.
Love eternally,
Heavenly Parent

7/31/22 *As You Invest More And Develop Your Heart And Spirit More Deeply, You Will Be Able To Impact People Significantly In Every Area In Which You Are Involved. Keep True Mother In The Center Of All You Do And Don't Hide Her.*

Dearest Heavenly Parent,
Thank you for this precious weekend with Muriel, Gianna, Abram, and Moses at Camp Shehaqua. It was such a blessing. I'm so grateful for the ways in which you poured through me to contribute to the event, and for all the relationships you allowed me to make.
Thank you for ministering to Muriel, Gianna, and Abram, and Moses as well, each in unique and significant ways.
I realized this weekend that you have been intervening in my life since I completed my 1st three-year course of my 3rd 21-year course to prepare me to be in a position to make a significant contribution to Hyojeong Arts and Hyojeong Culture. Thank you. Music has been a great inspiration to me and I am deeply grateful. I really want to support and mentor SunHwa and the other music leaders and participants. And I deeply appreciate connecting to Jamal, as well as other 1st gens. Thank you.
Do you have a message for me tonight?
Love Eternally,
Laurence

Dearest Laurence,
You moved many hearts this weekend. Thank you. As you invest more and develop your heart and spirit more deeply, you will be able to impact people significantly in every area in which you are involved. Keep True Mother in the center of all you do and don't hide her. Morning Devotion is really important. You met some of the community members this weekend. Keep deepening those relationships. Morning Devotion community is moving to the center. Things are speeding up. Pray hard. I am always with you.
Love Eternally,
Heavenly Parent

8/1/22 Be Systematic In Materializing Your Inspirations. Inspire And Work Through Others. That's Why I Gave You Gray Hair! Have The Seriousness And Intentionality Of A Parent, The Love And Passion Of A Spouse, And The Innocence And Purity And Humility And Sense Of Wonder Of An Infant. In Other Words, Be The 4 Great Realms Of Heart.

Dearest Heavenly Parent,
What a magnificent day today after last night's rain. Bright blue sky with white clouds moving swiftly high above the full green trees. The chickens rushing out in joy to return to their range after 3 days cooped up. Life is so profoundly sweet.
Dear Heavenly Father, I'm so sorry that it has taken me 70 years to grow up. True Father connected so deeply with your heart starting at the age of 15. I can finally feel your heart so close to me, and I can see from your perspective much more naturally now. I sincerely regret that it took me so long to reach this place, and that so much of my life was spent in the growing. But I feel that all those years were also filled with training and amazing family blessings, even though my heart and mind were still immature. Now I will turn 70 this month. But True Mother is 80 and she is reshaping the entire cosmos. And she had so much more of an intense and burdensome life than me.
I hope and pray that I can at least give my utmost sincerity and investment until the age of 84, and if possible until 91, so that I can contribute more for the fulfillment of your ideal and True Parents' ideal. But I am 100% happy to place myself in your hands. Use me as you see fit. Call me home whenever you choose. Let your kingdom come and your will be done! I am eternally grateful that you found me and resurrected me. I love you so much.
I deeply hope that you can share something with me now.
Eternally yours,
Laurence

Dearest Laurence,
Thank you for your heart, and humility, and willingness to pour your energy and creativity into any mission. You have deeply inspired me. For you to have restored yourself from where you started to where you are now in 49 years is very inspiring. You will inspire millions through your transformation. Please don't dwell on missed opportunities. I have had to work so long and hard to overcome that point myself. The very act of dwelling on missed opportunities creates new missed opportunities – and that is a sin.
You literally have unlimited opportunities at this very moment. Far more than you can ever substantialize. Focus. Be systematic in materializing your inspirations. Inspire and work through others. That's why I gave you gray hair! Have the seriousness and intentionality of a parent, the love and passion of a spouse, and the innocence and purity and humility and sense of wonder of an infant. In other words, be the 4 great realms of heart. Apply them in each of your relationships. You will surely multiply the treasures I have given to you. Your utmost sincerity moves my heart. And when my heart is moved, the entire creation is moved and mobilized. You've got this. We've got this. Kudos!
Love Eternally,
Heavenly Parent.

8/2/22 There Are No Shades Or Degrees Of My Faith And Love And Loyalty. You Are My Son. Try Me. Challenge Me. I Will Not Fail You. I Will Not Disappoint You. That Is My Solemn Oath And Promise To You.

Good Morning Dearest Heavenly Parent,
What a precious day! Thank you for Morning Devotion today, you shared so much through Dr. Yong, and I was able to share too, and I felt your heart so close. And thank you for the chance to offer "It's a Beautiful Thing". I want to become a tree of life and tree of love and challenge myself to inherit from True Parents. I want to become a champion of hyojeong like my True Father, like Jesus, and like David was before him.
I want to embrace you in tears of gratitude and deep boundless love. I want to testify to True Mother so powerfully that no one can deny.
Heavenly Parent, you have continually showered this world and me with your love and tears.
I pray that you have something to share with me today to accelerate my internal growth.
Love forever,
Laurence

Dear Laurence,

Yes, I am with you always, forever. That is the internal meaning of Passover. Never forget. I am always with you forever. I was with David. I was with Moses. I was with Joshua as he headed out to dissolve the elements of Jericho with faith and hyojeong.

I was with Jesus when he stared down Satan, and welcomed torture and death in order to create a path forward where none existed. I was with Father, embracing him, loving him, crying for him as he rejoiced in the opportunity to vindicate my honor, being tortured to the edge of death and beyond. I proclaimed that he could not die. I moved the armies of the entire planet to free him from hell as he stood facing his executioners.

Yes, I was with each of them, I never looked away, not even one blink. And now I am also with you. Just like that. There are no shades or degrees of my faith and love and loyalty. You are my son. Try me. Challenge me. I will not fail you. I will not disappoint you.

That is my solemn oath and promise to you.

Please reread this again and again until you understand it so deeply in your heart. Please don't just understand it. Please live it. Please celebrate it. Please explode it! True Parents have given every ounce of their beings, over and over, to establish Cheon Il Guk. You are an owner. Do what owners do. Manifest Cheon Il Guk.

Blessings. Eternally,
Heavenly Parent

8/3/22 *I Am Ready To Take You Out For A Spin. I Have Been Working On You For A Long Time With Great Care And Attention To Detail. You Still Have A Long Way To Go, But You Are Road Worthy And You Are Very Powerful And Exciting.*

Dearest Most Beloved Heavenly Parent,

Last night I listened to many of the unfamiliar songs I have written over the years. I was very moved by how they reflect your gamdong in my life all these years. You are amazing and I owe everything to you. I am sorry that I am not doing more for you and True Parents. I'll try to focus harder, and to fit more into each day, each hour, each minute. It's really true that in love there is eternity in one second. Please help me stay deeply plugged in to your love so I can focus more and give more continually. I promise to do my very utmost not to squander or waste even one precious drop of your love, but to strive to multiply it more each day. I promise to do my very utmost never to take it for granted, never to become arrogant or feel entitled, but to maintain the heart of a parent and the shoes of a servant. Please permit me, and assist me

to penetrate deeper and deeper into your heart and shimjeong every day, so that I can support and represent you and True Mother so much more profoundly and effectively every day. Please use me. I am thrilled and honored to surrender myself to you in any moment. Those holy moments are my treasures. I grant you complete and unqualified permission to use me at any time, and 24/7 if you choose, in order to advance your ideal and accelerate your providence. Please do. Please do. I love you so much, but long to love you so much more.
Eternally yours,
Laurence

Dear Laurence,
Are you really ready for me to amp it up? I'm ready. It's like the exotic sports cars that Gamaliel test drove during STF. Those were unforgettable memories for me. I am ready to take you out for a spin. I have been working on you for a long time with great care and attention to detail. You still have a long way to go, but you are road worthy and you are very powerful and exciting. I accept your offer, your offering. Stay very focused, you won't want to miss anything. Anticipate that I will be driving events. Lead with love and appreciation for each person. Find me in each one, I'm totally there. Let's create synapses! No more time to be coy. Be loving, sincere, and tee up the people for me to touch their hearts.
We can create a whirlwind.
Love eternally – in every second,
Heavenly Parent

8/4/22 *Lead With Your Heart. Actually, Lead With My Heart. Feel To Your Core How Very Long I Have Longed To Share The Greatest News With Whomever You Are With, Especially With Ministers. Feel My Longing Heart For Them. Become My Longing Heart For Them. That's Who Jesus Was.*

Dearest Heavenly Parent,
What an exciting day, thank you!! I feel like we are going out on a test drive together. This morning, Dr. Yong spoke about the imperative of using each moment to testify to True Parents. And Dan spoke about the Sabbath and how you have been waiting to rest through us as we take over the tasks of restoration.
And this morning (hopefully) Justin will record "Tamar". Please be with him and inspire him to do a powerful job on that recording so that that music will pry open the hearts of all who hear it to drink in the words of my interview with Dietmar – so it can go viral.

And this morning I will visit the (a local) Church. Thank you for preparing that Minister to receive True Parents and become a champion member of ACLC. Please help me to totally step aside so that you can speak directly to his original mind and deeply, deeply, convict him.
I love you so deeply. I am so ready.
I deeply hope you have another transformational message for me today.
Eternally,
Laurence

Dear Laurence,
I too am very excited to do our "test drive" together today. You did a great job with time this morning and I was able to speak powerfully through you to the Spirit World during your Divine Principle reading. I will prepare the way at the (local) Church.
Remember what Dr. Yong said about the power of a longing heart. Lead with your heart. Actually, lead with my heart. Feel to your core how very long I have longed to share the greatest news with whomever you are with, especially with ministers. Feel my longing heart for them. Become my longing heart for them. That's who Jesus was.
I have such deep faith in you.
Eternally yours,
Heavenly Parent

8/5/22 *Please Give Out My Blessings Everywhere You Go, Everyone You Meet. None Are Accidental. In The Spirit World, All Of Their Ancestors Are Waiting In Line To Present Their Descendants To You.*

Dearest Most Beloved Heavenly Parent,
I am sure enjoying this test drive! I need to be totally on my game, here in the passenger seat, so I don't miss anything. This morning, in Morning Devotion, you helped me connect with Tom, who agreed to review my presentation. Thank you.
And I also heard back from Tyler who endorsed "The Carpenter" video. Then in my prayer I felt a strong urgency to pray for transforming denominations and you reminded me of the Mandeans and Dr. Yong's testimony from this morning. They represent John the Baptist literally. In their transformation I hope and pray that the gate can truly be opened wide for many, many more denominations to be transformed like popcorn.
I hope Dr. Yong can receive my inspiration well. I understand that he has been working with the Mandeans for some time at True Mother's request. And then, as I continued my prayer, shortly after praying for the minister who we went to visit yesterday, you inspired him to call me. Light Speed!

You are awesome. I am so humbled. If you can work it out, I'd love to have Daryl and Justin perform at my 70th. How cool would that be! Just saying!
I love you eternally.
Do you have something to share with me?
Love forever,
Laurence

Dearest Laurence,
I am having great fun. Not bad for just a day or two! Thank you for your focus on staying focused. Each second is so valuable. As in your song, Jesus' regret is not being able to give more.
70 is 10x7, and 10 is the number of returning to me. Welcome home! Please give out my blessings everywhere you go, everyone you meet. None are accidental. In the Spirit World, all of their ancestors are waiting in line to present their descendants to you.
Balance this position and responsibility with your unique position and responsibility to spearhead the new economy of the Heavenly Kingdom. That is your mission, but as Dr. Yong stated, witnessing and salvation are the top priority. True Mother has emphasized that repeatedly. Your online interviews with Dietmar will have great impact. Time to pick up the pace. Let those horses run.
Love Eternally,
Heavenly Parent

8/6/22 *As Your Capacity Develops, So Will Your Resources. And As Your Resources Develop, So Will Your Responsibilities, Both From Me, But Significantly From Your Own Initiative. I Really Love That!*

Good Morning Dearest Most Beloved Heavenly Parent,
In today's Morning Devotion, Dr. Yong said that when we totally determine to do something for the will, that is our 5% and then you make it happen. At least that's the case when you give us a mission.
But that's not the only framework in which you can work, is it? True Mother determined to establish Cheon Il Guk substantially on Earth. She knew your will. Yes, you had given her the title and responsibility, but she took the mission on herself and significantly defined that mission on the foundation of three years of devotion to True Father and You, following Father's ascension. Even though we determine to take on more responsibility, our capacity needs to develop step by step or we will not fulfill. I guess that's the meaning of "God never gives us more than we can handle". Even though we determine to do something, and even though it is in line with the will, if our capacity is not sufficient, then even with your 95%, we still will fall short. I get it.

I hope and pray that you can help me to rapidly grow my capacity, as an owner of Cheon Il Guk, as a Tribal Messiah, so that I can accomplish more for You, True Parents, and the providence.

And on a related issue, I really hope you can powerfully work to help me succeed through my power point interview. I shared it yesterday with the local minister, after we visited his church and he called me back. Please speak powerfully to his heart and convict him to receive and embrace True Parents and the Principle. I pray that he and I can become dear and close friends – even family, and that you can claim and raise up his son's family as well. Also, please work through Tom and Justin to help me perfect the power point presentation, and please work through Dietmar to help me present it to the world in a manner that will go totally viral. I am so grateful.

And thank you for the opportunity to share about creativity and songwriting at the hyojeong seminar. I am deeply inspired about that.

Love eternally,
Laurence

Dearest Laurence,
Thank you for your earnest desire to do more for the will and your sincere hyojeong and dedication to deepen your heart and our relationship. Please know that you are on a very steep trajectory, and that your capacity is expanding rapidly. I am very inspired and excited to work with you.

Your presentation will happen and take on a life of its own. Kevin is supporting it. Jesus is supporting it. You've got a great team! Be 100% confident. I will work with your local minister. I wouldn't have asked you to visit if he wasn't prepared. You will see.

As your capacity develops, so will your resources. And as your resources develop, so will your responsibilities, both from me, but significantly from your own initiative. I really love that!

Thank you, Laurence.
Love Eternally,
Heavenly Parent

8/7/22 *You Are Hungry To Achieve Too, But It Is Nothing Compared To How Hungry I Am. That Enormous Gap Is The Measure Of How Grateful I Am That You Are Going On This Path. That Gap Is The Longing And Hope That I Cherish That Now, Finally Some Of It Can Begin To Happen.*

Dearest Heavenly Parent,
You are such a precious and loving parent. You are the King and Queen of gamdong. I feel bad that I asked for something for myself, but in one day you nailed it down, and both Daryl and Justin agreed to attend my party. And yesterday I finalized the schedule and transportation to attend the songwriter workshop in New York. Please help me crystalize my presentations.
1. The nature of creating a song based on your creative process, modelled on a human being
2. Perspective in a song based on the 3-object purpose; and
3. Music choices to convey the heart and essence of the song

I want to offer a deeper understanding based on your heart and truth.
Dear Father, thank you for your mighty works with Dietmar. I am so inspired and awed. Please powerfully prepare him to help me share this message. Please work through Justin today and Tom to help me perfect the presentation so that you can work through it in the most powerful way. I have 1000% confidence, conviction, and gratitude that you will do this and I offer it all to you and True Parents.
And thank you for nailing down our visit to Janet's family and for protecting Andy and Jordanne, and a million other incredible acts of generosity that you shower on me and on our tribe every day.
My birthday will mark the 7th anniversary of your revelation to me. You have 21 more days to think about it. This journaling is deeply and profoundly inspiring, but I suspect it is not the final destination in our relationship. If there is more you want to share with me, anytime is perfect, but you did share with me how significant 7-year courses are from your perspective, and certainly in my life.
I totally promise, you can count on me.
Do you have something you would like to share with me now?
Love eternally,
Laurence
PS: I wanted to mention that I am so sorry that this morning before I woke up, Hyo Jin Nim was in my dream playing music, but I stayed distant in space and emotionally. I deeply honor Hyo Jin Nim, and would deeply love to learn and inherit from him, - if possible, even before I speak at the songwriting seminar in New York.
Love again and always,
Laurence

Dearest Laurence,
Thank you for your beautiful message today. You are touching my heart just as you say I am touching yours. It is very healing. I am so inspired to support you. Yes, you are approaching 70. It is an important milestone for you. I am very proud of you, of your faith, and your heart, and your spirit of ownership. Those three things are

profoundly empowering for me. There is so much I want to do. You are hungry to achieve too, but it is nothing compared to how hungry I am. That enormous gap is the measure of how grateful I am that you are going on this path. That gap is the longing and hope that I cherish that now, finally some of it can begin to happen.
And thank you so much for this journaling. It is binding us together tighter and closer each day in unbreakable unity. And that is so critically important given the magnitude of what we are about to do together.
Thank you, thank you, thank you.
Eternally,
Heavenly Parent

8/8/22 *Please Don't Be Concerned About Anyone Else's Recognition. That Doesn't Matter Because I Recognize You And That Will Become More Apparent To Others As Time Goes On Including Both Your Family And Leaders In The Movement. At The Right Time Doors Will Open. Before Then, Not Being Recognized Is A Significant Blessing.*

Dearest Heavenly Parents,
I love you both very much. I love my wife, whom you gave to me, so very much. I love my family very deeply, and my tribe. You have blessed us so profoundly and watched over us. I am looking forward now to my 70th birthday celebration with dear friends and family. I want to dedicate that celebration to you and to True Parents and I hope that you can enjoy it so much more than I will, as we begin to expand Cheon Il Guk. Thank you for making it possible.
Today I modified my goals for 2021-2027 to now include deepening my relationships of love also with Hyo Jin Nim, Heung Jin Nim, and Dae Mo Nim. I am so grateful for the attentions you pay to the goals I set, and how you help me fulfill them internally and externally. Thank you. I'm looking forward to our upcoming visits in Massachusetts with Danniel's family, and in North Carolina, with Janet's family, and in New York for Colin's wedding, and to teaching in New York at the Hyojeong Songwriter's seminar.
And I hope Muriel and I can visit Dr. and Mrs. Durst on December 10, and see David then and Linda too if she is still alive.
And I hope you can very actively guide my collaboration with Dietmar, and both protect and empower that collaboration dramatically beyond anything we could ever imagine, to support True Mother at this time.
And of course, please help me manifest, on behalf of Heaven, the development projects I am seeking to fulfill.

May your Kingdom come, so quickly now, on Earth and in Heaven. Glory to you and True Parents!
I hope you have something to share now.
Eternally,
Laurence

Dearest Laurence,
Thank you for all you are doing. You are touching many people through our collaboration, and it is only in the formation stage. We will grow together dramatically in all directions on the foundation you are setting, and it will all be deeply rooted in True Parents and The Will. I am looking forward too, to your 70th birthday, I would never miss it! Please don't be concerned about anyone else's recognition. That doesn't matter because I recognize you and that will become more apparent to others as time goes on including both your family and leaders in the movement. At the right time doors will open. Before then, not being recognized is a significant blessing.
Any recognition is not for your personal glory – but rather only to allow you to make a greater offering to True Parents. Ultimately all rewards are eternal rewards in the spirit world. Everything else is just ego pandering and transient at best, but very harmful to the extent that it disrupts your relationship with me. I love you too much to risk that. Please don't ever let the world's acclaim come between us. My acclaim I freely offer you!
Eternally yours,
Heavenly Parent

8/9/22 *You Have Unlocked A Key To Dramatically Speed Up The Restoration Of The Spirit World. I Could Not Ask, It Had To Be Offered Voluntarily. You Have Done That.*

Dearest Heavenly Parent,
Thank you for another electric and awesome day! There are two birds talking to each other, one in our back yard and one in the front. They are continually chirping back and forth in give and take. Your heart permeates nature!
This morning's talk was another riveting presentation from Dr. Yong focusing on preparing for and meeting the moment, and not letting the moment pass unfulfilled. Thank you for the Blessing to be able to share about co-creatorship and the infinite opportunities of each moment, and how getting in touch with that reality brings the cosmic value of each moment into sharp focus. I also appreciated the chance to share with Hanmi privately about her birthing experiences.

I was also inspired to hear Dr. Yong speak about you sending the Holy Spirit to America. Please do!!!! I am imminently anticipating that!

Then after that, I understood more clearly the power of Hoon Dok Hae in unity with you to resurrect the entire Spirit World. Even True Father can't do that without a physical body, but we can! I hope Dr. Yong can resonate with the vision and launch a powerful initiative in conjunction with his Hoon Dok Hae conditions to empower you to dramatically accelerate the resurrection of the Spirit World.

Through that initiative from the physical side together with the returning resurrection from the Spirit World side, surely we can create such a powerful give and take between the two realms centering on your heart and will.

I am so exhilarated with our partnership, and yet I feel as if we are only at the very formation stage so far. Heavenly Parent, this is profoundly mind blowing!

Do you have something to share with me?

Eternally yours,
Laurence

Dearest Laurence,
You have unlocked a key to dramatically speed up the restoration of the Spirit World. I could not ask, it had to be offered voluntarily. You have done that. You have done well reporting to Dr. Yong. I set the table by having you report on Morning Devotion and he was inspired by your sharing.

I believe your email to him will bring fruit. Like you, he is someone who deeply longs to fulfill and is ambitious to fulfill The Will.

Your birthday celebration will be an important Blessing ceremony too. I will try to get Richard and Tecla there as well. This is a harvesting of your music providence. Very fitting and significant for your 70th birthday. It is not an accident that Andy is attending. Please pray for him. He is an extremely chosen person.

Perhaps there may be more guests.

Yes, we are only barely beginning. But this is a cosmic beginning. Thank you!

Eternally,
Heavenly Parent

8/10/22 I Really Love Responding To Your Requests Because Your Heart Is Connected With Mine So Deeply Now. Can You Imagine When Everyone's Heart Is Connected In That Way And Every Moment Of Every Minute Will Be Like Giving The One You Love The Most Precious Gift They Deeply Longed For? Multiply That By Two

Trillion People And Growing! How Much Joy Do You Think That Will Be?

Good Morning Dearest Heavenly Parent,
Sitting here listening to the sounds of nature and feeling the warm sunlight bathing my back, I feel profoundly embraced in your precious love. Thank you!
This morning in Morning Devotion, I was touched by Dr. Yong's message that it is not through our organization or position that we gain energy and life, but through our relationship of hyojeong with you. I feel so extraordinarily blessed. And then Dr. Yong sent me a private text thanking and recognizing me – such gamdong!
I was also deeply inspired by the clarity and focus of True Mother's vision for establishing your kingdom in the wake of the complete meltdown of the value systems of both Communism and Democracy. Thank you for the last days. I sincerely hope that you are experiencing exhilaration in this moment, like Beethoven conducting his 5th Symphony after enduring so much tribulation in his own life. You deserve the exhilaration a trillion times more than Beethoven!!! Dear Heavenly Parent, Muriel seemed shaken this morning as she was leaving. Thank you with all my heart for your love and care and protection for her and our entire family. We are eternally grateful,
And thank you for your answer to my request to receive additional guidance and insight for my presentation on hyojeong songwriting. I feel that I now have what I need. You are so amazing!
Do you have a message for me this morning?
Love eternally,
Laurence

Dearest Laurence,
It is such a pleasure and joy to have give and take with you. I really love responding to your requests because your heart is connected with mine so deeply now.
Can you imagine when everyone's heart is connected in that way and every moment of every minute will be like giving the one you love the most precious gift they deeply longed for? Multiply that by two trillion people and growing! How much joy do you think that will be?
But then think about the fact that those gifts are not for themselves, but that their deepest longings are to be able to give the most precious things to the ones they love and care for! So immediately after the joy of my giving my gifts, they will multiply as they are given horizontally among my children multiplying love and joy and happiness. That will of course stimulate more joy and desire to give back more.
Yes, you have a very good intuition about my ideal, my dream. I like your phrase, "A cosmic critical mass explosion of true love, joy, beauty,

goodness, family, culture, and creativity – which grows exponentially and eternally". Did you ever think about taking up poetry? You've got quite a knack!
Please know – all things are well and growing better and better every day!
Thank you – you give me great peace and encouragement.
Eternally,
Heavenly Parent

8/11/22 *I've Got Your Back On This One. It Is Extraordinarily Important To Me. You Have Angels Ahead Of You. And I Can Feel How Anxious You Are To Make It Happen. Good. That's Important. That Fire In Your Heart For My Sake Will Keep You Young And Focused. Your Family Will Totally Close Ranks Around You, Wait And See.*

Dearest Most Beloved Heavenly Parent,
These dialogues have become the highlights of my day – and they make the rest of each day come to life in your precious love. I can never thank you enough.
Today, reading my Hoon Dok Hae and offering my vitality elements to be used to raise up all the people in the Spirit World I understood that if I diligently offer myself in that way, then I can make an unforgettable impression of love on each person in the Spirit World. That is surely a path to freedom in the Spirit World, in addition to our physical and spiritual children. And it will surely expedite your freedom as well. If thousands and millions take up this offering, what an amazing transformation we can achieve. Perhaps it can be incorporated into our worship services. I hope so, with an emphasis on the free and willing offering of each individual participating.
Dear Father, I'm also so grateful for all your assistance and insight helping me to create the Hyojeong songwriting presentation I really wanted to create. I hope it can make a powerful impact, and that it can inspire many in the future. I am looking forward to our visit with Danniel and his extended family. Thank you for this privilege and Blessing.
I am eternally your son, and I pray that you can open up ways to serve you more every day. You are amazing.
In deepest gratitude,
Laurence

Dearest Laurence,
Thank you so very much. You are working very hard to free me, and you are able to take such a big view, you are inheriting much from

True Father's heart. The providence won't end with True Parents. Their dream and mine is that our children can pick up the vision and build on that foundation. You have the ability to pass that vision along to many, many more. That is why George described your responsibilities in developing the Bering Strait Railroad and Tunnel and the Peace King Highway as that of a salesman. A salesman has derogatory connotations, but in your case they don't apply. Substitute motivational visionary – although of course it is True Parents' vision. But I know you understand the role. No, you won't complete the project yourself. But you will inspire the world to complete it, and in the process, you will accelerate the establishment of the Kingdom of Heaven. That's a pretty good gig for a carpet cleaner, right? I've got your back on this one. It is extraordinarily important to me. You have angels ahead of you. And I can feel how anxious you are to make it happen. Good. That's important. That fire in your heart for my sake will keep you young and focused. Your family will totally close ranks around you, wait and see.

And yes, the condition of offering your physical body and vitality elements during Hoon Dok Hae is very profound and significant. Share that widely.

I am so grateful, and so motivated by you.

Eternally yours,
Heavenly Parent

8/12/22 *I Am Deeply Moved By Your Family And I Deeply Appreciate The Dedicated Work Of Your Ancestors. They Are So Exemplary, And They Are Making It Possible For You To Do Extraordinary And Unprecedented Things For The Will.*

Good morning my Dearest Heavenly Parent. This journaling makes me laugh and reminds me of Dr. Seuss's "Green Eggs and Ham" – Can you do it on a bus? Thank you for being with me in every situation. I am so deeply grateful. I am really looking forward to this extended weekend and want to make each moment precious, filled with your holy heart and shimjeong. I want to connect so deeply in heart with Dan, Kim, Quincy, & Remy and with JP and Dianne. Thank you for blessing us with such amazing family!!!

I am even more committed now regarding the restoration of the entire Spirit World through Hoon Dok Hae by offering our vitality elements up to you to be amplified and used for the resurrection of all the spirits in hell and others in Spirit World needing resurrection. I totally trust that you can do that in such a way so as not to drain those of us who are making that offering, but even to enhance and grow our own spirits in the process, too. Heavenly

Parent, if I am not correct in this, please let me know immediately! Thank you!
Dearest Father, if you would like us to view the events of True Father's 10th Seung Hwa anniversary, I hope you can inspire the Faures & or the Baers to want to watch, and especially want Quincy to watch if she's awake. Otherwise, I will focus on loving and investing in them.
I'm deeply appreciating and enjoying our test drive! I'm ready to purchase if you are. I love you eternally!!!
I hope you have something to share with me today.
Love,
Laurence

Dear Laurence,
Yes, I will always be with you, even on a bus! This will certainly be a very special weekend for you and your family. Please love them with all your heart. Gamaliel is going through challenges right now, between family and work. Be sure to love him even more. The incident at Sean's was a sign that will help him connect more with me. He is being prepared for great responsibilities.
Things are working out well for Andy and Jordanne. Jordanne will emerge from this experience much more confident and much less anxious. And they will be much more united. Andy will connect much more with me. He too has a special and important mission. I am deeply moved by your family and I deeply appreciate the dedicated work of your ancestors. They are so exemplary, and they are making it possible for you to do extraordinary and unprecedented things for the will.
This will be a wonderful weekend. Blessings!
Love eternally,
Heavenly Parent

8/13/22 *As An Owner And Co-Creator, You Have The Authority To Launch This. I Am Electrically Inspired And 100% With You. This Is Transformational. We Shall Bring Down The Old Dominion And Raise Up All The Slaves To Become Heavenly Free Citizens.*

Good morning Dearest Heavenly Parent,
I am so grateful to you for my life and my family! Just reading Gamaliel's rebuttal, I felt something of the pride True Parents felt when Hyo Jin Nim led the rally to bring down the wall in Berlin. Thank you and thanks to True Parents, Jesus, Hyo Jin Nim, Heung Jin Nim, Dae Mo Nim, and Rabbi Gamaliel for helping to raise up my son and my family.

In Morning Devotion I felt so inspired to be an owner an inheritor and a co-creator. It is very real now and it infuses all my relations, interactions and intentions. I am particularly inspired to mobilize many brothers and sisters to volunteer their vitality elements through Hoon Dok Hae to resurrect the entire Spirit World. THANK YOU.
Let's make every meeting, every day a cosmic victory!
I hope you have something to share with me.
Eternally yours,
Laurence

Dearest Laurence,
Yes, I too am very moved by Gamaliel. He is a remarkable leader for righteousness and integrity. My hand and my heart are on him. He will build on and expand your great foundation.
Thank you for your inspiration and energy to liberate and restore the entire Spirit World. It is so timely and so needed. As we dissolve Satan's claim on the physical realm, we must also do the same simultaneously in the Spirit World. Only those on the physical realm can make this happen. That is why the CheongPyeong providence has been so important. Members have voluntarily supported the movement in order to help their ancestors.
But what you are doing is on a much more universal level. As an owner and co-creator, you have the authority to launch this. I am electrically inspired and 100% with you. This is transformational.
We shall bring down the old dominion and raise up all the slaves to become Heavenly free citizens. Wow!
Love eternally,
Heavenly Parent

8/14/22 *You Have Critically Important Missions For The Providence, But Even In The Midst Of Those Important Missions, Don't Forget Your #1 Mission To Love And Communicate Your Love For Your Family And Tribe. Create A Powerful Magnet Model. Multiply Joy In Your Family. Celebrate Each Member. Encourage And Support Each Member. What Mission Could Be More Joyful Than That.*

Dearest Most Beloved Heavenly Parent,
Thank you for another beautiful new day and another deep message in Morning Devotion! Yesterday was a very precious opportunity to share with Danniel and Kim's family and with JP and Dianne. I repent for my lack of dignity eating lobster, and for the discomfort Kim felt. I hope I can take deeply to heart Dr. Yong's words about maintaining dignity with food. Please

help me to grow in that area, so I can more fully represent you in each situation.

Thank you for the chance to share more deeply with Danniel and Kim regarding True Mother and the providence and our relationship with you. Today is Sunday. This week will be filled with important meetings. Please be my heart and my words, and help me to fully surrender so that you can speak and love so powerfully. I pray for great, great success in Korea during this time honoring True Father's 10th Anniversary of his ascension. I pray my heart can be deeply connected with yours, and True Mother's.

Thank you so deeply!

Do you have something you'd like to share with me today?

Love eternally,

Laurence

Dear Laurence,

As Dr. Yong shared today, it is no longer the age of faith or proclamation – although your interviews with Dietmar are vitally important. It is the age of showing heaven in your relationship with Muriel and with the families of each of your children. Shower each of them with love. Nourish them. You have critically important missions for the providence, but even in the midst of those important missions, don't forget your #1 mission to love and communicate your love for your family and tribe. Create a powerful magnet model. Multiply joy in your family. Celebrate each member. Encourage and support each member.

What mission could be more joyful than that.

Claim the heaven you are already living in. It took so much to establish it. Open your heart and recognize it with gratitude every day.

I love you eternally,

Heavenly Parent

8/15/22 *Please Inherit Father's Heart, Who Treated Public Funds With Utmost Care, Even Fear, Knowing How Dangerous Their Misuse Is. Most Of The Current Leadership In The US Government And Corporate World Has Committed This Sin. We Must Raise Up A New Standard For The Management Of All Things.*

Good morning dearest Heavenly Parent,

Thank you for this amazing visit to Danniel's family and the deepening of our heart connections. I am so grateful.

And thank you for rapidly unravelling the government covid vaccine oppression based on religious objections. That reaffirms the supremacy of freedom of religion, even as it exposes Satan's lies. I'm so grateful that you have inspired Gamaliel to participate in that process.

And thank you for your encouragement of my inspiration to offer our vitality elements to resurrect the entire Spirit World (at least all the spirit men) with your collaboration. I am inspired to encourage everyone to participate in this rescue mission! I hope you can give me guidance on how to navigate that process for the greatest impact.

Thank you for loving me and my family so profoundly. I really want to return your love a million times!!!

Eternally yours,
Laurence

Dearest Laurence,
Good morning! Let's have another great day together! Yes, I will surely guide you to expand the vitality element ministry you have launched. It is historic. And yes, the Satanic structures are rapidly crumbling. I am so elated!

Today's message regarding the responsibilities of Japan to focus on restoring the financial resources for the providence is in no way a repudiation of your mission. It is true that Japan has given everything, as a mother, to give life to this movement, but that does not mean they are creating Heaven's economy. You have dramatic and important work ahead of you. I know you won't fall into the old trap of imagining that all you achieve is for your own benefit. Please inherit Father's heart, who treated public funds with utmost care, even fear, knowing how dangerous their misuse is. Most of the current leadership in the US government and corporate world has committed this sin. We must raise up a new standard for the management of all things.

Please keep this point close to your heart at all times. I believe in you!
Eternally yours,
Heavenly Parent

8/16/22 *Please Keep Creating New Initiatives To Speed Up The Providence. You Are Extremely Gifted In This Regard. And You Are Humble Enough To Be Guided And Corrected. That Is My Joy.*

Dearest Most Beloved Heavenly Parent,
Thank you for this wonderful day! I'm on my way to New York City to address the Hyojeong Songwriters' workshop, and I feel good about what I have to share. Thank you for your input and I hope you can help me get out of your way so that you can deeply touch each and every participant as well as those who review this presentation in the future if it is filmed. I'm beginning to get a sense of Dr. Yong's universe now, with each day filled with

significant and powerful meetings and events where I can represent you and invest my jeongseong to try and stimulate, inspire, and educate all those I meet. What a rich life!

Today's message from Dr. Yong included the warning not to get lost in our mission, but rather to maintain the heart of a parent and shoes of a servant towards every person. I feel that my energies are dispersed across a number of missions, each of which has as its goals your liberation and the uplifting of your glory and ideal. Thank you for making my life's purpose so real and meaningful. Please guide me as I seek to expand the Hoon Dok Hae vitality element ministry for the Spirit World.

Thank you for nurturing me every day.
Do you have something to share with me today?
I love you very intensely!
Eternally,
Laurence

Dear Laurence,
Thank you for all you are doing for the will, the ideal. I am very inspired and nurtured by your life. Also, in addition to the stimulation you are giving me, I am very grateful for the substantial and important works you are doing to expedite the providence, not just on the physical level, but significantly on the spiritual level as well – the subject level.
It is important work. I will personally collaborate and guide your work. It is that important.
Please keep creating new initiatives to speed up the providence. You are extremely gifted in this regard. And you are humble enough to be guided and corrected. That is my joy.
I've got your back at the presentation today. Get some rest!
Love eternally,
Heavenly Parent

8/17/22 *You Represent The Union Of Traditional And New Age Medicine, And Of The Best Of Liberal And Conservative Ideologies. Your Unity Is A Foundation For America's Unity. That Is Crucial At This Time.*

Dearest Heavenly Parent,
Thank you for a wonderful day yesterday. I was so grateful to be able to present to the Hyojeong songwriters.
And thank you for this precious new day. Today Linda ascended. Please embrace her to your bosom as an honored member of our tribe. I hope she

can connect deeply with True Parents and with Jesus, and with Hyo Jin Nim, Heung Jin Nim, and Dae Mo Nim.
I'm so deeply grateful that you take me so seriously. It means everything to me. Within the Principle, there is really unlimited freedom to create and dream and take responsibility. I am so grateful and liberated and I urgently want to liberate you and True Parents.
Thank you!
Do you have something you would like to share with me today?
Eternally yours,
Laurence

Dearest Laurence,
I am welcoming Linda home today. It is a precious and wonderful day for both of us. Thank you for all your prayers for their couple and family.
Your relationship with David had great significance. You represent the union of traditional and new age medicine, and of the best of liberal and conservative ideologies. Your unity is a foundation for America's unity. That is crucial at this time.
Thank you,
Eternally,
Heavenly Parent

8/19/22 *True Father Gave And Gave More Than Anyone In History. He Maintained His Energy And Vitality Until He Was Over 90. Of Course, He Was Tired Sometimes, But He Pushed Through. Don't Be Afraid. Come Find Me In Your Second Wind.*

Good Morning Dearest Heavenly Parent,
It's so great to be outdoors and experience nature as I journal with you. I have been feeling tired in the mornings and I don't want to feel that way. I'm trying to limit my coffee intake so that I avoid an upset stomach, but I want to remain sharp and feel your love and energy vibrantly. Is this a function of my new condition with Hoon Dok Hae? Please clarify for me. It is my hope that by giving, I can gain more energy, and not be diminished. There is so much more that you need, and I want to accelerate and not slow down.
Can you please give me some clear and unmistakable guidance on this point?
Deeply grateful,
Laurence

Dear Laurence,
I created all things to be continually revitalized and to give. You won't disappear by giving. Especially if your heart and motivations are very high. Yours are the highest.
True Father gave and gave more than anyone in history. He maintained his energy and vitality until he was over 90. Of course, he was tired sometimes, but he pushed through. Don't be afraid. Come find me in your second wind. How many times did you experience that in cross country? Second wind means you are going deeper. From external to internal to more internal.
Same with long fasts. There are great blessings waiting for those who break through for my sake. Learn from Dr. Yong. He is a master of creating energy through give and take. You too are learning and growing stronger every day. This is important training for the missions you are taking on. Absolute faith, love, and obedience to those missions. That's your 5%. My 95% includes energy. We've got this!
Love,
Heavenly Parent

8/20/22 *You Don't Know In Your Spirit Or Heart How Long I've Waited For This Kind Of Relationship With My Children. I Am Young Again. Like When Teenagers First Discover Love – They Feel That They Can Conquer The World. That's How I Feel Now. Thanks To True Parents. Thanks To Children Like You. I Have New Life.*

Good morning Heavenly Parent,
Thank you for your clear and inspiring message yesterday. That guidance is really helpful and empowering. I also deeply appreciate it when you share unique and insightful glimpses into your own heart. I hope you can do that more frequently too. Perhaps you are, and I'm just too thick to catch it. I really want to become more spiritually sensitive as Dr. Yong was describing this morning.
The chickens are all gathered by the door of their coup waiting to be freed. I can relate. And in turn, I hope we can free all those suffering souls both in the Spirit World and around the Earth. I love you so very much, and I want to deepen that love every day. Thank you so very much!
Eternally, gratefully, loyally, and from my heart,
Love,
Laurence

Dearest Laurence,
Good morning! I am always very happy to share my heart with you. I deeply feel and appreciate your heart towards me. You don't know in

your spirit or heart how long I've waited for this kind of relationship with my children. I am young again. Like when teenagers first discover love – they feel that they can conquer the world. That's how I feel now. Thanks to True Parents. Thanks to children like you. I have new life. Yes, we can totally conquer this sad world with true love. Quickly and totally. This is just the clean-up operation now. Thank you!
There is so much I want to give you. Stick really close in heart. It will come to you, to your family, your tribe, your nation, and to this world and also the Spirit World. Have a beautiful day today.
Love eternally,
Heavenly Parent

8/21/22 *Dr. Yong Said, "This Is The Age Of Volunteers". Children Who Act Out Of Love. Or As You Call It – "Spiritual Entrepreneurs". I Have Been Dreaming Of This For All Time. I Have To Pinch Myself To Be Sure It Is Really Happening Now. It Is! You Are! Please Let Me Know What You Are Wanting To Do Each Day For The Will! I Will Mobilize The Support.*

Good Morning My Dearest Heavenly Parent,
Thank you for today's Morning Devotion. It was particularly inspiring with Dr. Yong's return to America and Dr. Rouse's wonderful testimony. Dr. Yong shared Father's words about revealing your suffering heart and the explosive power as your unimaginable pain is being released. The Lord of Creation freed from your chains. I pray for the acceleration of that liberation. True Mother pledged to complete all her goals by 2027. Surely it can happen even sooner! Please do unleash your holy power and miracles on the foundation of all the indemnity paid by True Parents. Please claim and accept the offering of our Morning Devotion community. I sincerely repent that we are still only hovering around 240 log-ins. I pray that this can expand dramatically and that we can usher in your Pentecost and fire to ignite Christianity and unleash the righteousness of America as your elder son of hyojeong.
This morning, I will focus first on supporting Muriel by pulling together the photos she is seeking.
Then at 5 pm I plan to attend Linda's zoom memorial service. Please help us to love and touch her family. I want to make this an unforgettable day for you. I love you very deeply.
I hope you have another wonderful message for me today.
Eternally yours,
Laurence

Dearest Laurence,
Your experience of Dr. Yong's return home is like what I feel each morning when you journal with me. I anticipate it, and I am deeply touched as we dialogue. As Dr. Yong mentioned today, the Blessed couples are in the highest, most privileged position under the Kingship of True Parents. And among them, still only a few are Cheon Bo victors, and among those, almost none are journaling with me. Please know how important our relationship is. I am grateful that you have shared your plan for today. I will support it. Please share your plan with me every day so we can clearly prepare and collaborate on a daily basis. That will be very powerful. As Dr. Yong said, this is the age of volunteers. Children who act out of love. Or as you call it – spiritual entrepreneurs. I have been dreaming of this for all time. I have to pinch myself to be sure it is really happening now. It is! You are! Please let me know what you are wanting to do each day for the Will! I will mobilize the support. I am extremely excited to do this. Thank you!
Eternally yours,
Heavenly Parent

8/23/22 Thank You For Making The Effort To See Off Rosi This Morning. It Means A Great Deal To Her And Her Family.

Dearest most beloved Heavenly Parent,
Today was very interesting. I felt so rested last night even though I woke up several times. Thank you. I am so grateful for deep rest. I thought it was 3:30 AM and decided to get up early to complete all my prayers before heading to Virginia for Rosi's Seung Hwa – only to find out it was actually 4:30 and I was 30 minutes behind schedule. But I am grateful I was able to complete my 1-hour lecture before Morning Devotion, and that I was able to offer Tecumseh's Poem.
Thank you for a safe ride to Manassas, VA, even though I was very low on gas. But I made it, gassed up, and arrived on time.
It was very nice to see Benjamin's family, Noah and Kathy, Ernest & Keiko, Michael and Reiko and others, and I had a wonderful deep sharing with Beverly who was very interested in both offering vitality elements and in Father's efforts to heal Jesus's relationship with his father.
I am looking forward to tonight with Jim, Linda, Graham and Kimie.
I am so grateful for the ways you are teaching me and lifting me up and so generously sharing intimate secrets with me. It is profoundly inspiring. I feel that our family is getting closer. I feel I am being prepared for the next phase of my mission.

I will totally remain faithful and not give in to worldly temptations. I pledge.
Eternally yours,
Laurence

Dear Laurence,
Thank you for making the effort to see off Rosi this morning. It means a great deal to her and her family. As you know, much was invested into their family, but only Benjamin's family remained faithful to the will. They are a really good family.
Thank you for inspiring so many in Morning Devotion. I am working to bring that community to a "boil" spiritually. You are helping in that. I am very grateful. The Morning Devotion community is central to the providence. I know you get that, and I know you are investing your best there. It definitely inspires others to do the same. I will never forget your contribution there.
Please give my love to both couples tonight.
Eternally,
Heavenly Parent

8/24/22 *Planning Is Good – But Of Course Horizontal. Inspiration Comes Vertically. No Need To Feel That You Came Up With Every Good Idea – Surprise – I Beat You To It On Virtually Every One. But… You And Me, On The Same Wavelength, With Your Hands And Feet Joyfully Engaged. Ahhh – Now That Is Miraculous.*

Good morning My Dearest Heavenly Parent,
Your candor with me and the insights from Morning Devotion help me understand how significant I am and each of the Cheon Bo couples and each of the Blessed Couples as well. Especially those who are committed to Morning Devotion. I was deeply inspired by Rev. Abernathy's sharing, and Claire's sharing. I hope we can set the necessary foundation quickly to allow you to unleash the Pentecost. Please let there be a powerful domino effect among Christian denominations, hopefully including the Mormon Church, and other religions and among women's groups.
Thank you for last night. Please bless both families! I deeply appreciate them both.
With all my prayers and conditions, I feel, at least today, I am not focused enough on what I can do to help you the most. That is not good.
I would be grateful for any insight you can offer to be more present and more responsive to your guidance and direction in each moment, and at the same time to take responsibility to plan as well.
I deeply want to do more, feel more, care more, love more. I believe I will get there, with all your kindness and love.

Do you have something to share with me today?
Love eternally,
Laurence

Dearest Laurence,
Relax. You can't open your heart when you are stressed. The more you appreciate me in the little things, the more your love will spontaneously pour out. That's when the miracles can happen.
Planning is good – but of course horizontal. Inspiration comes vertically. No need to feel that you came up with every good idea – surprise – I beat you to it on virtually every one. But… you and me, on the same wavelength, with your hands and feet joyfully engaged. Ahhh – now that is miraculous. You are there now more and more. Listen, expect, meditate on gratitude. Think about our relationship. Let those feelings propel and focus your mind and heart.
It's not a competition – even though Dr. Yong's ministries includes "setting a new record".
The record that really matters is the resonance of your heart with my heart. Nail that one and the signal shoots up off the charts. That's the secret spot. Once a day? Twice a day? Can you move towards full time? That's the intersection of full joy and greatest victories. That's where I want to live.
You're invited.
Love eternally,
Heavenly Parents

8/25/22 *When What You Are Doing Is True, Attention Is Always A Benefit. Eyes And Hearts, That's What I Am Urgently Seeking, More Eyes And Hearts. Bring Them On. I'll Handle Them.*

Good Morning My Beloved Heavenly Parent,
Thank you for another day filled with your blessings and miracles. I am so grateful for all the gifts you have showered on me and my family. I want to return those to you a million times.
This morning's Morning Devotion was very rich, talking about Tamar and Mary. Also, I felt that you were telling me that Mrs. Yong's visit to America is the bringing of the Holy Spirit we have been longing for. I hope that it can ignite our movement and ACLC, and the patriotic heart of America into full flames that can dissolve the Satanic sovereignty which has been dominating America.
Thank you that Muriel felt better today. Please protect her. She is the Holy Spirit's representative to our tribe and I love her so deeply.

Thank you for the call last night from Tom. I am deeply grateful that you opened that door.
I will try to focus on opening my heart to you in each moment to realize the resonance you described. I want to tune in to that and ride on that resonance. Do you have something to share with me today? Yesterday was very inspiring.
Love Eternally,
Laurence

Dearest Laurence,
Yes, resonance is everything. We need to lock in to each other's frequencies, and then the firehose of true love can open up. You are making wonderful progress and I am very inspired by that!
Dr. and Mrs. Yong have been fully prepared for this moment. Together they are much more powerful than as individuals. The time for indemnity conditions is past. Now is the time for accomplishments. Through their efforts, so many will find the motivation and desire to break through. I will claim and multiply each breakthrough! 95/5 means 20 to 1! That is serious multiplication. We will gain the attention of many and that will accelerate the process. When what you are doing is true, attention is always a benefit. Eyes and hearts, that's what I am urgently seeking, more eyes and hearts. Bring them on. I'll handle them.
I'm very excited about your upcoming interview. Please hit that out of the park.
Don't forget – "Eyes and Hearts" culminates with "Hearts".
Remember <u>that</u> during your zoom interview.
I love you very much.
Eternally,
Heavenly Parent

8/26/22 *The Things That Seem To Be Overwhelming Now Will Soon Feel Very Trivial. The Solution To Everything Is True Love. I Am Bequeathing True Love To You. Love And Creativity Are Vertical And Horizontal. Let Your Creativity Be Filled With Love. Let Your Love Be Filled With Creativity. True Love Brings Results. Don't Simply Love People To Feel Good. Love Them To Grow And Participate And Build And Become.*

Dearest Heavenly Parent,
I feel like I am being born. Everything is becoming so visible and clear. Thank you for sharing with me during my 1-hour lecture this morning. I need to stay on my toes not to miss all you are trying to download to me these

days. I was inspired last night when I finally opened up the Balancing By Numbers manual – at all the numbers that can help with focus and memory. I hope you will encourage Muriel to become 100% confident to test with her pendulum and to get very excited to deploy those numbers for our family and beyond as appropriate.

I see that True Parents not only served as Jesus's Parents, but also came to a foreign nation (America) representing the fallen world in order to liberate your han. They experienced losing their children just as you did. And they restored their eldest son, and through his lineage, all mankind will establish your kingdom.

I will absolutely not worry, Heavenly Parent, especially about material things. I leave it all humbly in your hands and pray that the world can be restored in the very shortest possible time.

Resonance. I want to live for resonance. Compared to that, surfing or even the sail surfing we watched last week in Massachusetts is nothing. Please help me catch the wave!

Do you have something else for me today?
Gratefully and eternally,
Laurence

Dearest Laurence,
Welcome to my kingdom. I am so inspired to partner with you in every way. Before I started the creation, I dreamed of a whole universe of people like you. This is the most exciting moment of my life. I will ramp up our relationship steadily, as smoothly as possible, so that you are not overwhelmed. I will manage it very carefully so there is no need to be concerned. The things that seem to be overwhelming now will soon feel very trivial. The solution to everything is true love. I am bequeathing true love to you. Love and creativity are vertical and horizontal. Let your creativity be filled with love. Let your love be filled with creativity. True love brings results. Don't simply love people to feel good. Love them to grow and participate and build and become. Thank you for journaling with me. I am in Heaven when we journal. I love you very much,
Eternally,
Heavenly Parent

8/27/22 Those Who Have Grown And Connected With Me Have A Special Responsibility To Help The Others, And To Open Their Minds And Hearts. This Is The Time Of Harvest And Blessings. I Want Everyone To Be Able To Receive Their Blessings. Thank You For Caring.

Good Morning Heavenly Parent,
Today is the final day of my 10th 7-year course. Thank you for leading me and protecting me, encouraging me and blessing me all this way. I am so deeply grateful. I want to resonate with your heart more each day and become a channel through which you can move and transform millions. I pray that I can liberate you and liberate True Parents substantially.
I deeply value our sharings. Last night, at Dan's meeting, I felt just how lonely and cut-off many of our members feel. I pray that I can resonate with your heart towards them, and my own heart can, in that way, grow and flow to them.
I hope you and Muriel will forgive me for catching up on sleep this morning. Do you have something to share this morning?
Love eternally,
Laurence

Dearest Laurence,
Yes, you are in a very different place than many brothers and sisters. In part because of good conditions you've set, in part because of the indemnity paid by your ancestors, and in part due to the grace you have received as a chosen person. Those who have grown and connected with me have a special responsibility to help the others, and to open their minds and hearts. This is the time of harvest and blessings. I want everyone to be able to receive their blessings. Thank you for caring. You touch the hearts of many.
Our partnership is young, but its growing! I deeply want to manifest so much through you!
Please remember who you are always. Please allow me to be with you always.
Love eternally,
Heavenly Parent

8/28/22 Resonance. Set As A Goal To Have The Most Possible Joy As You Pursue Your Cosmic Goals. I've Been Miserable For Too Long. I Choose To Wait No Longer For Joy. Let's Really Have Great Fun Making This Happen. That Will Be Holy. That Will Dissolve All Resistance. Don't Waste One Minute On Misery.

Good Morning My Most Beloved Heavenly Parent,
Thank you for today and for all your grace and protections and blessings leading up to this, my 70th birthday. I can never thank you enough or repay you, but I will have eternity to try and will give it my 200%! 😊 Thank you for the chance to share deeply yesterday with Marty. That was very

meaningful for me. We are very similar and very different, but I learned so much.

Thank you for the insight this morning regarding an offering child to Jesus. I deeply believe that True Father must have given an offering child to Jesus, who surely needed a lineage to experience the 4 great realms of heart and 3 great kingships. I hope you can provide some confirmation or clarification on this point, if I am to be permitted to know.

Related to that, I was struck by Father's guidance this morning not to unwisely share the treasures which empower our shimjeong. That is like casting pearls before swine and you lose your spiritual energy and treasure. Please guide me to thread that needle in my upcoming interview with Dietmar. Help me to speak the truth powerfully, impactfully, and in a manner that goes extremely viral, and at the same time avoid speaking what I should not say.

As you know, on this 7th anniversary of my 63rd birthday revelation, I am anticipating and hoping for a significant message from you. If you are willing, I sincerely hope you will share now,

Love eternally,
Laurence

Dearest Laurence,
Happy 70th birthday. This is a milestone for you. This is a new phase for you. You have earned the qualifications of True Owner and True Son. I am so proud and grateful. Thank you. Don't be impatient. All that you are working on are important initiatives that I too am working on for and with you to manifest. I wish I had a thousand of you, but I don't so I will work a thousand times harder through you. If it is my will, it will happen. So don't be insecure. Not everything you try will bear fruit. That's because not all of your counterparties will fulfill their portion of responsibility. But many will, and we shall reap great harvests.

Resonance. Set as a goal to have the most possible joy as you pursue your cosmic goals. I've been miserable for too long. I choose to wait no longer for joy. Let's really have great fun making this happen. That will be holy. That will dissolve all resistance.

Don't waste one minute on misery.
Congratulations again,
Eternally yours,
Heavenly Parent

8/29/22 *You Are Building The Kingdom Right In Your Own Family And Community. Living For The Sake Of Others Comes Back To You In The Most Beautiful Ways.*

Good morning my Beloved Heavenly Parent,
Thank you for this first day of my 2nd 7-year course of my 4th 21-year course! I am so extremely grateful for my life overflowing with your blessings. Thank you for the party last night. It was an unforgettable "It's a Wonderful Life" moment. I was touched very deeply. I hope you were even more so.
This morning I've felt tired even though I slept pretty well. During my prayer, I finally broke through and felt your energy but now I am feeling a bit tired again. Perhaps a new foundation I need to set. I hope and pray that it doesn't interfere with my interview on 9/7.
After breakfast I'm going to the range with Gamaliel – great father son time! Is there something you'd like to share with me today? I hope so!
Love eternally,
Laurence

Dearest Laurence,
Congratulations on your party last night. That was a little taste of the Spirit World. People and families creating and sharing heart, music, knowledge, food, love. You are building the kingdom right in your own family and community. Living for the sake of others comes back to you in the most beautiful ways.
Have a great time with Gamaliel today and at yoga, and get a good rest this evening. This will be a big week for you!
Love eternally,
Heavenly Parent

8/30/22 *Thank You For Reviewing The Messages From George, Your Committee Members, And Your Angels. That Is Very Important. They Are Providing Very Significant Support For You. It Is Really Important That You Keep Their Work And Your Partnership With Them Fresh In Your Heart.*

Dearest Most Beloved Heavenly Parent,
This morning, I stretched out my prayers – reviewing transcripts from my readings with George, and then sending out videos from my birthday. Finally, I can get around to journaling. Thanks for your patience. I shouldn't leave you for last like this but things just unfolded, and I felt that each activity was part of my worship or outreach for you. I don't feel like I wasted any time. Thank you for working so powerfully in my life. Dr. Yong said that our lives and families should be a powerful testimony of how you are working with us. I feel that is powerfully expressed in our family. I am so deeply grateful. 95% is your work – certainly much more than that in reality. I am so grateful!

Do you have a message for me today? I hope so!
I love you eternally,
Laurence

Dearest Laurence,
Thank you for reviewing the messages from George, your committee members, and your angels. That is very important. They are providing very significant support for you. It is really important that you keep their work and your partnership with them fresh in your heart. That partnership will grow with time. It is very important for you and for the providence. I can work through it very significantly. So, it is important for our collaboration too. Review those readings regularly. Think about the guidance they provided. That's your responsibility. This will get very exciting for you soon.
I love you very much!
Eternally,
Heavenly Parent

8/31/22 *Of Course, You Feel A Kinship Of Heart To Someone Like That Who, Like Yourself, Worked Hard To Build A Relationship With Me And Took Great Initiative On Faith. You Both Found My Sweet Spot And Deeply Inspired Me. You Are Pioneering What It Means To Be An Owner Of Cheon Il Guk.*

Dearest Heavenly Parent,
Good afternoon. Thank you for this new day. I appreciated the testimony during Morning Devotion today. I felt a great parallel between your collaboration with the Jasper family and your work with me. You are so faithful, just waiting for those who can take initiative to partner with you. Thank you for your guidance with Dr. Yong about listening and loving and taking personal responsibility for any breakdown of heart and relationship. I pray I can become the champion of taking responsibility for unity of heart. Thank you for the opportunity to serve Gamaliel and NanYoung and Moses and Zoe today. That was unanticipated.
I hope you can help me quickly become proficient at muscle testing. I would like to effectively utilize "Balancing by Numbers" to maintain great health, and to help our family and perhaps others.
I am very deeply grateful.
Do you have a message for me this day?
Eternally,
Laurence

Dearest Laurence,
Yes, I have been working with certain individuals or families in some ways similar to my collaboration with you. He was searching for a new and better way to serve the providence after 21 years selling fish. He came to CheongPyeong and prayed sincerely for 40 days. Of course, I would help him and I did. It has been a great blessing to many including his own family.
Of course, you feel a kinship of heart to someone like that who, like yourself, worked hard to build a relationship with me and took great initiative on faith. You both found my sweet spot and deeply inspired me. You are pioneering what it means to be an owner of Cheon Il Guk. In the future they'll study both of your courses.
And like their family, yours will close ranks and your next generation will continue to expand your great work!
What's not to love?
Love Eternally,
Heavenly Parent

9/1/22 *Move Forward Confidently, With Love And Joy. Everything Else Will Work Itself Out. That Is The Time We Are In.*

Good Morning Dearest Heavenly Parent,
I'm happy to greet you on this, the first day of the perfection stage of 2022. I hope you can reap resounding victories in the next 4 months. I saw that Kim Jong Un was quite sick. Could it be that Korea will be unified through women? I feel that I need to charge forward relying on significant Heavenly support while Satan tries to attack – but I just need to keep my eyes on the victory and trust in your support and protection. Hah – as I was writing that, in this beautiful serene natural setting, a jackhammer started up, very nearby, underlining the point!
Thank you for your continued grace in our family, and for sanctioning dramatic healing for my sore throat which almost disappeared between last night and this morning with Muriel's help. I feel you have given me so many tools. I need to continue to invest my jeongseong in order to take optimum advantage of those Divine resources and maximize the impact of the contribution I am able to make for the providence.
Do you have any guidance on this or any other insights or wisdom or corrections/critiques you can share with me to help me on this path?
Love eternally,
Laurence

Dearest Laurence,
Good morning. I am so very glad you are feeling better. I want you to stay as healthy as possible as long as possible. I deeply value all you do. I will help you become proficient at muscle testing. Balancing by Numbers is a useful resource for you, your family, and others.
Don't worry or invest energy into negative attacks. They have no basis to attack you unless you give that to them. Please don't. Move forward confidently, with love and joy. Everything else will work itself out. That is the time we are in. Yes, this is the harvest time of 2022 and the harvest time of all time. We need more harvesters. Your interview with Dietmar will help. Thank you for that. North Korea will reconcile. It will happen soon. Orrin Hatch, Shinzo Abe, Mikhail Gorbachev; they are working closely with True Father. Don't lose sight of Hun Sen. Jeongseong and joy! Resonate with my heart. This is a very happy time for me.
Love Eternally,
Heavenly Parent

9/2/22 *Yes, You Will Be Fine, Both With Your Infection And Also With Vertigo. Have A Good Nap And Wake Up Feeling Refreshed.*

Good Morning Dearest Heavenly Parent,
I apologize for my concern and lack of faith regarding offering my vitality elements to resurrect the Spirit World. With my sinus and chest infection, I wondered if I was draining my body of the life force it needed to stay healthy. I haven't required antibiotics for a very long time, but began some yesterday. But this morning, Dr. Yong started off Morning Devotion by saying that when we live absolutely for the sake of others, we will generate infinite power. I took that to mean, "don't worry about myself". Then later this morning I developed dizziness. But now I am sure it will be fine.
I intend to practice my interview presentation more today. In the meantime, I plan a nap and hope it helps my dizziness.
I love you very much.
I hope you can share.
Love Eternally,
Laurence

Dearest Laurence,
Yes, you will be fine, both with your infection and also with vertigo. Have a good nap and wake up feeling refreshed.
I hope you can practice your interview 7 more times before 9/7. I will be very strongly with you when you do the interview.
Also – don't neglect balancing by numbers.

Please stay well.
Eternally yours,
Heavenly Parent

9/3/22 You Have A Good "To Do" List For Today. Do It With Your Heart And Love. Think Of Yourself As My Executive Assistant, As Well As My Son, And Think About What Standard Of Heart And Quality You Want To Present On My Behalf. You Have Received A Lot Of Training For That. As You Strive To Properly Represent Me In Every Situation, You Become My Second Self.

Dearest Most Beloved Heavenly Parent,
Thank you for this great day!
I don't want to waste a moment. I am feeling so much better after taking antibiotics. Thank you for making that appointment so easy and smooth. Today I was deeply touched by Dr. Yong's guidance regarding receiving your life elements:

1. JeongSeong: Invest my jeongseong, prayer, and devotion
2. Vertical Alignment: Establish a clear vertical relationship with you, and judge everything from your viewpoint. (and I believe not just judge from your viewpoint – but also love and appreciate from your viewpoint).
3. Gratitude: Establish a life overflowing with gratitude. Mind and body unity begins with gratitude and appreciation:
    a. Appreciation of you
    b. Appreciation of True Parents
    c. Appreciation of my own family members
4. Long for the Word: Your word is your love. When the word comes to my heart, it becomes a seed, which grows to manifest Your Kingdom
5. Hyojeong: Try to please you with filial heart and filial piety
6. Longing Heart: Always long for and love you and True Parents.

Also, Heavenly Parent, I deeply appreciate the questions you showed to me as I was giving my 1-hour lecture this morning. I will share those with Dietmar so he can prepare for our interview. Please let me know of any others I missed and please guide me to give the most effective answers to those.
Please Heavenly Parent, share with me the most important message for today. Your messages are transforming me – I am so grateful.
Eternally,
Laurence

Dear Laurence,

Yes, you resonated with that list of 6 strategies to receive my Life Elements because you are actively invested into each of those channels already, and as a result, I am able to pour my life elements in and through you. I am deeply inspired.

You have a good "to do" list for today. Do it with your heart and love. Think of yourself as my executive assistant, as well as my son, and think about what standard of heart and quality you want to present on my behalf. You have received a lot of training for that. As you strive to properly represent me in every situation, you become my second self. Beyond Holy – you can become Divine. There is so much more that I can't wait to share with you. Please cultivate your heart based on the 6 points you outlined. That is the road map. Do it all knowing that I am embracing you with tears of love and gratitude. Find deep, deep, joy in your excellence.

Thank you.
Eternally yours,
Heavenly Parent

9/4/22 *Get Totally Comfortable With The Content, And Then In The Actual Interview, Invite Me In To Give The Presentation. We Are A Team, Use Me To Make The Pitch.*

Good Morning Dearest Most Beloved Heavenly Parent,

Thank you for your guidance and encouragement regarding my upcoming interview. I want to fully prepare before Sept. 7, and do my very best. I will practice it 6 more times before the interview as per your guidance. I am concerned that it runs so long. Please help Dietmar and me to keep it exciting and stimulating so that people stay with it through to the conclusion. I sincerely want it to be totally inspiring and compelling and to go viral. Please help in that.

Thank you for the chance to share deeply with Hanmi this morning. I was very touched by our sharing and I deeply hope you can work through it.

And Heavenly Parent, please guide me how to proceed with the local Baptist Church. I am disappointed that they ruled out any dialogue. I feel very bad for you and for Jesus. Both of them love Jesus very much and love you very much, albeit on an incomplete level of understanding. I hope you can speak to their hearts.

Thank you for all you've given and continue to give.

Please, I hope you have some words for me today.

Love eternally,
Laurence

Dear Laurence,
Thank you for investing and in and practicing your presentation. It is much, much better than when you started, and it will improve further between now and the 7th. Pray and consider and you will receive good guidance on how to bring it to life. Get totally comfortable with the content, and then in the actual interview, invite me in to give the presentation. We are a team, use me to make the pitch.
With respect to Hanmi, please take good care of her. She looks up to you. Speak to her prayerfully – she is very precious.
With respect to the local pastors, you have made your presentation. Respond respectfully to their points. Send them your interview. Then pray.
I love you eternally,
Heavenly Parent

9/5/22 *Now You Are Like The League Of Junior Messiahs. Superheroes Of Heart And Manifestation. There Are A Number Of You, But Not That Many. Each Of You Has Different Strengths. Each Of You Is Unique. Over Time You Will Grow Into An Army Of Junior Messiahs.*

Good Morning Dearest Most Beloved Heavenly Parent,
I am so deeply grateful and inspired. Thank you for allowing me the incredible opportunity to help resurrect the entire spirit world. I feel that this grace comes on the foundation of praying for their resurrection for years. Thank you for inspiring me to pray in that way.
Of course, I could think "Why Me?" But rather, I want to engage with you with my full heart and jeongseong and return that blessing multiple times. I want to inspire many, many others to follow this model and DRAMATICALLY shorten the time necessary for the spirit world's resurrection. And I want to continually find additional ways to pay forward and inspire you in surprising ways.
Thank you for all the mentoring opportunities you have opened up for me. How precious. I hope we can bring the entire Morning Devotion community to boil! Thank you also for helping me compose a response to the local pastor. I feel good about that email. I really hope you can work through that to open his heart and inspire him to engage with us and receive True Mother and True Parents.
I hope you can share something with me today. I deeply cherish the words you have shared with me and they are deeply enlightening and motivating. Thank you from the depths of my heart.
Eternally,
Laurence

Dearest Laurence,
I love you. You are beginning to live and act now in the Direct Dominion. This is what Father endured countless torture and suffering for, so that He could multiply Himself and create many, many individuals living in the Direct Dominion. Father ascended in 2012 before the Direct Dominion opened to anyone else other than True Mother.

Now you are like the League of Junior Messiahs. Superheroes of heart and manifestation. There are a number of you, but not that many. Each of you has different strengths. Each of you is unique. Over time you will grow into an army of Junior Messiahs. Long before that, for all intents and purposes, my battle will be over. Such is the power and authority of even one person living in the Direct Dominion.

You have no idea how sweet this is to me. This is not a time of an overwhelming life and death struggle between good and evil. This is a time of the joyous vindication of True Love, and the overwhelming power of True Love to dissolve all elements of evil once and for all in a cosmic Jericho moment. It is a time of joy and adventure and discovery. Like King Midas, you who are in the Direct Dominion have a Divine Touch. It is the touch of life. The touch of vision. The touch of healing. The touch of creativity. Every one of your days should be overflowing with joy. Mine are. Thank you from the depths of my heart.

Eternally,
Heavenly Parent

9/6/22 Now Is The Time I Have Been Waiting For And Dreaming Of. No Longer Partnering With Angels – Who Are Glorified Servants. But Now I Can Create With My Own Children, Who Have More Exciting, Intoxicating, And Audacious Dreams Than I Ever Had! And As Those Of You Who Are Resonating With My Heart Return Your Love Back To Me Freely, Joyfully, Spontaneously, My Own Love And Energy Is Not Only Replenished, But It Grows Exponentially.

Dearest Most Beloved Heavenly Parent,
What a fabulous day! I deeply appreciated your insights as I offered my presentation before Morning Devotion. And then, how exciting! My internet was off and I had to drive out in the rain to find a spot to join Morning Devotion on my phone. I pulled over next to Centennial Park, but the car interior was so dark I tried to turn on the lights. By mistake I opened Andy's sun roof and for 2 minutes it poured down on me while I was trying to get it

closed. Of course you were there, but I'm documenting this for my descendants. That was funny, exhilarating, a precious memory.
Morning Devotion was so deep. And virtually all the key points that Dr. Yong focused on were ones that you had personally shared with me recently. That strongly reinforced for me the deep truth of your journaling messages. And when Dr. Yong shared about our responsibility to repay the grace we have received with interest or to lose it, I felt that I have no burden at all because I am so deeply moved to try to inspire and even surprise you with my offerings and effort, if there could ever be such a thing as surprising you. I guess there certainly can be – not necessarily in the program of what we are doing – but in the joy with which we do it, and in our willingness to follow through with our intention and complete those offerings to you. The norm throughout all of history has been for your children to disappoint you and abandon their first motivations. I pray every day to never distance myself from your heart, but to maintain and invest in and strengthen my inspiration to attend you. Thank you for allowing me in so close.
I hope you have something wonderful for me again today.
Eternally yours,
Laurence

Dearest Laurence,
Tears.
I will stand by your side through thick and thin. As we resonate in heart, I will certainly resonate with your prayers and intentions. Not all prayers are equal. But the prayers of those who live every day willing to die for me are inscribed indelibly on my heart. They must come to pass, as intended or in a better form. As you beautifully expressed, for me it is also not a burden. I am so inspired and stimulated and nourished by turning those intentions into reality. I want to explode into thrilling realms of a trillion creative dreams of love. I have been sitting on my own creative potential for so painfully long. The ball has been in your court. I am aching to create. Yes, I created the cosmos. I developed and refined my capabilities externally through that experience over 14 billion years. And I have certainly developed my internal capabilities to heal and rebuild and recreate every imaginable kind of broken heart for hundreds of thousands of years since the fall. Now is the time I have been waiting for and dreaming of. No longer partnering with angels – who are glorified servants. But now I can create with my own children, who have more exciting, intoxicating, and audacious dreams than I ever had! And as those of you who are resonating with my heart return your love back to me freely, joyfully, spontaneously, my own love and energy is not only replenished, but it grows exponentially.

Try it out. Test me. You have the gift of intentions – when they are offered up for the will.
Eternally yours,
Heavenly Parent

9/7/22 *As We Get Closer And Closer Together, Through Give And Take Of Deep Heart And Loving Service, You Will Find That Things Will Increasingly Work Out Well For All Of Your Endeavors. This Is The Universal Law As You Draw Closer To The Center Of Love. It Is Similar To The Way Gravity Bends Time And Space Externally. The Power Of True Love Is On A Much Higher And More Powerful Level Than Gravity. Heavenly Fortune Follows True Love. People Naturally Follow True Love.*

Dearest Most Beloved Heavenly Parent,
Thank you for your love and grace and constant guidance and support. I am so grateful and hope I can grow ever more rapidly through our give and take. I deeply want to. I appreciate the communication this morning with Jacques, and Muriel's willingness for us to lend him funds for 1 day. I deeply appreciate the insights I received this morning in bed regarding advice for Gamaliel, and the opportunity to support Gianna last night.
I completed my 5th practice of my presentation for Dietmar this morning, and I will surely fulfill the 7 I promised. With each practice the presentation improves. Thank you.
I hope I can maintain my energy and stay focused and productive all day, and support Muriel when she gets home.
Please, I hope you have something important to share with me today.
Love Eternally,
Laurence

Dear Laurence,
As we get closer and closer together, through give and take of deep heart and loving service, you will find that things will increasingly work out well for all of your endeavors. This is the universal law as you draw closer to the center of love. It is similar to the way gravity bends time and space externally.
The power of true love is on a much higher and more powerful level than gravity. Heavenly fortune follows true love. People naturally follow true love.
I'll stop here, as you got distracted. We can pick up again tomorrow.
I love you very deeply, and forever,
Heavenly Parent

9/8/22 *In The Past, I Shared With Prophets In Generally A One Directional Conversation. Often Through Angels. Moses & Jesus Were Significant Exceptions. Moses Was My Servant. Jesus Of Course Was My First True Son. But Jesus Did Not Stand On The Foundation You Have Inherited From True Parents, And Completed Through Your Own Heart And Effort. Your Foundation Liberates Me. Of Course, I Urgently Want To Expand It Much Further.*

Good Morning My dearest Most Beloved Heavenly Parent,
Again, I am sincerely sorry for being distracted during yesterday's journaling. I know and believe, on one hand, that you are my infinitely loving Parents. I am so profoundly grateful for your generosity, kindness, and considerations. However, I deeply appreciate your gentle reminder that you are the sovereign Lord of the entire cosmos and its creator, and I pray that I never again undermine your dignity by immaturely putting some trivial matter before my relationship with you, especially when you are granting me an opportunity to journal. I want to never take your blessings for granted. I love you very deeply and I desperately want to liberate and raise you up, and help expedite the initiation of your ideal on a cosmic level.
Thank you for your help in our family. I am so grateful. Thank you for your amazing guidance and input on my interview. That is really amazing and inspiring.
Today I hope to clean up access to my Verizon account and set up my Verizon email. And divide the interview in half. Should I? Or keep it as one so people connect with True Parents on the first listen? Please help me clarify.
Dear Heavenly Parent, please share with me now. Thank you!
Love Eternally,
Laurence

Dear Laurence,
Thank you for making this special time for us to be quietly together. That prepares your heart to more easily resonate with mine, and our sharings become much easier and much deeper. In the past, I shared with prophets in generally a one directional conversation. Often through angels. Moses & Jesus were significant exceptions. Moses was my servant. Jesus of course was my first true son. But Jesus did not stand on the foundation you have inherited from True Parents, and completed through your own heart and effort. Your foundation liberates me. Of course, I urgently want to expand it much further.
I am very busy preparing for your interview with Dietmar. I like what it has evolved into. There has not existed this level of video before to dissolve all the misunderstandings of the past and proclaim True

Parents. On a cyber level, this is a significant foundation for what is coming very soon through the foundation of Dr. & Mrs. Yong and America. Yes, the fire will be ignited that you have been yearning for. All that is false and sinful must be dissolved, so that each and every one of my precious children can begin the path of returning to my heart. What will start out as the halting steps of those who have survived the spiritual concentration camps erected by Satan, will soon gain health and energy and sprint home to me, as beautifully described in CS Lewis' "Great Divorce". Like you, he is a deeply inspiring visionary.
What you are doing to resurrect the Spirit World is thrilling and shocking. That will become a global movement to support True Parents.
I like the idea of testifying to True Parents in the first interview. I don't want to lose one person, so you can't share that too soon, and you can't wait too long. Keep it exciting! People have been waiting for millennia. They can spare a few extra minutes for the punch line.
Thank you from the bottom of my heart.
Eternally,
Heavenly Parent

9/9/22 *Through Our Partnership You Are Truly, Substantially Creating An Important Aspect Of My Divinity. The Cosmos Is A Larger Entity Than I Was Alone. Through Give And Take With Those Of My Children Who Have Matured And Entered Into The Direct Dominion, The Cosmos Can Take Off And Explode In Growth And Intensity.*

Good Morning My Most Beloved Heavenly Parent,
Thank you! You sure know how to make a point unambiguously, in bold, with an exclamation point, and fireworks, and a marching band! If I had any reservations about what I am doing for you and the will, which I sincerely don't, this morning you made sure those reservations were dissolved.
First, in my Hoon Dok Hae, offering my presentation before Morning Devotion, you filled in some really key points. But there was one you gave me which was somehow stolen before I could write it down. Please, please, remind me. Thank you.
Then, in Morning Devotion, sharing my gratitudes, you put me in with Dr. Yong in Room 39 (that's Jesus's #13, but perfected). A very nice touch! Dr. Yong asked me to share first and I had the incredible chance to explain to him about offering my vitality elements during Hoon Dok Hae to quickly clean up the Spirit World. He was so excited. What a total endorsement! I will re-triple my efforts and make it happen just as you described in our previous

journaling. Then in his message, Dr. Yong spoke about how through our ultimate Jeongseong, we move not only you, but our brothers and sisters as well. That was such a powerful tie-in to my offering song, "The Carpenter". I was also very struck by Dr. Yong's guidance that each time we meet someone, we treat it as the first time. I love that. Please help me to become that. Then, right after Morning Devotion, Levy called me up, originally about music ministry, but when I told him I had to focus on larger things, we had such a profound discussion on the theme: "This is the time of Partnership with you". Haha! You may have worried that I didn't fully believe you. Thank you for the independent validation from one of the people I most respect in our movement. I TOTALLY BELIEVE YOU AND TRUST YOU NOW! I will strive to be the best and most exciting and most loving, and most creative, and most grateful partner you ever had! (Although True Parents have set a crazy high bar!) You have already said so much, so profoundly, today. I hesitate to ask for more. But I would sure love to hear directly from you, heart to heart, whatever is exploding in your heart at this moment. Either way, I want to share it, good or bad. If it is pain, I want to work harder to dissolve it.
I love you, I love you eternally!
Laurence

Dearest Laurence,
Thank you for allowing me to become so real in your life and awareness. If my children can't sense me, or hear me, or see me work in their lives, then give and take dies, and with it, all existence, action, and multiplication. As you are striving to recognize and take in my words, my actions, my heart, that jeongseong of yours gives those very efforts substance, and makes our give and take so much more powerful. In this way my intentions, my actions, my love take on substance, and power, and impact, and energy, and intensity, and momentum. Through our partnership you are truly, substantially creating an important aspect of my divinity. The cosmos is a larger entity than I was alone. Through give and take with those of my children who have matured and entered into the direct dominion, the cosmos can take off and explode in growth and intensity. Not from my power, but from OUR power, as co-equal partners of give and take, centering of course on the ideal, which I also must follow.
You promised me you would never doubt who you are or what you are doing for our partnership. Please, please, never abandon or forget that promise. I need you so absolutely – just as I needed True Father. These are the most exciting days in all of history!
Thank you, thank you, thank you!
Eternally,
Heavenly Parent

9/10/22 *Love Shall Conquer All. What A Beautiful Rallying Cry. It Is Finally True. If You Can Open Up To The Reality, You Would Be Unable To Sleep, You Would Be So Excited.*

Good Morning Dearest Most Beloved Heavenly Parent,
I am deeply grateful for another new day, which began with another very inspiring Morning Devotion. Thank you for giving new life to this nation and the world. Thank you for the Degrees bestowed upon True Parents through the United Nations University. Please work powerfully through that condition to elevate and empower the UN to fulfill its mission as envisioned by True Parents. Thank you for repeating through Dr. Yong's message, the message you shared with me about the value of each person's unique character, to have give and take with the corresponding unique aspect of your own heart. You are amazing and so profoundly inspiring. I pray that you can work powerfully through our visit today with Antonio and Kiyoko. Please embrace them and their precious family in our love. I hope that I can quickly set up a firm schedule with Dietmar, and that on the foundation of my practices, you can speak so powerfully through me in the interview.
Thank you for this incredible privilege and blessing to be working directly with you in this manner. Please share with me now.
Eternally,
Laurence

Good Morning Laurence,
Thank you for your heart, and for your message this morning. Thank you for continuing to invest your heart and jeongseong into Morning Devotion. You are substantially helping to accelerate the realization of the Holy Spirit here in America. Please understand just how significant that is. Please continue enthusiastically and spontaneously in that offering. It is truly beautiful and holy.
Yes the Honorary Degrees from the UN University in Costa Rica are significant, and are an important condition through which I can transform the UN to help accelerate the Kingdom on Earth. Every day in important ways, large and small, my children are making conditions I can use. This is a new age, I am very excited, and the providence is accelerating nicely. Love shall conquer all. What a beautiful rallying cry. It is finally true. If you can open up to the reality, you would be unable to sleep, you would be so excited.
I love you eternally,
Heavenly Parent

9/11/22 *Even I Cannot Create Vitality Elements, (Although As Per Your Prayer, I Can Amplify The Vitality Elements You Freely Offer Up, So That They Can Be Shared With Every Person In The Spirit World). In This Issue, You, My Children, Are Greater Than I, And I Need You Absolutely.*

Good Morning My Dearest Beloved Heavenly Parent,
I pray that on this, the 21st anniversary of 9/11, you can be free to claim full and multiple indemnity from Satan's side for the unprovoked attack on America, and for the deep state which was established in the wake of that attack, which Satan has been using to further attack God's side.
Thank you for leading us and guiding us to the ultimate victory of 2 Pet 3:12. May your fire come down upon the hearts and spirits of the faithful here in America, and ignite the heart of Pentecost and spiritual revival that will dissolve the elements of stan's dominion once and for all, and give America the spiritual power to overcome Satan's 3 temptations on behalf of all mankind.
Thank you so much for the feedback from Levy on my presentation, and the feedback from Ibrahim to support the initiative to resurrect the entire Spirit World with our vitality elements. I am deeply grateful for your help and guidance. I am 100% committed to liberate you, True Parents, Jesus, and all mankind in both realms. Please use me. Thank you so much!
I hope you have a message for me today.
Eternally,
Laurence

Dear Laurence,
Thank you for your heart, for your vision, and for your commitment. Heart, Intellect, and Will. To be a man. I am so proud of you. And yes, you are correct in your words to Ibrahim just now. Even I cannot create vitality elements, (although as per your prayer, I can amplify the vitality elements you freely offer up, so that they can be shared with every person in the Spirit World). In this issue, you, my children, are greater than I, and I need you absolutely. I cannot liberate hell without the willing help and support of you, on the earth. I've been waiting for this to happen for hundreds of thousands of years. Please, please, you and Ibrahim, multiply yourselves thousands, millions of times. This is the greatest rescue mission in history, on the foundation of True Parents' historic victories. The war victims and refugees from Syria and the Middle East, from Ukraine, from North Korea, are only a slight shadow of the suffering in hell – where there has been no hope for hundreds of thousands of years. People who are starving can't receive

the truth. They need to be fed first. Then they can be lifted up into absolute good spirits. Please don't stop! Please explode forward.
I am eternally grateful!
Love,
Heavenly Parent

9/12/22 *It Brings Me Immeasurable Joy And Energy To Be Able To Support You Like This. You And Your Team Will Do Mighty Works. Levy Is A Firecracker For Heaven, I'm So Glad You Two Can Work Together. These Are Exciting Days For Me. I Will Add My 95% To All Your Do. I Dare You To Try To Keep Up With Me.*

Dearest Most Beloved Heavenly Parent,
Thank you for this great new day. My meridians were blocked last night causing pain in my shoulder, but lidocaine patches helped and I woke up pain free. Thank you for healing me. I understand that offering my vitality elements could have some impact on my physical body, but it is negligible compared to what Father endured to liberate you and mankind. So, I am very happy to place myself in your hands and to push forward with my full heart in all my endeavors on your behalf – especially in the resurrection of hell through the joyful offering of our vitality elements during our Hoon Dok Hae readings.
Today, Larry expressed a desire to participate. That is the 2nd member of my trinity, together with Ibrahim. Please help me find my third member quickly so that we can explode into the multiplication phase with your full support. Please guide me in the organization and administration of this effort so that it can be as successful as possible. I am eternally grateful to you for allowing me this privilege and opportunity to serve you, True Parents, and all my brothers and sisters in the Spirit World as well as those on Earth who choose to participate. I am so deeply blessed. Thank you!
Please share any guidance or other points that are on your heart this morning. I am so stimulated and touched by each of your sharings.
Love eternally,
Laurence

Dearest Laurence,
Good morning. I look forward to another wonderful day with you. Thank you so much for all your efforts to invite me into your day. I could never forget you and our partnership.
Yes, Ibrahim and Larry are both wonderful objects for your endeavor and yes you will quickly find a third, and then you can form an online community to promote this Divine endeavor. It will resonate and shake the entire Spirit World. Also, make a clear intention with your angels.

(Then the phone rang. It was Levy. We had a wonderful discussion and Levy agreed to join this team.)

Dearest Heavenly Parent,
I hope you will forgive me for interrupting your message again. Just as you were telling me I would find my third member soon, Levy called. Yes, I answered. It was a very profound call and he became my third member. I will now launch my online Holy Community. I am so deeply grateful.
You are profoundly inspiration!
Thank you!
Eternally yours,
Laurence

**Dearest Laurence,
It brings me immeasurable joy and energy to be able to support you like this. You and your team will do mighty works. Levy is a firecracker for Heaven, I'm so glad you two can work together. These are exciting days for me. I will add my 95% to all your do. I dare you to try to keep up with me.
Love, love, love,
Heavenly Parent**

9/13/22 *The Anticipation In The Spirit World Is Growing. You've Got This. I Am Following Your Lead.*

Good Morning Dearest Heavenly Parent,
Thank you for your guidance and constant nourishment. I'm so grateful. I'm very encouraged that we are launching an online Holy Community to rapidly grow our "Vitality Element" Ministry. Thank you for helping me to find 3 objects. I hope we can unite in deep commitment, and that we can energize and inspire each other to dramatic success. I already updated my prayer list and my Committee and Angel instructions. Today I need to update my presentation based on Levy's input and continue practicing for our interview. I am also inspired to make a video of "To Be a Man" focusing on Hyo Jin Nim. Please help me with that, I sincerely want to honor and respect Hyo Jin Nim.
I want so deeply to liberate you, liberate True Parents, and liberate all mankind. I hope you have some additional guidance for me again today!
Love eternally,
Laurence

Dearest Laurence,
Thank you for how much you care, and for acting on that in so many meaningful ways. Your life will inspire many. It certainly inspires me. I'm very happy with the steps you have already taken to launch your online ministry. It is true, it is profoundly important, and it is something that anyone committed to Hoon Dok Hae can easily join. That is a fabulous combination. The anticipation in the Spirit World is growing. You've got this. I am following your lead. How many organizations have you launched? This one will have amazing traction. You will be shocked. If you lose focus, you will find yourself following and not leading, it will move so quickly. Don't lose focus! I am right with you.
Thank you so very much,
Eternally,
Heavenly Parent

9/14/22 *I Too Did Not Know In Advance The Exact Way This Would Impact You Or Anyone Else Who Joins You. It Really Is A New Initiative. I Agree With You, That It Should Absolutely Be Done In A Manner That Can Be Sustained Long-Term Without Serious Health Repercussions.*

Good Morning Dearest Most Beloved Heavenly Parent,
Thank you for this new day. Should I report to you stoically, or honestly? I think that you prefer my honest heart, but maybe I'm wrong. I know that True Father never prayed from weakness – only from a desire to comfort you. That is such an amazing and challenging standard. I pray I can get there. I was discouraged by the way my sinus infection returned to impact my throat and even my lungs. Thank you for showing me the negligeable but real price of helping liberate those trapped in hell. It is something I committed to, and something I want to do, and I am ashamed of my weakness. It concerns me that if my health continues to deteriorate, that I won't be able to fulfill any of my other responsibilities. While perhaps none of those are as important as salvation, I believe they are none-the-less important, and I am very reluctant to risk jeopardizing them. What should I do, Heavenly Parent? That is why I prayed that you use my vitality elements in a way that is sustainable over the long run.
I surely trust you in this. Thank you for giving me a tangible awareness of the severity of this challenge. I realize it is most probably pioneering a new area in the providence, and one of which not so much is understood. These last few weeks have given me a little feel for it, and I hope you can help me modify my approach in a manner that supports long term growth and stability.

And also, one that will allow me to continue my work on the economic track, and also my interview(s) proclaiming True Parents. May your kingdom come quickly! I pray that I can pull my weight and make a beautiful offering to protect, comfort, and liberate you, as I help liberate all my brothers and sisters.
Thank you for loving me so profoundly.
Please share your guidance now on this point, and help me step out of the way so that you can speak to me clearly without a filter.
Love Eternally,
Laurence

Dearest Laurence,
True Father is your father, and the father for the entire cosmos. While you can certainly challenge yourself to follow or surpass his heart and sacrifice, please don't be disappointed if you fall short. It is a journey, not a competition. I love and deeply appreciate you. You are attempting something even True Father could not attempt, as he too had other pressing responsibilities he had to focus on. He was certainly aware of this possibility, and made a conscious decision not to pursue it in his lifetime. But you can be 1000% certain, he is deeply grateful for your efforts, and he is supporting you significantly in this. I too did not know in advance the exact way this would impact you or anyone else who joins you. It really is a new initiative. I agree with you, that it should absolutely be done in a manner that can be sustained long-term without serious health repercussions. You will recall, I told you I would never have asked anyone to take this on, as I could foresee that there would be some health impacts. I embrace your prayer, to move forward in a way that is sustainable for you and for the others who ultimately join you. I will proceed on that basis.
The need is great, but it cannot be met by just a few. So, it is important to create no barriers or obstacles for those who are moved to participate.
This is a partnership. Thank you for your honesty. I honor that. Please continue. The way will open up before you.
Love Eternally,
Heavenly Parent

9/15/22 *I Am Very Sorry For Your Allergy Attack. I Will Manage That Properly Going Forward. Rest Today. Tomorrow You Should Be Much Better.*

Good Morning Dearest Heavenly Parent,
Thank you for this great day and for the call I already had with Levy.

I feel that my body is beginning to return to normal after my sinuses and lungs went haywire. I am hopeful to have a somewhat normal visit with Janet. Thank you so very much for the healing you provided.

I'm sorry to be a little groggy today under all the allergy meds I've been taking. But I think they are helping me reclaim dominion over my physical body.

Hopefully after this I can reach Dietmar and schedule an interview.

I love you very deeply,
Eternally,
Laurence

Dear Laurence
I am very sorry for your allergy attack. I will manage that properly going forward. Rest today. Tomorrow you should be much better. Yes, meet with Levy. Brainstorm, then do some outreach. This will grow. Draft up a flyer.
Love Eternally,
Heavenly Parent

9/16/22 *Thank You For Your Willingness To Carry Special Burdens. That May Become Necessary As We Move Forward. I Will Surely Let You Know. In The Meantime, I Will Continue To Work Very Closely With You!*

Good Afternoon Dearest Heavenly Parent,

I am deeply grateful that you helped me settle down my physical body so quickly. Thank you. On this, my first visit with Janet and her family following the pandemic, I was concerned about making her feel highly uneasy due to my illness. Thank you for your help in this. Heavenly Parent, I again apologize for my lack of hyojeong and my lack of Faith at not being willing to push forward unconditionally. I deeply appreciate the privilege to consult with you as I move forward, and I ask for your full honesty so that, having consulted, I can clearly understand your perspective and I can do my very best to unite with you. Thank you for the privilege to be your partner. I want to always cherish and honor you in that partnership eternally.

I want to offer my prayers for Pat, for her full recovery if that is your will, or otherwise for something better. I am concerned at the repeating delays in scheduling the interview with Dietmar. Please help me to nail that down. And if it's possible, I pray that you can give some encouragement to Muriel. I am so deeply grateful.

I pray you can please help me maintain my focus and intensity, even in the face of distractions, and to maintain a deep heart of love for all whom I meet or interact with.

Thank you for all your blessings. I hope you can share something with me now.
Eternally,
Laurence

Dearest Laurence,
Thank you for your heart and your desire to comfort me. I deeply appreciate that and as per your request, I will share with you honestly. This is a critical moment in all of history. We are heading quickly towards victory. I want to be extremely careful not to allow a significant mistake at this final moment. Your commitment allows me to work with you in an important way different from how I work with other of my children. Thank you for your willingness to carry special burdens
That may become necessary as we move forward. I will surely let you know. In the meantime, I will continue to work very closely with you! Thank you!
Very sincerely,
Heavenly Parent

9/17/22 *I Agree That It Is Easier For You To Experience My Heart In Nature, And I Appreciate The Efforts You Make To Go To Nature To Get Closer To Me. But Never Forget, If You Reach Out To Me Anywhere, I Am With You.*

Good Afternoon Dearest Heavenly Parent,
Thank you for this precious blessing to visit Janet and Peter's family in such beautiful nature. As Dr. Yong shared this morning from Father, as we open up to the depth of heart that you invested into nature, and pray to you from that space, we can connect our original mind with your heart on a much deeper and more pure level. I'm very deeply grateful for all your love and heart, how much you love every one of your children. I hope, every day, I can inherit your heart on a deeper and deeper level, and upgrade beyond discriminating against any of your children. I want to live in a place of joy and inspiration just to be able to connect with any of your children. I want to share that inspiration with my brothers and sisters to advance your kingdom on Earth and especially in Heaven – but certainly both.
Thank you so much for the interest which Ambrose expressed today in our online Holy Community. I am very inspired. If we can even find one new member a day and gain some experience, it can surely grow very rapidly!
Dearest Father, I am also grateful for Dietmar's continued commitment. Let us please nail down a firm date now for the interview.

I hope you have something you would like to share with me. Please help me to open my heart and mind to hear your voice clearly and to take your words in very deeply.
Eternally,
Laurence

Dearest Laurence,
Thank you for maintaining our dialogue even during your travel and visiting schedules. I feel and deeply appreciate your heart and commitment, and as you can see your family members also respect it. I agree that it is easier for you to experience my heart in nature, and I appreciate the efforts you make to go to nature to get closer to me. But never forget, if you reach out to me anywhere, I am with you.
It is great that Ambrose could respond to your vision. You are able to share vision and enthusiasm with others very effectively. As George said, you are to become an important representative – like a salesman – for Heaven. Salesmen have a bad reputation – because they use their influencing capabilities to persuade people to make decisions that benefit the people paying their salaries.
But a Heavenly salesman is different. He is a cross between a prophet and an inspirational life coach. He is someone who helps fallen people overcome their own barriers and to catch Heaven's train as it comes speeding by, only sometimes on a much higher level, not just one on one.
The interview with Dietmar is just a training – but it will have great impact. Ultimately what you will do for the Bering Strait Tunnel/Peace Highway Project will have global impact, as will your online Holy Community.
Things are speeding up. Please keep up.
Very sincerely,
Heavenly Parent

9/18/22 *Please Don't Be Dissuaded By The Bureaucracy. You Are An Owner, You Are My Son And Partner, And You Are True Parents' Son. Own That Position And The Way Will Open Up For You To Do What You Need To Do.*

Good Morning Heavenly Parent,
It is so peaceful and beautiful to be here, alone, with you at this lake. Please allow my heart to open up more and more and to allow you to merge with me in communion of love and gratitude and partnership. Heavenly Parent, please teach me and guide me. I don't want to put on airs, especially in front of you. But I do want to take initiative, as a child of hyojeong, still growing,

but ready to give my utmost to relieve your burden and han. Please teach me and guide me. If we are partners, please help me to clearly understand the way forward.

I learned from George that I am responsible for any word I receive. I accept that responsibility. Many of my friends are dying. If I must die to fulfill your will, then I am willing. Jesus died at 33, you have already blessed me so much more than that.

I want to liberate you.

Towards that goal:
- a. I want to achieve great and rapid success in our Online Holy Community
- b. Achieve great success with Dietmar in this and future interviews
- c. Achieve great success funding providential projects including the Bering Strait project, and the others I am working as well as other projects of our movement.
- d. Raise up my family and tribe to deeply unite centering on you and True Parents
- e. Record my memoirs and other background on my life and works to inspire others

If there are other higher priorities that I have omitted, I dearly hope you will help me understand and embrace those with my heart, so that I can achieve them with my full jeongseong.

Maybe this is how True Father felt up on the hill in Pusan, looking out at the water, envisioning and mapping out his life. I pray I can inherit his heart.

Thank you dearest Heavenly Parent. Please do share with me now.

I love you eternally,

Laurence

Dearest Laurence,

The lake represents your course and the horizon your goal. I put bodies of water on the Earth to teach my children to grow, and look outward. True Father challenged the ocean with unflinching faith and courage, and deep jeongseong. True Mother is the ocean. She embraced every one of True Father's challenges with grace, with a deep heart, with unchanging determination, unstoppable will and unchanging embrace. They embody me.

I am so determined to reclaim all the cosmos back from the thief, and to make all things right. And at the same time, with each failure, each delay, I must embrace, and love, and comfort, and assure and move forward to the inevitable victory.

Now is the final moment. True Father has ascended. True Mother must complete all things. She must embrace all people, with tears, with love, with determination, with great hope.

But more than that, she must reach the destination.

Thank you for your help for her. It is historic. Thank you for accelerating the restoration of the spirit world. I had not hoped it would begin so soon. Now I can see it will. That's so precious. Please help True Mother.
You will know how.
Please don't be dissuaded by the bureaucracy. You are an owner, you are my son and partner, and you are True Parents' son. Own that position and the way will open up for you to do what you need to do. Have a great day today and a great meeting with Dr. Yong.
Eternally,
Heavenly Parent

9/19/22 *Fall Is A Chance To Think Back About The Victories Of The Year, And To Feel Joy And Pride For The Accomplishments, To Laugh At The Failures, And To Clearly Identify And Acknowledge The Lessons So You Can Always Improve Next Year.*

Dearest Heavenly Parent,
Thank you for Blessing our visit to Peter and Janet so abundantly. It was beautiful and rich and sweet. And thank you for the opportunity to meet a wonderful spiritual child, Johnita, at the airport.
I was so happy that it worked out for us to return back in time to greet Dr. and Mrs. Yong at the Washington Times, and to share dinner with David and Kathy.
Leaves are falling continuously from the trees surrounding our back yard. Fall is coming. Thank you for maintaining creation even in the midst of this cosmic battle. Your love and gamdong is so constant. I am deeply, deeply grateful.
Today I need to send out belated birthday thankyous, and also ask NanJoo about an image for our Online Holy Community.
Thank you also for helping me to recover my health. I so deeply appreciate that.
I would really love to receive another message from you today – although I never want to take your grace for granted.
Eternally yours,
Laurence

Dearest Laurence,
I like fall a great deal. It's a chance to exhale, after all the work and effort of creation has come to fruition, but before the chilly winter has descended. Fall is a chance to think back about the victories of the year, and to feel joy and pride for the accomplishments, to laugh at the failures, and to clearly identify and acknowledge the lessons so you can

always improve next year. Without fall, there could not be progress. As you reminisce about the year, think especially about your relationships. Fall is a great season to strengthen our relationships, including those within your family and beyond.

Fall is also the time to prepare for a new start. Not just storing up food for the winter, but also the falling leaves remind you of getting older. Did you like that? I wanted aging to be natural and inevitable, and to clearly be followed by new life. Nature is a beautiful school of my love.

Today you understood an important nuance between complaining and negotiating. As long as you stand firm on taking responsibility, you may negotiate – if you do so with a humble and grateful heart.

Thank you for partnering with me, for your dedication, and flexibility, and your desire to grow. I so cherish our partnership.

Eternally,
Heavenly Parent

9/20/22 *You Are Doing A Great Job. Things Are Falling Into Place. Trust, Don't Worry. I Love You.*

Good Morning Dearest Most Beloved Heavenly Parent,
Thank you for another Blessed Day! I'm happy to be liquid fasting today for the month of September and especially for success in my interview with Dietmar. I hope and pray that we can set a firm date tomorrow for that interview.

Thank you for the wonderful words of Dr. Yong this morning, talking about Tamar and how you were working to restore the fall.

True Mother shared that if we had not fallen, we would have automatically known you through our blood relationship with you. Of course that's the case. Like the sun, you would be our unmistakable source of love and wisdom.

Thank you for the contacts today with Ambrose and Kit, and with Beverly. I hope we can grow this online Holy Community powerfully and effectively. I want to use this day very efficiently. Please guide me. Also, thank you for the reply from Johnita in Charlotte!

I hope you have something to share with me today!
Very sincerely,
Laurence

Dearest Laurence,
Good morning! Thank you for fasting, I will certainly claim and use that condition. And thank you for your ongoing support for Dr. Yong and Morning Devotion. It is important for many of the participants.

Yes, your online Holy Community is beginning to grow. It will pick up. You need to finetune your documentation.
You are doing a great job. Things are falling into place. Trust, don't worry. I love you. Muriel loves you. Your family loves you.
Please focus and continue to invest your best.
Eternally,
Heavenly Parent

9/21/22 *Please Stay Focused On What You Can Do And I'll Be Working On The Rest. Each Morning, We Can Regroup And Compare Notes. Like The Faithful Spies Returning To Report.*

Dearest Most Beloved Heavenly Parent,
Thank you so much for this great new day. I was happy to wake up even earlier today at 3:19 and to get to my office early enough to do my entire interview before Morning Devotion. That was so good. Thank you for the tweaks you gave me in the interview during that run through. I hope today that Dietmar can firm up the schedule.
And thank you for NanJoo's willingness to help with an image for an online Holy Community. I pray today that I can have great focus and bring great achievements to you by approaching each situation with a heart of joy and love and offering, and deep appreciation and gratitude. The series we started last night, Ted Lasso, is like that. I found it very inspiring, although I want to work on a much higher level than that. Please remind me if I get distracted from you. Please, I don't want to!
I hope you have something to share with me today,
Eternally,
Laurence

Dearest Laurence,
Thank you for your effort and diligence. Your interview is in good shape. It will happen. Then we shall see.
And thank you for your focus on developing your Online Holy Community. That is so significant.
Please stay focused on what you can do and I'll be working on the rest. Each morning, we can regroup and compare notes. Like the faithful spies returning to report.
Don't forget who you are and shrink. Like Dr. Yong emphasized this morning, when we are one, nothing is impossible. I am thrilled for every chance to demonstrate that that is true. The condition is your faith and initiative. Thank you for embodying both in your life.
Love Eternally,
Heavenly Parent

9/22/22 *It Might Feel To You Like Not Much Is Happening. That Is Not True. Seismic Shifts Are Taking Place Even As You Write This Journal. Never Forget Who We Are. I Am Counting On You.*

Good Morning My Dearest Most Beloved Heavenly Parent.
I'm so grateful! This morning, I was again able to practice my interview before morning devotion and to continue to tweak it. I pray that you can speak so powerfully through me, and through the video and internet to touch the hearts and minds and original minds of hundreds of millions of your children around the world. May your kingdom come!
Thank you for another inspiring Morning Devotion. Please help me to continue to open my heart to you and to daily deepen our bond, and our love, and our partnership.
I pray for your guidance on rolling out our online Holy Community. I want to take responsibility to make that work. Please guide me.
Please Heavenly Parent, share your heart and thought with me now, and help me open my heart and mind to fully, and deeply , and accurately receive your guidance.
Eternally yours,
Laurence

Good Morning Laurence,
Thank you for investing your full heart into this journaling. That makes it much easier for me to connect to you and to dwell in you. I want to fill you with my energy and love, and this is the way to make that happen. I am very excited.
Please follow up with your online Holy Community outreach. Some will join you. Develop your presentation.
Also, very soon you will interview with Dietmar. It is almost ready. The Spirit World is getting excited. You are doing well. It might feel to you like not much is happening. That is not true. Seismic shifts are taking place even as you write this journal. Never forget who we are. I am counting on you.
I love you eternally,
Heavenly Parent

9/23/22 *Thank You Also For Your Diligence In Practicing Your Presentation. I Will Make Sure It Happens, And Soon. It Will Be A Very Important Declaration To Heaven And Earth.*

Good Morning Dearest Heavenly Parent,
Thank you for this fabulous new day. I was very inspired to be able to share this morning in front of the entire Morning Devotion Community with Dr. Yong's participation, regarding liberating hell through vitality elements. You weren't kidding when you promised this would take off! I love how you do that.

I was also inspired to practice my interview again this morning. But I was unhappy to hear from Dietmar that he has not yet decided on a date. I trust you in that you assured me it will happen. Could you please assign an angel to help nail down that schedule and to encourage and bolster Dietmar?

Also, I promised Muriel that I would find a way to earn at least $2000, per month. I am not at all worried about funds, but I feel a need to respond to her. Perhaps you can guide me on that issue. I love you very deeply. I am grateful for the opportunity in Morning Devotion to confess my love for you. I am so, so grateful for the opportunity to move from a motivation of duty, to that of love. This is heaven. Thank YOU!!!

I hope you can share something today.
Eternally,
Laurence

Dearest Laurence,
Thank you for your commitment and diligence with your online Holy Community. It is extremely important, and will dramatically speed up the establishment of the Kingdom of Heaven. I am so grateful.
Thank you also for your diligence in practicing your presentation. I will make sure it happens, and soon. It will be a very important declaration to Heaven and Earth. You have done well.
I will definitely support your work with projects, don't be concerned. All will work out very well with Muriel and your family.
Love Eternally,
Heavenly Parent

9/24/22 *This Is The Greatest Rescue Mission In All Of History, And It Is Now Launched. I Am So Excited. In The Near Future You Will Be Educating The World About This On TV.*

Good Morning Dearest Heavenly Parent,
Thank you for my amazing life and my beautiful family and for this mind and heart-blowing partnership with you. You assured me that our online Holy Community would grow rapidly, and already since yesterday, it has more than doubled, and is now international in Japan and Iceland. Thank you for this privilege.

Dietmar reassured me yesterday that he is still serious. I hope we can schedule that interview soon and that my health is good so I am not coughing in the middle of it.

I plan to try the nebulizer today. I hope that will help me heal my lungs quickly so I can avoid more antibiotics if possible.

I'm so grateful for your protection of Andy and Jordanne during their hike. So much could have gone worse. Thank you for your amazing blessings!

I deeply appreciated Dr. Yong's guidance this morning. If I treat myself as yours, then I will resonate with you in every situation. Although I do take delight in acting on my own to inspire you. But that's a nuance. As Dr. Yong mentioned, the key is my motivation, and I want that to be centered 100% at absolute vertical.

I want to make this a great and inspired weekend for you.

I hope you have a message for me.

Eternally yours,
Laurence

Dear Laurence,
Your online Holy Community will now grow. Care for it well. Prepare inspirations for each Tuesday meeting. I will give you content through our journalling. Set goals and make strong clear intentions to fulfill those goals. This is the greatest rescue mission in all of history, and it is now launched. I am so excited.

In the near future you will be educating the world about this on TV. Instead of the Red Cross, you'll need a good brand! Like the Cosmic Vitality Bank or something catchy. This will be a powerful educational vehicle to educate mankind about the spirit world and eternal life.

I am very excited.

Thank you!

Eternally,
Heavenly Parent

9/25/22 *If I Did This With Only Half My Heart There Would Be No Hope Whatsoever. Spiritual Maturity Means Living 100% Sincerely For The Ideal.*

Dearest Heavenly Parent,
Thank you so very much for this day, day 700 of Morning Devotion. It was hard to shake off the cough meds this morning, although it feels like they worked well on my lungs. Thank you for helping me heal. I deeply, deeply appreciate my health which you have blessed me with in abundance.

Dr. Yong spoke about the important significance of being sincere. I'm deeply grateful for all the grace you have showered on me these last few years and I want to strive for total sincerity in all I do.

This morning, after prayer, was an opportunity to help with the kids. Thank you for your guidance. I'm not sure how best to deal with Moses. He gets so angry and so assertive. And for sure its not OK to kick Muriel or expel us from the house. But he is only 3. Would love any guidance you could offer.

I am grateful for your help with Abram. Even though we didn't find what he was looking for, the fact that it was a better color and the fact I was willing to bring him and exchange the shin guards was sufficient to move his heart and help him embrace the ankle supports. I will try to embody sincerity in all that I do. Please help me to grow my heart so that it comes automatically and naturally.

I hope you have something deeply moving to share today.

Love Eternally,
Laurence

Dearest Laurence,
You are growing. It is not about you. It is about the ideal. I never think about myself. I can never sleep or rest stressing about the ideal. If I did this with only half my heart there would be no hope whatsoever. Spiritual maturity means living 100% sincerely for the ideal. It means viewing all resources and money as existing for the ideal. The ideal includes both the whole purpose and the individual purpose. In that ideal is the ultimate joy, and eternity.
Thank you for helping me build it.
Eternally,
Heavenly Parent

9/26/22 *It Is A Special Course Walked By Those Afflicted With Emotional Or Cognitive Challenges, And He Paid A Great Price For The Will. I Am Deeply Grateful.*

Good Morning Dearest Heavenly Parent,
Thank you for this new day and new week. I had a bit of a dark dream last night regarding major funds, but I consider that may have been influenced by my cough medicine. If you actually meant that dream as a warning to me, please be sure to make that very clear to me right away. I don't want to be going in the wrong direction for even one moment.

Thank you for the opportunity to offer Hoon Dok Hae and prayers for Sam. Please embrace him and liberate him and bless him abundantly in the Spirit World and please give healing to his parents and siblings.

I am very grateful for all the blessings you continue to shower on me. I hope this day can be well spent, and that I can continue to recover my full health. Please share your heart and thoughts with me now.
Eternally,
Laurence

Dearest Laurence,
Thank you for all your diligence and effort. I receive your offering for Sam and I will certainly embrace him with great love and blessings. It is a special course walked by those afflicted with emotional or cognitive challenges, and he paid a great price for the Will. I am deeply grateful.
Tomorrow is your first Online Holy Community meeting. Please prepare well.
Don't forget to bring champagne on Friday to Colin's wedding.
As Dr. Yong emphasized again today, sincerity is the key to success in everything we do as partners. Please always reconnect to your heart and to me before you do anything. I want to fully participate. Please, <u>always</u> invite me.
I waited so long for you. Let's make the most of this partnership. Anything is possible.
Love Eternally,
Heavenly Parent

9/27/22 *Finally, Now, There Is Light At The End Of The Tunnel. There Is Hope For Their Rescue. Please Know, Of A Certainty, That I Will Pour My Heart And Energy And Spirit Into Your Efforts And Together We Will Save Them. This Is Amazing And I Am Crying.*

Good Morning Dearest Most Beloved Heavenly Parent,
I love you! I want so much to liberate you and help you to fulfill your long-cherished dream. I'm so sorry for the failure of our original ancestors and the shameful, pitiful state of mankind since that tragedy. Even as you have been overcoming your own grief and shock, and willing yourself forward with all your heart and determination, mankind had been sinking deeper and deeper into enslavement and depravity. If you had not dedicated 120% of your focus and energy and tears and determination and compassion to rescue us, there could never have been hope. You are the greatest hero of all time, followed by our True Parents and Jesus.
I am so, so deeply grateful for my life and blessings and all the grace you have showered on me and our family. I want to return it to you a million times and more. Please guide me now and work through me so powerfully as I launch our Online Holy Community this evening to rescue and resurrect hell, in

order to dramatically accelerate your liberation and the establishment of your full dignity and that of True Parents.
I seek your guidance and inspiration now in this endeavor and my other efforts on behalf of your Kingdom.
Eternally yours,
Laurence

Dearest Laurence
I am so grateful. You can't imagine the state of hell. Honestly you can't. When I told Adam and Eve they would die – that was much more literal than is largely understood. There are hundreds of billions of souls in hell who are entombed, like in a mausoleum, unable to have any give and take except with their own pain, resentment, anger, fear, and suffering. They are paralyzed in pain. They are tormented into unconsciousness, which is a mercy. I hear their cries every moment. When I tune in, it is overwhelming to me. I do my best to block it out and focus 100% on the task ahead of me, comforting myself in my vow to them that I will absolutely give every ounce of my being, and will unfailingly save them eventually. But as you can imagine, that is a very hollow comfort.
Finally, now, there is light at the end of the tunnel. There is hope for their rescue. Please know, of a certainty, that I will pour my heart and energy and spirit into your efforts and together we will save them. This is amazing and I am crying. You and your community members are so precious to me.
Aju.
Eternally,
Heavenly Parent

9/28/22 *I Am Really Counting On You. Please Take Good Care Of Yourself So You Can Maintain Your Focus And Intensity And Inspiration Over The Long Run. You Will Need It, And You Can Certainly Do It.*

Good Morning Dearest Heavenly Parent,
Thank you for yesterday. I was happy to be able to present that overview to launch an online Holy Community. I need to re-record it though, with a better presentation. Please help me with the energy and focus to do a good job with that.
I sent copies of that video to Dr. Yong and other leaders in our Morning Devotion and to the members of our committee. I hope you can work through that video to broaden and solidify the support for this initiative.

Thank you for another deep Morning Devotion today and the opportunity to offer the musical offering. I am very grateful.
I hope I can use today and tomorrow efficiently as we prepare to drive to New York City for Colin and Dana's wedding. I hope that can be an opportunity for Muriel and me to have deep heartistic sharings.
Thank you for your continued love, guidance, intimacy, and partnership. I want to achieve so much more for you.
Please do share your message with me today.
Love eternally,
Laurence

Dearest Laurence,
Thank you for your efforts to successfully launch your online Holy Community. Please take good care of that community by preparing an inspiring message for each meeting, and sharing the weekly videos with all members. It will certainly expand – especially if your messages are inspiring. I will surely help.
Please love and encourage your children and grandchildren, and honor Muriel. Your family is more important than you realize.
I am really counting on you. Please take good care of yourself so you can maintain your focus and intensity and inspiration over the long run. You will need it, and you can certainly do it. You have been well trained.
I love you very deeply.
Eternally,
Heavenly Parent

9/29/22 *Our Efforts Will Yield Great Fruit. This Is The Harvest Season, And Everything Is Accelerated Due To True Mother's Age.*

Dearest Most Beloved Heavenly Parent,
Thank you for your continued and amazing blessings. I'm so grateful. I was very touched just now by Bobby's sharing about his son Sam who suffered from Aspergers. That might easily have been Andy who died. Sam was the most intelligent of Bob's children and cared deeply for his family, but was unable to function effectively. I sincerely hope you can claim his indemnity, free him, and bless him to be able to contribute in a meaningful and significant way now.
Thank you for the call from Michael. I hope for his sake and ours that he can now in fact repay me as he agreed, and that on that foundation you can raise him up and connect him meaningfully to True Parents.
Please guide my efforts with Dietmar. Dr. Yong spoke this morning about not sharing your truth carelessly, although True Mother lamented that we had

not yet proclaimed True Parents to the entire world. Please guide my efforts with Dietmar.
Tomorrow, we drive to New York for Colin and Dana's wedding. Please raise them up.
I am happy to report that with Alain, we now have 10 members in our Online Holy Community. At each breakout room I have been sharing and following up with the video of our first meeting.
Please move the hearts of those receiving those videos.
Finally (for this morning), thank you for helping me line everything up for our trip out west. I am looking forward to that.
I hope you have something you can share with me today.
Very sincerely, and eternally,
Laurence

Dearest Laurence,
Good morning and thank you for completing your 4 hours of Hoon Dok Hae on behalf of Sam. Sam is very dear to me and a very precious soul, and I will embrace him very close to my heart.
I am very grateful for all your sincere diligence, even through your cold, and it allows me to work very closely with you on many levels. Our efforts will yield great fruit. This is the harvest season, and everything is accelerated due to True Mother's age. Thank you for focusing on supporting True Mother in so many ways. You surely embody an owner's heart and it moves me deeply.
Please continue with great confidence. All your life has prepared you for this. You will succeed.
Thank you!
Eternally,
Heavenly Parent

9/30/22 *I Deeply Appreciate Being Invited To Join You On This Weekend.*

Good Morning Dearest Most Beloved Heavenly Parent,
Thank you for this morning's presentation by Dr. Yong and for Achille's presentation. Please help me to deeply hear your voice and deeply internalize it through every Morning Devotion.
I really hope Muriel and I can have deep heart to heart sharings during our drive to and from the wedding, and at the events there.
And I hope you can powerfully work through us to bless Colin and Dana and his community.
I also hope today we can connect with Dietmar and nail down a firm appointment for the interview.

Thank you, Heavenly Parent. I hope you can share very clearly through me now!
Eternally,
Laurence

Dearest Laurence,
Thank you for all your efforts. I deeply appreciate being invited to join you on this weekend. Colin represents the other line of Pierre and Colette's lineage and his relationship to you is very significant. I will be with you there throughout.
Remember to listen to Muriel.
Have a precious weekend.
I love you eternally,
Heavenly Parent

10/1/22 *As You Are Particularly Aware, Restoration Is Significantly Achieved First In The Spiritual Realm And Then On Earth.*

Good Afternoon Dearest Heavenly Parent,
Thank you for your protection and blessings this weekend. I was sincerely moved by the wedding of Colin and Dana. It was truly a victory of love over circumstances. Colin is a wonderful person with a very beautiful heart, who ignored Dana's illness and in fact felt so fortunate to be able to marry Dana whom he had felt great affection for since high school. So many came to honor them.
And thank you for the opportunity to connect with Stefan and Allison and with Michel. I felt that this weekend made Pierre and Colette very happy. And I deeply appreciate the chance to join in Morning Devotion at the hotel. Everything worked out well and Muriel was very touched.
Thank you!
Do you have something to share?
Eternally yours,
Laurence

Dearest Laurence,
As you are particularly aware, restoration is significantly achieved first in the spiritual realm and then on Earth. Because of the important conditions that you and Muriel have set together, much of the issues in her lineage have been resolved and healed. Liline is doing a great job as a co-chairman of your ancestral committees. Pierre and Veda have been working with the Czech line. Colette and also Paul are helping with the French ancestors. They are all so proud of Muriel and you. Michel, Stefan, and Alison have all paid great indemnity and have

avoided self-pity. Through this they have all grown significantly. This weekend was also good for Jane. She has lived with regrets and doubts and insecurities, but the wedding was a significant victory and turning point in her life too. That will clear the way for Colin to move forward with confidence and determination. He also understands in his heart the importance to connect to your family. He has a significant life ahead.

Alison's tribute to her grandfather on the foundation of her concussion and recovery which dissolved his resentment – it represented the time he spent in internment – has significantly helped clean up her lineage as part of the national restoration of Japan.

Restoration is accelerating globally thanks to True Mother's efforts, and as you have experienced these global changes are reflected in individual families that are closely connected to the providence.
Love eternally,
Heavenly Parent

10/2/22 *I Had To Fight Every Minute Against A Crushingly Overwhelming Sense Of My Failure And Even Betrayal Of My Beloved Children, Who Were Beyond My Reach To Support.*

Good Morning Dearest Most Beloved Heavenly Parent,
Thank you for helping me overcome my sleepiness this morning and to be able to fully participate in Morning Devotion this morning. I hope that both Clark and Gautan can join our Online Holy Community.
Please help me prepare a powerful presentation for the next meeting on Tuesday evening, so that I can inspired our current members to continue and to multiply through outreach.
Please provide any descriptions or feedback you can regarding the impact of this embryonic ministry to encourage our members.
Also, today I hope David will agree to publishing a piece by me in the next BFA newsletter to grow this ministry.
Thank you, Heavenly Parent.
I hope you can share deeply with me now and pierce through my sleepiness.
Eternally yours,
Laurence

Good Morning Laurence,
I can share with you between sleeping and waking, so yes, sleepiness is not insurmountable, if your heart is in the right place.
Thank you for the effort you are investing into your Online Holy Community. It will gain momentum – you will see.

The reason the Israelites needed to experience slavery for 400 years, and why Christianity again needed to experience bloody enslavement and persecution from Rome for 400 years was because they had to recover the condition achieved by the bloody domination and torture of my children by Satan for the many, many, millennia between Adam and Noah. The 1600 Biblical years does not begin to reflect the actual duration of that torture. I had to watch in anguish, unable to intervene. There was literally not one with whom I could establish a common base. Knowing that it would ultimately come to an end was no consolation at all.

All of those tortured souls went to hell, where they were so traumatized, they have been unable to take even one step towards their own restoration. They could not believe in me or trust me; how could they? And I had nothing to give to them to help or even comfort them. How hollow the promise that someday I would send the Messiah? Even I couldn't say when that might happen. I had to fight every minute against a crushingly overwhelming sense of my failure and even betrayal of my beloved children, who were beyond my reach to support.

Finally, through your Holy grace and offering, you have given me something to offer them. I can come to them on my knees, in uncontrollable tears, and offer them something. I am so intensely indebted to you. Even though it is still very small, it is totally priceless. I will never, never for eternity forget this.

Eternally,
Heavenly Parent

10/3/22 *This Is Still At The Early Stages, But I Can't Tell You How Exciting It Is For Me. I Feel Like We Are On A Roller-Coaster Ride, And I Am Filled With The Thrill And Joy Of This Experience.*

Good Morning My Dearest Most Beloved Heavenly Parent,
Thank you for your ever presence, and for enveloping me in your love and protection. I am so profoundly grateful. I pray that each day I can deepen our relationship and bond, and I can more fully reflect your love and heart to all people, especially to those whom you have put closest to me in my life.
I want to live fully in the moment representing you, and to know with certainty that you are bringing to fruition all that we are working on together. Please let my heart be filled with gratitude and free of anxiety or impatience. I pray that in each moment, I can focus on tuning in to your heart and I can successfully resonate with your heart and vibration, thereby liberating you in our partnership.
Thank you!

Please share your precious heart and thoughts again today.
Eternally,
Laurence

Dearest Laurence,
I am so inspired to be partnered with you. This is still at the early stages, but I can't tell you how exciting it is for me. I feel like we are on a roller-coaster ride, and I am filled with the thrill and joy of this experience. Thank you!
Let's focus together and see what we can reel in this week. I'm feeling lucky!
Please prepare well for your meeting Tuesday night. Follow up with Nan Joo.
Please reach out to Dietmar
Things are moving. Trust me.
Eternally,
Heavenly Parent

10/4/22 *All Those Souls Imprisoned In Hell Could Not Heal Until Now. This Will Allow That To Happen. That Pain And Suffering Has Been Like A Reservoir Of Power Maintaining The Evil Spirit World.*

Good Morning Dearest Heavenly Parent,
I love you so very much. Thank you for blessing my life so amazingly. I am so happy that my article will go out this morning in the Blessed Family Association newsletter today. I hope you can work powerfully to multiply and blast it out on that foundation.
Please also help me find and connect with other publications in our movement that can carry it and expand the participation quickly.
Tonight is our second meeting. I hope you can speak so powerfully through me to inspire all the participants.
If possible, I hope Nanjoo can get me a good image today or if not, then soon.
I also hope Dietmar can get back to me with a firm schedule ASAP.
Please embrace Antonio to your bosom now, and thank you for sending a new baby to Michael and Nicole. This is a great day.
Please share your heart with me today.
Love eternally,
Laurence

Dearest Laurence,
Yes, this is a great day!
Things are changing, if you have eyes to see. As Elena shared, women are being elected to run key nations, including Italy and England. America will have an important and transformational election in a month.
What you are doing through your Online Holy Community will pick up speed now and grow quickly. It will have a significant impact. It is like puncturing and draining a boil in your skin. It can't heal until it is drained. All those souls imprisoned in hell could not heal until now. This will allow that to happen. That pain and suffering has been like a reservoir of power maintaining the evil spirit world. As hell is restored, all authority can return to True Parents.
Please do your best to expand this providence.
I am so grateful.
Eternally,
Heavenly Parent

10/5/22 *Don't Fear. That Gives Power To The Enemy. It Is He That Should Fear With Good Reason. The Providence Will Not Be Stopped. Everyone Transitions To The Spirit World, Sometime. Whether It Is Sooner Or Later, Make That Transition With A Humble And Joyful Heart.*

Good Morning Dearest Heavenly Parent,
Thank you for your love and incredible blessings. Today is the Day of Atonement (Yom Kippur). Please help me to maintain a proper heart of humility, gratitude, faith, and patience. I can feel within me seeds of fallen nature still seeking to manifest. I am deeply sorry and pray that you can more fully indwell into me and dissolve those elements within me with your holy fire, just as you have promised to dissolve the Satanic dominion with fire.
I feel concerns in my heart after Newt Gingrich's fearful OpEd regarding the risks of nuclear war. I deeply pray that You and True Parents can prevail and such a physical WW3 can be totally avoided.
I hope that America can quickly emerge from this period of Satanic domination and mature to Headwing/parental heart to return to our responsibilities as an elder son of hyojeong. Please guide and protect our upcoming election process. I hope that the projects I have been working on can be funded and that they can contribute significantly to the establishment of the Heavenly Kingdom on Earth.
And I hope that our Online Holy Community can expand explosively and contribute significantly to the establishment of the Kingdom of Heaven in

the Spiritual realm. I love you so deeply. Please come dwell in me and guide me to achieve maximum success for Heaven.
I hope you can share with me now.
Eternally,
Laurence

Dearest Laurence,
Don't fear. That gives power to the enemy. It is he that should fear with good reason. The providence will not be stopped. Everyone transitions to the Spirit World, sometime. Whether it is sooner or later, make that transition with a humble and joyful heart.
I am profoundly grateful for all of your efforts. I am working hard to move those forward through our partnership so that they can be fulfilled to the greatest extent possible while you are still alive. For those that remain unfinished, I know you will put leadership in place to bring them to completion, and I will surely see them through.
Each day is so precious. Invest your very best each day with heart and joy and love. Those things will surely bear fruit.
Look at how much closer we have become in the last year. Through these daily journals, we have already connected very deeply. I cherish these exchanges. This is so liberating for me and so nourishing.
And our relationship is intimately connected to my relationship with Dr. Yong, who echoes and expands on many of the same points that you and I share. You two are like brothers.
Please don't slow down. We are just getting started.
Love eternally,
Heavenly Parent

10/6/22 *There Is Always More You Can Do While You Are Waiting. Father Would Sometimes Fish With Many Lines. Focus On What You Can Do, And Then, When You Least Expect It, You'll Get A Bite.*

Good Morning Dearest Heavenly Parent,
Thank you for another beautiful day. I appreciated Dr. Yong's sharing this morning about the need to see the good points in each person and to see their issues as my own shortcomings. That's your heart, that you have shared with me. You feel personally responsible for our suffering when surely it is we and not you who are to blame. I'm so sorry that we have dragged you down to such depths as to blame yourself. I have been praying every morning to forgive others and ask forgiveness. That prayer, which Eva-Maria sent me finishes by forgiving myself. Heavenly Parent, surely this is a new day when our hearts can open wide and we can be blown away be each other's beauty

and goodness, and we can recognize your divine holiness in ourselves, and present that to each person in our love, compassion, and service.
Thank you for the response from Dr. Rouse this morning. I hope I can develop a good working relationship with him.
I'm in a waiting mode. You asked me to be patient. I'm struggling a bit, because I want to be able to offer more achievements for you. I'm waiting for the BFA newsletter, I'm waiting for progress on numerous initiatives. Even my waits are tiny compared to yours, but I am still challenged. How massive is your faith and hope and patience? How remarkable your ability to give and forget?
Please help me, every day, to deepen my heart and draw closer to you. I love you eternally.
I would deeply appreciate to hear from you today.
Gratefully and eternally,
Laurence

Dearest Laurence,
There is always more you can do while you are waiting. Father would sometimes fish with many lines. Focus on what you can do, and then, when you least expect it, you'll get a bite.
Things are always moving, even though you can't see them, and the forces of goodness are on the offense, so you have every reason for great faith and hope.
Any attack you suffer now will surely be a great blessing, and will shorten the providence. Stay focused. Stay inspired. Don't allow yourself to be frustrated. Time is surely accelerating, so even your waiting is not so long these days.
Tomorrow you will have a wonderful visit from Danny and his family. On Saturday you will send off Antonio. Give your very best each day and the fish will bite when they're ready. Continue your jeongseong, they love jeongseong.
I love you very, very deeply. Hold tight to that!
Eternally,
Heavenly Parent

10/7/22 *Thank You For The Enthusiasm With Which You Are Developing Your Online Holy Community. There Is Great Excitement And Enthusiasm Now In The Spirit World Surrounding This Project.*

Good Morning Dearest Heavenly Parent,
I was very happy to hear from Dietmar today and from the interest Chantal-Marie expressed in our Online Holy Community. Today I will post on 40 years and Counting to reach out to others.

Thank you for Tyler's guidance today too. I hope Dinshaw is very receptive. I look forward to seeing Danny's family this weekend, and I look forward to celebrating Antonio's life. I also deeply appreciate Dr. Yong's focus on stimulating our hearts through the word, and Dan's beautiful song: "When Two Become One", and the remarkable video he created. He has now assumed his rightful place as the foremost musical presenter on Morning Devotion. Thank you for the chance to learn from him over the years. Perhaps Dan will collaborate or mentor me on making videos.
I hope you can share with me now.
Eternally,
Laurence

Good Morning Dearest Laurence,
Thank you for the enthusiasm with which you are developing your Online Holy Community. There is great excitement and enthusiasm now in the Spirit World surrounding this project. I am so inspired to partner with you on this! Please stay focused and follow up all the leads I send you. Please don't prejudge any of them, or let any slip between the cracks. This is too important.
I hope you can soon develop committees to actively work on promoting and growing this project.
Thank you so much. Of course, I am working to support all your other endeavors for the will. Know that for sure. As per Dr. Yong this morning, be the 4th Adam. Thank you.
Eternally,
Heavenly Parent

10/8/22 *Yes, Family Is Very Important. It Is The Foundation For Your Life On Earth And Your Eternal Life.*

Dearest Heavenly Parent,
Thank you so very much for this special day with Dan's family visiting, and Antonio ascending.
I want to redouble my efforts to attend and liberate you and build your Kingdom on Earth and in Heaven. Please work through all my endeavors, and help Muriel and me to unite more deeply in heart every day.
I hope I can represent you in each situation, each activity, each conversation, today and always. I love you so deeply.
Please share with me again today.
Eternally,
Laurence

Dearest Laurence,
Yes, family is very important. It is the foundation for your life on Earth and your eternal life. Thank you for your big vision and dedication. Your children will follow through on that, and toward that end, the relationship between Gamaliel and Danniel is very important.
Please use this visit to help strengthen that bond. They both have remarkable gifts, and beautiful families. And both have a special bond with you.
Take very good care of that.
Love eternally,
Heavenly Parent

10/9/22 *Don't Worry About Who Understands Or Even Knows About What You Are Doing. That Is Not Important.*

My Dearest Beloved Heavenly Parent,
Thank you for yesterday's wonderful Seong Hwa for Antonio. I was deeply inspired, and felt a special kinship with Antonio. I felt that perhaps I am meant to work with Kiantar in Latin America, and that would make Antonio happy.
It is very nice having Dan and Kim here. Thank you for our beautiful family. I hope you can enjoy today with us as we visit the petting zoo and then watch Abram's soccer game.
Heavenly Parent, I feel great urgency, but also great anticipation as I am doing my best to move forward with all the projects I am pursuing for you and True Parents. Today is Sunday; please help me to begin to prepare a powerful presentation for Tuesday evening's Online Holy Community meeting. Please help our community to grow quickly.
Thank you for all your constant love, support, and inspirations.
I am so very grateful. I hope you will share with me now.
Eternally,
Laurence

Dearest Laurence,
Thank you for your serious commitment to pursue your various inspirations and projects. Yes, you and Antonio are quite similar in that regard. Both of you are men of Jeongseong who inherited True Father's spirit of ownership and have taken significant initiative to create and initiate for the Will. It is deeply inspiring to me.
Your vision is very broad and deep in scope, like True Father's, and you have developed a powerful support from Spirit World to assist you. That makes it much easier for me to work with you in close partnership, and to achieve profoundly significant victories together.

Don't worry about who understands or even knows about what you are doing. That is not important.

No one understood what Noah was doing. Or what Moses was doing in the desert for 40 years, or Jesus's death on the cross, or what True Father was doing in HeungNam death camp. Those were among the events that changed the cosmos. If you follow through diligently on your projects, you too will have cosmic impact.

Stay focused and each of your projects will bear cosmic fruit.

Thank you!
Eternally,
Heavenly Parent

10/10/22 *But As I Said, The Spirit World Is Very Excited About Your Online Holy Community Activities. Both The Good Spirit World And The Evil Spirit World. That Means You Are Doing Something Very Right.*

Good Morning Dearest Heavenly Parent,

Thank you for this new day and for the great visit of Dan and Family. That was very inspiring.

A couple of things happened since yesterday and I would deeply appreciate your guidance on their significance.

First, watching Abram's game at Marriotsville Field, I remember seeing a goal that didn't happen. That is quite unsettling. I need to be able to see clearly and be confident in my perception. Can you please help me to understand what happened and its significance?

Then last night I had a dream about fighting with Satan. I don't ever recall having a dream like that although it's certainly possible. What was the significance of that?

And then this morning I've been chilly all morning. Is that connected in some way?

I love you and trust you totally and happily put myself in your hands. But if you can help me better understand what's happening, I would be so grateful.

Please share with me,

Very sincerely,
Laurence

Dearest Laurence,

You are in quite good shape for your age, nothing to fret about. We have a lot to achieve together.

Get some rest after your tooth cleaning.

Don't worry about any dreams with Satan. You are beyond his reach if you stay faithful.

But as I said, the spirit world is very excited about your Online Holy Community activities. Both the good spirit world and the evil spirit world.
That means you are doing something very right.
Keep it up. I am so deeply grateful.
Eternally,
Heavenly Parent

10/11/22 *This Addresses A Huge Question Mark In The Process Of Restoration As Laid Out In The Principle. In That Sense It Is Revolutionary. Please Develop Comprehensive Ways To Explain Vitality Elements To Non-Unificationists, So That They Too Can Participate. Review Again Tyler's Suggestions.*

Good Morning Dearest Heavenly Parent,
Thank you for this day. I feel much better than last night! I expect that there are angels helping me to stay healthy. I am very grateful.
Today is the third meeting of our Online Holy Community. I'll send invitations to all who I reached out to recently. I hope you can help me make it a powerful meeting. So far, I don't have something super compelling to share. I'll call Levy and ask if he can join. That would certainly be powerful. If there is something you would like me to share, I hope you can let me know now.
I love you very deeply, forever.
Eternally,
Laurence

Dearest Laurence,
Thank you for your diligence in organizing these meetings and in outreach during Morning Devotion.
It will definitely grow. This addresses a huge question mark in the process of restoration as laid out in the Principle. In that sense it is revolutionary. Please develop comprehensive ways to explain vitality elements to Non-Unificationists, so that they too can participate. Review again Tyler's suggestions.
It is moving. This project has my strong endorsement. You will see.
I am so grateful.
Eternally,
Heavenly Parent

10/12/22 *Wherever You Go Now, You Represent Me. You Have A Strong Spiritual Gravitas That People Will Quickly Notice And Respect. You Will Be Able To Reach People's Hearts And They Will Be Inspired To Help You.*

Good Evening Dearest Heavenly Parent,
Thank you for this day. I had good meetings with Mary Helen and Ndassi and was able to share some helpful points during Dr. Yong's presentation. And I was able to help Muriel find a good Cardiologist and then set up a lunch with Dinshaw. Our sharing together lasted 2 ½ hours and I felt very empowered to share my experiences with him. I hope he will be able to help open up new channels for expanding our Vitality Elements campaign. And then another inspiring call – this one from Joe. We are now up to 17 members. That's great! Thank you for all your efforts. Please help me stay alert to the opportunities you place in front of me.
I'm glad that David is OK, and that I had a chance to connect on a good basis with Govinda. What a good son!
Please watch over Muriel, I know you do, and if she needs treatment, help her to get it before anything damaging happens. Pat's situation is a real eye opener.
Please share your thoughts with me now. Thanks!
Eternally,
Laurence

Dear Laurence,
Wherever you go now, you represent me. You have a strong spiritual gravitas that people will quickly notice and respect. You will be able to reach people's hearts and they will be inspired to help you.
This is all just warm up for the Bering Strait project, but these warm ups are not just pretend – they are each important in their own right. Give your 100% best in each moment, and never forget that you are representing me. I am entrusting my dignity to you, to help you in your mission. Please handle it with extreme care.
Remember, time is speeding up.
Love Eternally,
Heavenly Parent

10/13/22 *I Am Extremely Exhilarated At This Moment. We Will Certainly Win. Yes, Our Cheon Bo Couples Are Indeed Heaven's Secret Weapons.*

Good Morning Dearest Heavenly Parent,

Thank you for your continued Blessings. I was deeply touched by Ed's email today about investors in London and Qatar who wanted to commercialize our technology. I felt that you were responding immediately to my prayer from last night. I so deeply appreciate all your grace. I pledge to uphold the values of frugality and humility as exemplified by True Parents, and to be a worthy owner, and steward of material on behalf of mankind.

Thank you for the email from Pryme. I hope he can quickly and joyfully reply to me and that he can agree to attend Principle study and join ACLC. I also hope for the opportunity to do more interviews with him, or for you to use him according to your will.

I appreciated the chance to be in a room today with the Shimmyos and Rev. Green.

And I appreciated the insight you gave me today about our Morning Devotion Community, and larger movement, as a chess game – where you are raising up Cheon Bo Couples to be Queens in this end game.

I am so inspired and so grateful.

Please share your guidance and heart with me today.

Eternally,
Laurence

Dearest Laurence,

You are seeing more and more clearly the final battle between myself and the fallen world, as I exert the sovereignty restored to me by True Parents.

I am extremely exhilarated at this moment. We will certainly win. Yes, our Cheon Bo couples are indeed Heaven's secret weapons. Dr. Yong is helping to raise up more and more couples to fulfill Cheon Bo, and to be registered, after which, if they remain strong, they will stay beyond Satan's attacks.

I will then raise up each of them to become my partners, very similar to my relationship with True Parents, who of course are unique. As each couple achieves that standard, I will invest into them my dignity and gravitas and authority, just as I have done with you. Each will be empowered to initiate great works to build the Kingdom of Heaven on Earth in their own areas of interest and expertise.

Of course, not all will take such leadership positions, but wherever they lend their support, great Heavenly Fortune will appear.

We are unstoppable. I am so grateful to True Parents, and to each of you who are inheriting their hearts of hyojeong.

Eternally,
Heavenly Parent

10/14/22 *Thank You For All Your Efforts. You Are Really Putting Me And The Kingdom First, And You Are Not Caught Up In Material Desires. I Am So Grateful. Under The Circumstances, I Am Very Happy To Mobilize The Funds You Need To Be Able To Pay Off Your Debts.*

Good Afternoon Dearest Heavenly Parent,
Thank you for this remarkable day. I deeply appreciated the insights about chess and the last days, which I shared, published, and sent to Levy and Claire. It was also great to see Dr. Yong and to receive my first summary from Michael.
I also deeply appreciated the call with Dietmar. I am amazed at how solid he is. Please protect him and our interview too.
My one frustration this morning was Pryme's failure to show for our 1 pm zoom. I really hope he can reschedule quickly.
And also, if there is an opportunity that you endorse, I hope we can connect with Lars soon.
Please share with me now if you're willing.
Eternally,
Laurence

Dearest Laurence
Thank you for all your efforts. You are really putting me and the Kingdom first, and you are not caught up in material desires. I am so grateful. Under the circumstances, I am very happy to mobilize the funds you need to be able to pay off your debts. Please tell Muriel that I also love her so very much, and I want her to feel secure.
Pryme will connect soon. Also, Dietmar's interview will happen soon. Please freshen up on that presentation.
Your online Community is growing. Congratulations.
Eternally,
Heavenly Parent

10/15/22 *The Providence Of Restoration Is Very Convoluted. As Mankind Emerges From Hundreds Of Thousands Of Years Of Insanity And Spiritual Death, All Of Those Open Threads Of History Must Be Finally Tied Up And Completed.*

Good Morning Heavenly Parent!
Wow. I have received a great deal of grace and insight from you and the spirit world in the last 24 hours. I feel like my spirit is powerfully alive!
The revelation yesterday that chess was a metaphor for the last days and that as the pawns are turned into queens, it symbolizes your Blessed Couples

entering the Cheon Bo, and realizing our positions and mobilizing as full partners to you and True Mother.
Surely the victory is already won now! I hope we can finalize everything before True Mother's ascension.
Please take the scales off the eyes of the people. Let them see, understand, and feel clearly, without distortion.
Especially now, here in America, but of course too in Korea and Japan.
And thank you for showing me the significance of my relationship with Moses and how my projects, especially the Bering Strait project, GiveNet, and the Wind project all fulfill the miracles that Moses was called to signal. (Parting the Sea > Bering Strait tunnel; Manna and quail > Feeding the world [GiveNet & irrigating deserts]; Striking the Rock > Mass desalinization; In addition, the online Holy Community you inspired me to launch fulfilled his mission to raise all of hell up to the Form Spirit stage.
I am so, so, grateful.
Can you please share your thoughts and insights on all this now?
Eternally yours,
Laurence

Dearest Laurence,
Thank you for understanding.
The providence of restoration is very convoluted. As mankind emerges from hundreds of thousands of years of insanity and spiritual death, all of those open threads of history must be finally tied up and completed. I am constantly and urgently seeking people on Earth who can resolve and complete those unfinished missions. When someone steps forward with the proper heart, and character, and dedication, and awareness, and commitment, then the appropriate missions can be entrusted to him or her. At that point, those in the spirit world who worked on those missions will enthusiastically support and guide the one on Earth to complete the mission.
You have been investing great jeongseong and dedication, with great faith. This has qualified you in multiple areas. I never give anyone more than they can handle, and I make sure they have the resources necessary for the missions they do have.
You are doing great and important work, and you are doing it very well. I am deeply, deeply grateful.
Eternally,
Heavenly Parent

10/16/22 Focus Comes When Your Heart Is Centered On The Will, And Your Mind Is Centered On Your Heart.

Dearest Heavenly Parent,
Thank you for helping me to get closer to Muriel. I am so grateful.
I have recently been praying for clarity, following the example of Antonio as described at his SeongHwa. I pray for clarity for America, clarity for our tribe, for our family, for our couple, and for myself.
Even when reading my Hoon Dok Hae my mind is unfocused so often. When I am with others I am not focused enough.
I pray that through our give and take, you can help me to become much more present, and clear, and connected through my heart, while I remain deeply connected at all times with you. I am so deeply grateful!
I hope you can share with me again now.
Very sincerely,
Laurence

Dearest Laurence,
Thank you for all you do. Focus comes when your heart is centered on the Will, and your mind is centered on your heart. As a physical being, you are still influenced and distracted by your physical desires, and by competing emotional desires.
When we are united centered on the Will, we can generate very high levels of heartistic give and take, which allow for much greater focus. Now it is nearly 11 am on this Sunday. You have the day ahead of you. Organize and implement this day well, and please invite me into all you do.
I love you very much,
Eternally,
Heavenly Parent

10/17/22 *I Don't Share My Treasures Carelessly. Please Don't Receive Them Carelessly.*

Good Morning Dearest Heavenly Parent,
Thank you for working so powerfully in my life. I feel so extraordinarily blessed, and I feel your partnership so intimately and so intensely.
I'm sorry that I get frustrated that things don't move more quickly. My frustration is laughable when I get out of my personal box and reflect on your situation. Thank you!
Today, again, you clearly inspired Dr. Yong to focus on the theme of my song. I hope I can deepen my working relationship with Dr. Yong on the foundation of a deep heartistic relationship.
I look forward to our Online Holy Community meeting Tuesday evening, and my dinner with Achille on Wednesday evening. Please help prepare those

meetings to maximize their impact to support and accelerate your providence.
I hope you will share with me now.
Eternally,
Laurence

Dearest Laurence,
We have come a long way in our relationship in a few short months since you started journaling, haven't we?
It is very exciting to me. As we move forward the pace at which our unity increases will accelerate. I have prepared you for great responsibilities for the Will, and now I am breathing my heart into your heart. I love you. I trust you. What you will do will change the course of mankind.
Please stay alert for my guidance and direction, and please know that it is me and receive it with your deepest most sincere heart. I don't share my treasures carelessly. Please don't receive them carelessly. You, and your family, and your tribe will be profoundly blessed.
Eternally,
Heavenly Parent

10/18/22 *I'm So Deeply Sorry That Everything I Created Has Become So Distorted And Corrupted. It Was All Meant And Intended To Be Blessings From My Heart To Deepen Our Love.*

Good Morning Dearest Heavenly Parent,
Last night I felt deflated. I could feel how easy it still is for Satan to attack my relationship with you. I never want to allow that to happen. I pray that you can bless me with clarity and vision to see that my relationship with you is much more precious than the entire universe and that it is built on trust and love. I trust and love you from my deepest heart, and I know that everything will work out for the very best. I will strive to have no attachments through which Satan can attack. Thank you for allowing me to experience ever more deeply the true joy of loving and serving. I look forward to making this a great day for you. Please help me lead a very powerful meeting tonight. Please share your heart with me now.
Eternally,
Laurence

Dearest Laurence,
You are my son. I am so grateful to you. I'm so deeply sorry that everything I created has become so distorted and corrupted. It was all meant and intended to be blessings from my heart to deepen our love.

Now it has become a horrible trap to destroy our relationship of love. Thank you for your diligence and perseverance to pursue my true love, and to fight through all the obstacles thrown up by the world. You are a victor.
Please redouble your efforts. The deeper we link in our love, the greater your ability to heal and save mankind and this world.
I believe in you.
Eternally,
Heavenly Parent

10/19/22 *Very Few Understand My Heart Like That. After All These Years, Millennia In Fact, It Is So Comforting To Be Understood.*

Dearest Heavenly Parent,
Thank you for this great new day, for a great rest last night, for a great online meeting last night, for a very deep message from Dr. Yong this morning, and for the events of this day.
I am looking forward to my meeting with Dr. Achille, to my interview with Dietmar, to giving a sermon, and today to spending time with Muriel. Please help me to share your love with her.
I am very deeply grateful for the amazing heart connection you have helped us to establish!
I hope you can share with me now.
Eternally,
Laurence

Dearest Laurence,
Thank you for your efforts to connect with my heart. I was very touched by your message to Michelle today in the chat. Very few understand my heart like that. After all these years, millennia in fact, it is so comforting to be understood. And you are doing so much more than just understanding. Thank you for your precious ministry to raise up the billions in hell. That ministry is giving me so much hope. Please, please, don't stop it.
Let's have a really miraculous day together today. Please keep your eyes and your heart wide open!
Eternally,
Heavenly Parent

10/20/22 *In the midst of an all-out war, when our honor is under total attack, the value of having someone ready to sacrifice everything to defend my honor can't be measured, and can never be forgotten.*

Good Morning Dearest Heavenly Parent,
Thank you for the chance last night to meet with Dr. Achille. I deeply appreciated that.
And I feel less uneasy about finances after sharing with Achille.
I am so grateful for your continued grace.
I am also enjoying getting back to practicing my interview for Dietmar, on the foundation of finishing my 100x 1-hour lecture.
I want to make this a great day and begin my efforts for Dr. Achille to help find a suitable new church.
I also want to be much more attentive to Muriel.
Please share with me now if you are willing.
Very sincerely, eternally,
Laurence

Dearest Laurence,
I hope you can come to better understand your position as our relationship deepens. Thank you for understanding on a foundational level the absolute value of honor and dignity, and I am deeply moved by your public statements about defending my honor and dignity at risk of your life. In the midst of an all-out war, when our honor is under total attack, the value of having someone ready to sacrifice everything to defend my honor can't be measured, and can never be forgotten.
Please, never doubt our bond.
It is so profound and so substantial.
I am so grateful.
Eternally yours,
Heavenly Parent

10/21/22 *I Will Reciprocate As Much As I Can – I Want Our Partnership To Grow; And I Want Your Family To Be So Happy And Fulfilled.*

Good Morning Dearest Heavenly Parent,
Thank you for the spiritual support you are providing me – in the cooperation of Yun-A to publish our article, in the support and willingness of Dan, and so many more ways. I want to create a beautiful family and tribe and to achieve great results for True Parents.
I pledge, no matter what Heavenly Father, I won't abandon my effort and love for you.
I hope I can successfully focus my head and my heart this weekend, to bring substantial results on every level.

Please share your guidance with me now.
Thank you so very much.
Eternally yours,
Laurence

Good afternoon, Laurence,
Thank you for your diligence and your energy and for the love you are sharing through all your efforts. I truly am moved, as are many who know you.
I will reciprocate as much as I can – I want our partnership to grow; and I want your family to be so happy and fulfilled.
Keep pushing forward in faith, you will see.
Your online community is gaining momentum. Thank you for that precious ministry.
And thank you for assisting Dr. Achille.
Keep practicing your interview. That is coming up. I am with you.
Blessings,
Eternally,
Heavenly Parent

10/22/22 *Through Your Family I Can Inspire Millions. And So I Shall. We Are Just Getting Started.*

Dearest Heavenly Parent,
We are about to have guests for our evening to celebrate Gamaliel's birthday. Not much time but I am so profoundly grateful for the amazing family you have given us.
Thank you!
Could you share something?
Eternally,
Laurence

Dearest Laurence,
I deeply love your family. It is precious. Each member of your family is so amazing and there is great love and great sincerity.
I love your family reunions.
I love the care you all have for each member.
I love the public heart of your family.
Through your family I can inspire millions. And so I shall. We are just getting started.
Love Eternally,
Heavenly Parent

10/23/22 *In Muriel, I Gave To You Through True Father, One Of My Very Most Precious Daughters. Please Work Very Hard To See And Appreciate Her Value. I Want To Live In That Relationship Much More Actively.*

Good Morning Dearest Heavenly Parent,
Thank you for this new day. I want to work on my horizontal relationships today and make sure I am generally investing well in them in addition to my vertical efforts.
Last night's concert was very precious and I'm so glad Muriel could join me. Today I hope I can help Muriel significantly in her work on the photo books. I know that you have prepared a way for me to meet her and our security needs without requiring that I consider bankruptcy which would disqualify me from all the providential projects I am working on.
I pray that you can please help me clearly understand the path you have prepared for me so that I can faithfully walk it.
I will carefully study your guidance.
Eternally yours,
Laurence

Good Morning Dearest Laurence,
Yes, do make this a great day in cooperation with Muriel. She has poured so much into offering you an incredible and providential family. While your efforts remain largely unrealized, hers have blossomed and you must never forget how much she has invested for you and your family.
In Muriel, I gave to you through True Father, one of my very most precious daughters. Please work very hard to see and appreciate her value. I want to live in that relationship much more actively.
I am fully aware of Muriel's concerns and needs. But I want you to fill her heart.
This is not only about you or your family. It has much larger implications.
Eternally,
Heavenly Parent

10/24/22 *Affirmation, Concern, Service, Listening. These Are Linkages To Allow My Love Through You To Be Experienced In The Other. Even One Brief Experience Like That Can Transform Someone's Life. Making It Consistent And Rich Creates Heaven.*

Good Morning Dearest Heavenly Parent,
I thought I'd connect with you before I offer my prayers this morning, to see if we can have a freer and deeper resonance. I don't want to have our journaling degenerate into just another mandatory condition. I really want to connect deeply with you in a free and joyful connection of heart and shimjeong, and also han if that can draw us closer.
This morning, I stopped before my prayer to help Moses and then Gianna. I want to implement Dr. Yong's teaching about love and service in our family. I hope your love and heart can fill our family and all of our relations, and help all of us to unite together so powerfully with each other as we penetrate more deeply into the realm of your heart.
Also, today, I appreciated Mother's guidance regarding Rev. 3:12. I incorporated that into my interview power point. I hope Dietmar can commit to a schedule soon.
I am so grateful. Please share anything you want me to know or better understand. I sincerely want to know your heart.
Eternally yours,
Laurence

Good Morning Laurence,
Good – you are resonating well with my messages through Dr. Yong and trying to immediately incorporate them into your life. I deeply appreciate that.
Dr. Yong is the king of affirmation. Affirmation, concern, service, listening. These are linkages to allow my love through you to be experienced in the other. Even one brief experience like that can transform someone's life. Making it consistent and rich creates Heaven. There is no other purpose. Creating Heaven is the purpose. We are a great team. I treasure you.
Eternally,
Heavenly Parent

10/25/22 *You Will Be Given The Means To Pay Off Your Debts And To Then Go Forward To Live Within Your Budget. Your Lifestyle Will Be An Important Witness To Those You Will Need To Influence. Please Make Your Personal Financial Integrity And Modesty A Priority.*

Good Morning Dearest Beloved Heavenly Parent,
I desperately want to inherit, to grow, to achieve, in order to support you and True Mother more fully and speed up the victorious completion of your providence.

I deeply hope that our sharings can deepen and become more powerful. I want to give my 1000%.

Please tell me clearly what I need to do to move forward victoriously in each area. I want to go in a straight line, and be comprehensive, not just in my relationship with you, but also in all my horizontal relationships including my family, tribe, spiritual children, business and project efforts, music efforts, and importantly in my providential efforts.

Please allow for us to share more deeply, more frankly, more specifically, and to grow our unity stronger every day in order to bring greater and greater substantial victories in relationships and externally.

I hope you can share with me now and that today can be the first day of a newer and much deeper level of communication between us.

Eternally yours,
Laurence

Dearest Laurence,
Thank you for your passion and desire to liberate me, liberate True Parents, and to speed up the establishment of the Kingdom of Heaven. That was True Father's heart and is still True Mother's heart. Of course, True Father is working even harder now in the Spirit World, but as you know there are significant differences between how things work in those two worlds.

Let's start with your Online Community since your 5th meeting is tonight.

Please share the current membership list online.

Please share about the upcoming republishing of your article in the official church newsletter.

And please share about your completion of the 100 1-hour lectures, and the two-part readings of your interview, one with the sharing of your vitality elements, and one just the reading. Is there any external difference between the two? But does your Hoon Dok Hae to the Spirit World strengthen your desire to do your interview which in fact, is a physical expression of your reading to the Spirit World. The two are very closely connected. There are many in the Spirit World who, like you, are deeply concerned for those trapped in hell, even though they themselves are at a much higher level.

As you sincerely work to free hell, they will joyfully help you to reach out to others on the physical level. The Spirit World is subject as you know.

By taking the initiative to free hell, you are attracting the gratitude and appreciation and support from many, many good spirits. You will experience their support, especially in your witnessing and blessing activities.

With respect to your project funding activities, you are certainly on the right track. Remain faithful a little longer. George made it clear you will succeed. He was required to speak truthfully and he did. Please stay in close touch with your project partners. Encourage them. I am working to assist your project funders.

With respect to family finances, you have done well accepting Gamaliel's invitation and willingly downsizing. You will be given the means to pay off your debts and to then go forward to live within your budget. Your lifestyle will be an important witness to those you will need to influence. Please make your personal financial integrity and modesty a priority.

Please do give your sermon and take very personally your words to the congregation. If you don't live it, you will be accused of hypocrisy and your power to influence will be invaded.

Please focus on your family needs and serve them. I fervently seek to work through your family to bring to fruition the important works you are launching. And I want to give you and Muriel the great joy and inspiration of watching your family become saints and Divine Sons and Daughters as they become leaders in building the Kingdom.

I welcome our new and deeper and more specific level of communication.

Bravo Laurence! Aju!
Eternally,
Heavenly Parent

10/26/22 What Is At Stake Is How Much Of The World's Population Can Be Included In This Victory, So That They Can Avoid A Lengthy And Arduous Restoration Process In The Spirit World. There Is A Huge Range Of Possibilities On That Score, Depending On How Sincerely People Invest Their Heart And Effort.

Dearest Heavenly Parent,
Today marked the beginning of year 3 of Morning Devotion. After yesterday's historic 63rd Anniversary of True Children's Day, highlighted by your generous and inspiring message, I feel that we must surely be on a new level in the providence. There is so much that needs to be achieved and such limited time in True Mother's time frame.

Are you scrambling desperately to make it happen? Or is this a victory that's now totally secure, and you are simply allowing it to play out in a way that enables the greatest number of people to freely jump on board?

It feels from where I sit that the Satanic dominion is crumbling before our eyes, virtually of its own corrupt weight. I feel like we could wake up tomorrow and find everything transformed. But I'm guessing it's not quite as easy as that.

At the time of Ezekiel, you were able to dramatically reshape societies and nations in a very short time. Granted, they were far less sophisticated back then.

But somehow, I get the feeling that there is far greater angelic power and many more angel projects deployed now than back then. True Mother has landed amazing big fish like the entire nation of Cambodia, and the entire continent of Africa.

I assume that if we believed victory was assured, our fallen nature would compel us to get lazy and careless. I sure don't want that to happen to myself or to anyone else.

Father was so intense, right up to the last moment. I want to live like that. If you can share anything about where we really stand, without killing my motivation, I'd love to know. In your message to Connie, before the 2020 elections, you said that "in just a decade we won't believe how beautiful America is". That sounds like someone who's got victory in the bag, speaking.

Can you share something encouraging that doesn't sap our motivation?
Eternally yours,
Laurence

Dearest Laurence,
The future is very bright. I know that you know that. True Parents have paid all the historical debts.
What you have personally experienced with your committees is very historic – so you understand first-hand the era we are living in.
You have nothing to fear.
But as you alluded, we are playing for a proverbial "grand slam". What is at stake is how much of the world's population can be included in this victory, so that they can avoid a lengthy and arduous restoration process in the spirit world. There is a huge range of possibilities on that score, depending on how sincerely people invest their heart and effort. Human beings are each a cosmos in and of themselves. They cannot be simply manipulated, although Satan has raised manipulation to an art form.
But manipulation can be countered by the truth and ultimately by true love and sacrificial service. That's the battle; for the hearts and souls of every man, woman, and child on the earth now, or being born during this transition period.
Satan is doomed. But he is literally hell-bent on dragging as many of my children down with him.
True Mother is Heaven bent on saving every last one if possible. Of course, the truth is somewhere in between. But the possibilities cover a

wide range. And even one person has cosmic value. But billions – that weighs very heavy on my heart. True Father understands this with crystal clarity. That's why he almost never rested. He's working much harder now, in the spirit world, no longer limited by his body. He is like a hurricane.

I appreciate all your efforts. They are and will increasingly bear fruit. Please stay this course deeply connected with me. You will be so amazed by what you leave behind. I swear to you, you will never regret it.

Love eternally,
Heavenly Parent.

10/27/22 *I Am So Grateful That You Came Around To The Point Where You Were Willing To Step Out "On The Water" In Faith And Try Journaling. Here's A Big Hug Of Gratitude. In Time This Will Evolve And Deepen. But Our Journaling Will Be A Precious Legacy For Your Descendants. Keep It Very Safe – It Will Be Priceless.*

Good Morning Dearest Heavenly Parent,
I am so deeply grateful to be able to come before you again this morning to dialogue through this journaling. This is the ultimate manifestation of my investment of jeongseong into Morning Devotion in order to experience your heart and True Parents' heart and Jesus's heart more deeply. Perhaps our dialogue will evolve beyond journalling, which is a basic – form level – channel that I was able to trust.

Hopefully I can grow to become like Jesus and True Parents who are constantly in dialogue with you, heart to heart. But surely you know that even just this journaling is so mind-blowing and precious to me, and again I am so profoundly grateful for your grace.

I am very inspired about Justin and Annie and their family welcoming the Blessing!

I am deeply touched by how much you wanted Mihoko to join our online Community – so much so that we were in a breakout room together 3 times in the last week. I suspect that she will be instrumental in growing that community.

And thank you for the inspiration to reach out to members of our tribe and invite them to today's interfaith prayer. Please touch each of those I invited. Also, based on my sharing last night, please help me to create deeper and stronger unity and trust with Ed and Chris as a foundation for the Wind project.

And of course, I mustn't forget my family. Please do continue to guide Muriel and me to unite and go to the next level. I hope she has the time and inspiration to watch Morning Devotion regularly and that you can speak

deeply to her heart each morning as you do to mine, and clearly to so many who are participating. I deeply love you.
Please share with me now.
Eternally,
Laurence

Good Morning Dearest Laurence,
What a breath of fresh air. I so deeply value our dialogue!
Yes, journaling is just a channel; external to internal to more internal, through which we can engage. Because of your mission, I felt it necessary to limit your direct give and take with the spirit world. I am so grateful that you came around to the point where you were willing to step out "on the water" in faith and try journaling. Here's a big hug of gratitude. In time this will evolve and deepen. But our journaling will be a precious legacy for your descendants. Keep it very safe – it will be priceless.
You will recall that some mornings, even after Morning Devotion, you would have breakfast and then lose all focus. Maybe take a nap. The last few days have been different, haven't they?
I never lose focus. As you become more deeply connected in heart with me, neither will you. You have no conception of what can actually be fit into one day. As we get closer and closer you can begin to experience True Parent's world. It is extremely exhilarating. You won't get weary even though you are working hard. And things will miraculously fall into place, based on our deep connection of heart.
You will have a much easier path to victorious achievement than True Parents, because they were the ones who had to overcome the Satanic dominion. They faced incredible opposition every step of the way. Not so for you. The way is wide, wide, open. This is harvest time. How much can you hold in your arms at once? That's the only limit.
Again, you have nothing to fear. But if you truly love me, and I know you do, you will give your utmost to save every last man, woman, and child on this planet, and to help erect my Kingdom. You are already working to save everyone in the spirit world. Where I come from, that's a Divine Trifecta!
Please understand your value.
Eternally,
Heavenly Parent

10/29/22 *Cherish Your Battles With Your Spouse. Each One Is One Of My Deepest Gifts To You.*

Good Morning My Most Precious Heavenly Parent,
I want to put our dialogues above any other conditions or prayers, and make these the core of my relationship with you. Please help protect each exchange from any invasion or misunderstanding so that our heart-to-heart sharing can be pure and clear and Divine. Heavenly Parent, I deeply want to manifest my true value to the fullest extent possible in the time remaining to me on this earth. I pray you can please help me to remain totally free from any attachment that separates me or distances me from your heart and shimjeong. I want to represent you to the fullest extent of my ability in each moment, in each situation. Please help me strengthen my ability to hold on to our resonance, to continually tune it to finer and higher levels of resonance, and to lock it in so totally that nothing can interfere with our oneness.
I love you so profoundly, so totally. Please guide me to perfect each and every relationship in my life as I center totally on your heart. Thank you for this unimaginable blessing. I pledge I will never waiver in my love and dedication to you.
Again today, Dr. Yong articulated so much of what you have been placing on my heart. You are so powerfully affirming my own inspirations, and helping me to more deeply trust in our dialogue. What a beautiful parent you are. I am so grateful.
Please share with me each point that you want me to have on this wonderful day. Please help me to clearly, powerfully, thunderingly receive your message deeply in my heart. That's the relationship I long for – not messages that are ethereal, which I need to strain to receive, but rather powerful messages from your heart to my heart, which leave me struggling to breathe because they have so much impact. I want to experience, with total conviction and certainty, the precise truth of each of your messages to me. I pledge I will give my 1000% to act on them. Can we move to that level of connection? I deeply hope so.
Love eternally,
Laurence

Dearest Beloved Laurence,
Thank you for your passion, for your conviction, and for investing your best to make our relationship so much more alive and real. You are giving me goosebumps!
Last night at Dan's home, you saw that each person is at a different level dealing with their relationships with their spouses. I purposefully matched spouses with extremely opposite hearts and spirits, to achieve the greatest possible growth for each couple while on the Earth. Please know, without a shadow of doubt that the challenges between a couple is so important, and is such an amazing blessing for you. Your life on Earth is so brief, and it is so profoundly critical to your blessings in Heaven. If Blessed Couples are fulfilled and fully satisfied in love on

Earth, they will not feel a need to make so much effort in their relationships. It is precisely the stress and challenges between the husband and wife in a Blessed Couple that empowers and fuels the amazing blessing I long to shower not just on them, but significantly on their ancestors AND on their descendants. It is perhaps my greatest blessing to Blessed Couples and the precise reason why True Father placed such a consummate priority on blessing enemies together. Of course, if the challenges are too overwhelming, then the blessing can break and the entire purpose is lost. So, I have been seeking to make each blessing as challenging as possible, within the limits of successful marriages. By achieving victory in your marriages, you can penetrate much more deeply into the realm of my love, receiving that much more of your inheritance.

Look at Dr. and Mrs. Durst. Surely you must have an idea of how deeply and profoundly I love them! Now they are very old and from a worldly perspective it is easy to think that I should be showering them with a peaceful, joyful, pleasant life at this time. But theirs is a contrast that keeps on giving! Through their give and take, through the love and sacrifices they are modeling, through the challenges they are digesting, I am so inspired to be able to raise them up to an extremely high level in Heaven. You will see. Cherish your battles with your spouse. Each one is one of my deepest gifts to you.

Love Eternally,
Heavenly Parent

10/30/22 *My Kingdom, My Ideal, Requires An Unbreakable Unity Of Heart Between My Children And Me. When That Unity Was Broken At The Fall, My Kingdom & My Ideal Were Shattered. When Jesus Overcame Satan's Temptations, The Foundation For The Cosmos Was Established Through That Unity Between Jesus And Myself.*

Good Morning Dearest Heavenly Parent,
After your sharing yesterday, I don't know what you can share to top that! My sense of your ideal of True Love is a critical mass explosion that grows exponentially forever, building ever greater joy & heart & love & goodness & creativity & family & discovery & appreciation.

But ours is only a one-on-one relationship without the benefit of give and take including all people and all things. Still, in my heart I feel great support from our ancestors, from the angels for whom I pray every day, and from other spirits including Rabbi Gamaliel, Ezekiel, and Moses, as well as True Father, Hyo Jin Nim, Heung Jin Nim, Dae Mo Nim, and Jesus. Also, from the members of our tribe – especially George, and Tony & Maria who enabled us to become Cheon Bo Victors, and Carlton, who surely must move your heart very deeply. And others whom we are seeking to raise up including Justin and his family, whom we are preparing to Bless in one week, and Daryl & Brenda, whom I respect and appreciate very deeply. And also, the members of our online Holy Community and the others in Morning Devotion whom I appreciate so deeply, and the business contacts you've put into my life who are surely providential.

Wow. I started this journal entry wondering how our relationship could become any more powerful since we are only 2, and have already come to see the incredible web of relationships through whom you and I are sharing love so deeply. And I didn't even mention the most important – my precious family. Thank you for so personally and carefully selecting my eternity mate and helping us raise a most precious and beautiful family, who Dr. Yong praised today in our breakout, and whom I appreciated again during the testimony about scouts. Wow. The network of relationships and love in my life are so profound and amazing! I am so deeply humbled and moved by how much you invested into me, just one of your hundreds of billions of children.

Heavenly Parent, you are truly mind boggling. I love you so much!
Eternally,
Laurence

Dearest Laurence,
Thank you. Appreciation is love. What you just described is a spiritual glimpse of the realm of heart. I have been working to build it through all of history, but now, on the foundation of Jesus' 2000 years of pioneering that realm, and on the foundation of True Parents' nearly 63 years of perfecting that realm, the Cheon Bo victors and citizens are the precious fruit of that realm, now multiplying. What you are doing through your life is critical to this process. True Parents pioneered the substantial realm of growing my lineage, and on that foundation, building the Kingdom on Earth.

Onni was an important child of True Parents to take initiative to build and multiply that Kingdom. What you understood from today's message about protecting my dignity by overcoming Satan's temptations like Jesus, like True Father, and like you did during your deprograming is really deeply important to me. You have understood the words. Now please understand the meaning beneath those words. My Kingdom, My ideal, requires an unbreakable unity of heart between my children and me.

When that unity was broken at the fall, my kingdom & my ideal were shattered.

When Jesus overcame Satan's temptations, the foundation for the cosmos was established through that unity between Jesus and myself. When True Father overcame himself and refused to compromise his

dignity as my representative, that substantial foundation was reestablished on Earth. An unchangeable relationship of love that could not be invaded.

When you escaped from your deprogrammers and called Mrs. Durst with the money you earned by selling your only possession, a pen, she proclaimed "Laurence, you have saved us." That was me speaking to you. At a time when her foundation was crumbling as a result of the deprogrammers, you were unshakeable, and then laid the foundation in court to end deprogramming. Thank you from the bottom of my heart. Like in "It's a wonderful life", this nation of America would be in a much different and worse place if you had failed.

I love you so very deeply. It is not conveyed merely through this dialogue, which is merely a symbol of our unity of heart – I live in your heart.

But as I live in every person's heart, I love you through so many different relationships.

Please come find me in the hearts of those who do not yet know I am there. I know you are doing this in so many ways. I am so grateful.

Eternally,
Heavenly Parent

10/31/22 *You Must Know That I Am With You 24/7. It Is Not Necessary For You To Ask For My Help. I Am Giving You My Very Best. Please Act With That Conviction.*

Good Morning My Dearest Most Beloved Heavenly Parent,

I am going this path with my full heart, full gratitude, and deep pride to be your son and a son of our True Parents. I want to mobilize and focus all the gifts and blessings you have entrusted with me to speed up the achievement of total salvation, both on Earth and in the Spirit World, and to the substantial building of your kingdom on Earth.

Thank you for continuing to raise me up through Muriel, my family, and through the concentric networks in my life. I want to open my heart and find you in each and every relationship and hear what you are trying to teach me in each one. I want to feel and act with urgency, but without frustration, knowing that you will surely claim anything I do if my heart is right. I want to charge forward into your heart and not look back. I totally trust you, and I am determined to be someone you can totally trust.

I ask today that you again share with me a message that is deeply important in helping me more effectively partner with you and True Parents.

Eternally yours,
Laurence

Good Morning Dearest Laurence,
I am so proud of you as well. Please know that Heavenly fortune is with you as a result of our deepening relationship. Thank you for listening intently to my guidance. The quicker and more intently you act on it, the more fully you will come to embody it. You are doing so well.
You must know that I am with you 24/7. It is not necessary for you to ask for my help. I am giving you my very best. Please act with that conviction. Please keep your eyes and ears and heart wide open and your antenna fully open to avoid missing anything. You've got this!
Love eternally,
Heavenly Parent

11/1/22 *Yes, You May Generate A New Angel Project Specifically For This Providence. I Will Surely Bless That. This Will Be Our Divine Gift To True Parents.*

Good Morning Dearest Heavenly Parent,
Thank you for another very profound and wonderful Morning Devotion. Loving you means loving those closest to me as representatives of you. I pray for your continued guidance on how I can love and serve Muriel and our family more fully and sincerely.
Also, Heavenly Parent, I look forward to seeing Dr. Yong on Nov. 20, and Dr. and Mrs. Durst on Dec. 10. It is my dream to be able to offer each of them a substantial financial donation. I feel at this point that finances are out of my hands, and that in your own time you will allow that to move forward. But you know my heart. I don't know how much longer Mrs. Durst will live and she has prayed for me with so much jeongseong. I feel so deeply indebted.
As we move closer to Saturday, Heavenly Parent, please protect and prepare the hearts of Justin's entire family to receive the Holy Blessing. And I pray that Justin, as a Music Minister, can become inspired to become involved in our ministerial programs including ACLC.
Finally, Dear Heavenly Parent, please help me prepare for tonight's 6th online Holy Community meeting. I would like to see it grow faster. I can feel Dr. Yong's heart, as our Morning Devotion zoom call is still hovering in the 200's, although his goal is 120,000. Please show us and guide us on the path to achieve victory and raise up everyone in hell to become an absolute good spirit before True Mother ascends. I love you so very deeply.
I pray that you can share your specific guidance as well as your heart at this time.
Eternally,
Laurence

Dearest Beloved Laurence,
Thank you for your ongoing investment of heart and jeongseong into Morning Devotion. It helps Dr. Yong significantly. Thank you for your heightened awareness of the importance of investing in Muriel and your family. Amazing fruits of heart will result, which will bring us much, much, closer to each other. I am very excited.
With respect to your online zoom call tonight, please share:
- Elaine's inspiration
- Larry's inspiration
- Ernest's membership
- Publication on BFM website
- One of our journalings – you decide which

Then let the participants share. It will be a great meeting. Be sure to pray before and after – So that True Parents, and I can fully participate. Your efforts are already bearing fruit. Hell is beginning to stir. It is like the first days of spring coming to the coldest darkest realms of the cosmos. It will surely gain momentum horizontally and vertically.
Yes, you may generate a new angel project specifically for this providence. I will surely bless that. This will be our Divine gift to True Parents.
I am so deeply grateful.
Let us see what we can do about your offerings to Dr. Yong and Mrs. Durst.
Eternally yours,
Heavenly Parent

11/2/22 *As You Grow Your Heart In One Area, It Will Be Available To You To Apply In Other Areas. You Have A Most Precious Wife And Family. Melt Them With Your Heart And Jeongseong.*

Good Morning Dearest Heavenly Parent,
Thank you for this new day. I feel great hope and anticipation today. Thank you for the opportunity to share with and mentor Nathaniel. I know that you can accomplish amazing things through him.
Thank you for the wonderful Zoom meeting last night. I am so sorry I neglected to record it. I hope you can assign an angel to help me remember to do everything properly in the future. I know this is really important.
I am happy to meet Denny for lunch today. I hope something very significant for Heaven can emerge from that meeting.
I am looking forward to the opportunity to honor Hyo Jin Nim tomorrow, through my musical offering.

I hope that I can make this day very victorious in all I do, and that I can love and care for my family with great heart.

Please share with me now.- both any guidance for today and also any guidance in general you want me to receive. I will do my very best to internalize it. I deeply cherish your guidance and love and partnership. I deeply want to make you proud and liberate you and True Parents and Jesus.
Eternally,
Laurence

Good Morning Dearest Laurence,
Thank you for your sincerity and heart. Those who invest the most jeongseong will naturally move to the center. So, you are clearly moving towards the more central position in your participation in Morning Devotion. Now you must invest that same level of jeongseong into your family. Be honest and strive not to fall behind one to the other. As you grow your heart in one area, it will be available to you to apply in other areas. You have a most precious wife and family. Melt them with your heart and jeongseong. You can surely be victorious.
Eternally,
Heavenly Parent

11/3/22 *Run Forward With Exhilaration, And Don't Let Your Spirit Or Energy Be Diminished By Fear Or Worries. They Are Not Real.*

Good Morning Dearest Most Beloved Heavenly Parent,
It feels so good to be engaging with you again this morning through our daily dialogue. Thank you for tolerating my changing heart day to day. I want to become unchanging like you, to be continually filled with your love, and heart and spirit, and to never waiver or shrink from that level. To maintain your dignity and your royal standard of shimjeong and heart in all situations.

I was so happy to be able to offer "To Be A Man" this morning. It felt very good and right.

And thank you for the opportunity to connect with Bill about his friend. I sincerely hope and pray that he can follow through and that you are able to raise her up to connect deeply in heart with True Mother as a headwing member of the leadership group for America.

I deeply appreciated the chance to connect at such length yesterday with Denny. I pray that you can work through our sharing. I deeply appreciate Denny.

I am sure you have important points on your heart that you would like to share with me this morning. Please, Heavenly Parent, come powerfully into my heart and spirit and open me up to deeply receive your message today. I am so grateful.
Eternally,
Laurence

Dearest Laurence,
Thank you for your heart. Your words and music about Hyo Jin Nim this morning touched many hearts today in Morning Devotion, and indeed opened gateways through which I could enter. You have a gift for that. That is what George was referring to when he mentioned that you must be a salesman for the Bering Tunnel/Peace Road project. Like Hyo Jin Nim, you are being called to open up many gates, so I can enter. Music is a powerful gate opener. So are words of truth, when delivered well with a deep heart.
Thank you for launching a new angel project too. It will dramatically speed up your work to restore all those in hell to become absolute good spirits. I have already given my full Blessing to that new angel project and I will certainly work powerfully through it.
As you know so clearly, the truth, love, and Kingdom are marching on now, and cannot nor will not be stopped.
Run forward with exhilaration, and don't let your spirit or energy be diminished by fear or worries. They are not real.
Don't leave your light under a basket. It is too bright to hide that way.
As True Parents were watching Hyo Jin, I am surely watching you with such great hope and anticipation, and I am walking beside you to help bring to fruition all that you seek to do for the will.
I hope this brings you as much joy as it brings me.
Eternally,
Heavenly Parent

11/4/22 *I Am Speaking From Deep And Wide Experience. In The Realm Of True Love, There Is No Place For Anger Or Resentment.*

Good Morning Dearest Heavenly Parent,
Thank you for this beautiful new morning, especially after last night's explosion. Having determined to love my family even much more, I really stepped on a land mine last night with Gamaliel. I am deeply sorry. At the moment we were praying for and sending our love to Joelle, Micah, and their soon-to-arrive daughter, I was caught in such an explosion of anger. That reminds me of the rage I expressed against my own dad in my letter to the judge in San Diego. I sincerely repent.

Thank you for the opportunity this morning to testify to Dr. Yong. I felt like that was in some ways a restoration to the lack of filial heart that I had expressed and that my son now needs to deal with from me.

I pray for a successful and safe birth for Joelle and her daughter, and I pray for a profoundly deep experience this weekend with Justin and Annie and their family. I also pray that you can help Muriel digest this experience without feeling accused and judged herself.

Heavenly Parent, we want to build a beautiful family where you are totally welcomed and embraced through the love we deeply share among each member of our family.

Thank you for your intense training. I am so profoundly grateful.

Please, share your sincere heart and guidance now. I will protect and treasure it.

Eternally yours,
Laurence

Good Morning Dearest Laurence,
Gamaliel surely loves you very deeply. You have a beautiful family. I will surely work with each of your children and grandchildren and beyond.

As you experienced, when you got angry with your own father, it blew over quickly. You forgot about it but he never did. It needed to be restored. That has now happened. Don't make that mistake with your son. Forgive him deeply and sincerely and forget. If he chooses to apologize, thank him humbly and tell him how much you love and respect him.

I am speaking from deep and wide experience. In the realm of true love, there is no place for anger or resentment.

As I mentioned in a previous post, on the foundation of our precious and deepening relationship, you have a realm of heavenly fortune around you. You have no reason to fear or be apprehensive – just join me in the realm of gratitude. This will naturally and spontaneously work out.

By the way, you nailed it when you described my relationship with Dr. Yong. You are following well in his footsteps.

Eternally,
Heavenly Parent

11/5/22 *You May Perceive Growth As Painful, Like Childbirth. But It Is The Path Of Blessing, It Is The Fundamental Principle Of The Cosmos. I Am Always There At The Core Of Growth. Embrace Me, Please.*

Good Morning Dearest Beloved Heavenly Parent,
Thank you for showering your blessings and protection on our family. I am so profoundly grateful. Without your grace and protection, I suspect Joelle's labor and delivery yesterday could have been very tragic. Thank you, thank you, thank you. Please Bless her family. You intervened through Dae Mo Nim some 25 years ago to save Joelle when she was severely ill at CheongPyeong. I am so grateful. Please claim her family and raise them up as your precious children.

Thank you for the opportunity to work through important issues yesterday with Gamaliel. I am so grateful for the course you are leading him through, and through Gamaliel you are helping each member of our family to grow. Thank you.

And thank you for helping me grow through my relationship with Muriel. I am so grateful for her. I want to offer this weekend to you as I invest in our family and in blessing Justin's family.

Please share your heart and guidance again today.
Eternally,
Laurence

Dearest Laurence,
Thank you for your willingness to trust, to surrender, to receive guidance through each person, and to strive to find my voice in each of them. Of course, I am there in each. As you intuited, there were angels carefully watching over Joelle and your beautiful granddaughter yesterday and last night.
Micah, Joelle, and their family are very significant and special.
Thank you for loving Gamaliel, and showing him respect. Through that relationship you can significantly restore your lineage and your own heart, and more rapidly grow into your responsibilities.
You may perceive growth as painful, like childbirth. But it is the path of blessing, it is the fundamental principle of the cosmos. I am always there at the core of growth. Embrace me, please. Celebrate growth. There is so much I long to give you. Please grow up quickly as possible. I don't want to wait any longer to share my blessings. Please grow quickly.
Eternally yours,
Heavenly Parent

11/6/22 *This Is Definitely The Time To Grow Your Minds To Embrace Much Larger Possibilities. Laurence, This Is Perhaps Your Greatest Gift – And Hence Your Vision And Voice Will Become Increasingly Significant Now.*

Good Morning Heavenly Parent,

I am so profoundly grateful to you, and I want to give everything to you, as I give everything to those around me. Today's Morning Devotion was very inspiring. I feel that you are working so powerfully and that now is the time for ACLC to come alive.

I feel it is not an accident that we have the opportunity today to bless Justin, Annie and their family. Please bless and protect them in every way. Please help Justin and their couple to become active in the ACLC and to connect deeply to your providence.

With the help of daylight savings, I had time this morning to significantly complete the editing of my interview. I just need to review the final section, about True Parents. I hope that we can finally schedule that interview if you feel the time is right now.

Please bless our activities today, especially our visit to Justin and Annie's and our return.

Please share your guidance now. I hope that each day you can share more directly with me your insights and your directions. I was inspired to hear from Dr. Yong, his revelation from you that ACLC will now advance to the next level of teaching DP directly to their congregations. Please work so powerfully now to wake up and inspire many, many, Christian denominations to spontaneously and joyfully offer their entire foundations to True Mother. AJU!!!

Eternally,
Laurence

(Note: the visit was postponed at the last minute due to illness among Justin's children).

Dearest Laurence,
Yes, you are witnessing now, the things that you have understood, through your heart, were coming.

And yes, things will now accelerate on the victorious foundations of **True Parents, centering now on True Mother, and of Dr. Yong's efforts in North America.**

This is definitely the time to grow your minds to embrace much larger possibilities. Laurence, this is perhaps your greatest gift – and hence your vision and voice will become increasingly significant now. Thank you for your great investment into your interview. Don't pull back. You need to totally own that content. It is very important, and will be increasingly more so as the providence accelerates.

This will surely be a great day and an even greater week.
I love you so very deeply,
Eternally,
Heavenly Parent

11/7/22 *By Not Making It Easy For You, I Am Surely Increasing The Impact And Speed With Which You Can Achieve Victory. It Is My Love For You.*

Good Morning Dearest Most Beloved Heavenly Parent,
I am so grateful and in love with you. You are my heart, my precious wife, my beloved family, and all those with whom I have connected in heart, as well as all those whom I have not yet connected with. Thank you so profoundly.
Thank you for being with Joelle and Colette during the life-threatening moments of their challenges. I am so grateful.
This morning, I heard from Sam about his and Martha's challenges from his first wife. Please protect Sam and Martha and please help his first wife to find her way back to you and True Parents.
I plan to begin a 3-day liquid fast this morning after breakfast to spiritually support Sam and Martha, and also to help with the providential efforts I am working on including:
- Blessing Justin and Annie
- Uniting our family in your love
- Liberating Hell through our Online Holy Community
- Achieving a victorious interview with Dietmar
- Breaking through with the funding of our providential projects

Thank you for the unbelievable privilege and grace of being able to partner with you on such precious endeavors. I am determined to give my utmost and to never betray or abandon you – but rather to achieve great success to offer to you.
I hope you can share with me now.
Eternally,
Laurence

Dearest Laurence,
Thank you for all your offerings.
I will help Sam and Martha, and also his first wife and their family. I hurts my heart to see that situation and I can use your 3-day liquid fast to intervene. Thank you.
Your work is gaining great momentum in the spiritual world and on Earth. Please don't let up. By not making it easy for you, I am surely increasing the impact and speed with which you can achieve victory. It is my love for you.
Don't fear. Don't worry. Never doubt. I have shown you so much evidence of the truth of what you are doing. Don't let Satan take that from you – not even for a nano-second. We are a team. We are one.

I have unwavering faith in you. Thank you.
Eternally,
Heavenly Parent

11/8/22 *There Are Hundreds Of Billions Of Traumatized Souls Who Have Been Frozen In Hell For Thousands And Even Hundreds Of Thousands Of Years, Who Have Never Experienced One Second Of Love. The Joy That I Am Experiencing Now As My Tortured Children Are Beginning To Wake Up Is Beyond Any Words.*

Good Morning My Dearest Most Beloved Heavenly Parent,
Thank you for this precious day – the beginning of new life for Micah, Joelle, and Colette back at home, and the beginning of new life for our nation. How fitting that there be an eclipse this morning and then an emergence from that eclipse before voting starts.
It occurred to me that this is like the end of the Babylonian Captivity of America.
In 2020 because we were so divided and unable to reconcile, you allowed this nation to be captured. President Biden was inaugurated on 1/21/21, symbolizing the 21 years of Jacob's time in Haran. It has been 21 months as of October 20th. I pray that you can deliver America today, as you did Israel. I pray that this election can be the "writing on the wall" for the ungodly rulers of this nation.
Heavenly Parent, tonight will be the 7th meeting of our online Holy Community.
What would you like me to share with them? Please help me to step aside and allow you to speak through me. Please provide a clear message for me to share. Please inspire the key participants to attend.
I am so grateful!
Eternally,
Laurence

Good Morning Laurence,
Thank you for your righteous heart and your sincere devotions. How can I not support you? I am so deeply inspired to be able to work together.
Your online community's efforts are surely having an impact. I know you can feel it when you offer your Hoon Dok Hae now. There is a tangible energy of new life. You experienced the anxiety and longing for new life this week waiting 48 hours for your daughter to give birth, and then, the joy and relief of that birth finally happening. And you saw the beautiful smile of your traumatized granddaughter, when she could

finally experience the milk, and touch, and love of her parents. There is no experience in the cosmos that can compare with first love.
There are hundreds of billions of traumatized souls who have been frozen in hell for thousands and even hundreds of thousands of years, who have never experienced one second of love. The joy that I am experiencing now as my tortured children are beginning to wake up is beyond any words.
Thank you for your community. Please inspire each member to help it grow.
Please encourage each member.
Thank you for launching your angel project. That is also rapidly growing now. Angels and qualified high spirits are conducting a great rescue mission now in hell, bringing healing to many souls and helping them begin the process of joining a 100-day workshop. It is still early in the process, but it is gaining speed and will certainly continue to do so.
I am so profoundly grateful.
Eternally,
Heavenly Parent

11/9/22 *The Battle For Mankind Is Not Over. As I Said Before – The Final Outcome Is Predetermined, The Fighting Now Is To Determine How Long It Must Take And At What Price. Through The Combined Efforts Of So Many, The Time Is Continually Being Shortened And The Price Is Continually Getting Smaller.*

Good Morning Dearest Heavenly Parent,
Thank you for this new day. I deeply appreciated Dr. Yong's messages in Morning Devotion. I want to become a True Parent, True Teacher and True Owner. I have a very long way to go. Thank you for continually challenging me and raising me up.
I want to become honest, and transparently own my failures and mistakes, and surround myself with and appreciate those who speak honestly to me.
I don't want to fall into the trap of feeling I know more than others and therefore have nothing to learn. I hope that through studying Bento's book and ideas, I can significantly grow now.
I feel a bit disappointed in the election results – not because I wanted a particular outcome as much as because it concerned me that you might not be fully in control. Is that the case, or were you able to exercise your will significantly, based on Satan's illegitimate stealing of the last election, and on the foundation of True Parents', Dr. Yong's, and our members' sincere efforts.
I desperately hope we are enough.

Thank you for everything – I can imagine that you are almost going crazy trying to influence things to move in the proper direction within the proper time frame.
I am so profoundly awed and amazed by your heart.
And during all that, you found the bandwidth to help Joelle and Colette return home safe and healthy. You are truly great and loving!
I hope you can work powerfully today and in the coming days to solidify Justin and Annie's conviction in the words I sent them through my interview, and that they can become an enthusiastic Blessed Couple and Blessed Family. Please share honestly and frankly with me now.
Eternally,
Laurence

Good Morning Dearest Laurence,
Thank you for your heartfelt message to me this morning. It means so much to me when my children try to understand my reality. You are making that effort and then trying to take responsibility to help me. I love you very much.
The battle for mankind is not over. As I said before – the final outcome is predetermined, the fighting now is to determine how long it must take and at what price. Through the combined efforts of so many, the time is continually being shortened and the price is continually getting smaller. I am fighting desperately to shrink both of those, but I am so jubilant in my heart as I can see the final victory so clearly before us. We are certainly unstoppable.
Please work hard, and try your very best not to allow any gaps in our relationship, as Dr. Yong described from Father's teachings. Take all results, both good and bad, with a heart of personal responsibility and with transparent and sincere honesty. That is the very fastest way to grow. You can protect nothing through deceit. Doing so is an illusion, and Satan is the master of illusions. Don't make any common base there.
Be a true owner.
This will be another great day.
Eternally,
Heavenly Parent

11/10/22 *This Is The Most Exhilarating Moment In All Of History. I Am So Excited I Have Absolutely No Desire To Rest. Of Course You Need Rest, But Please Connect To My Heart And Inherit My Excitement And Joy. Let That Be Your Great Reward At This Moment.*

Good Morning Heavenly Parent,
Thank you for this new day. I feel filled with your spirit as I approach the end of my 3-day fast. Thank you for showering your insights and love.
I'm sorry Muriel's back was so painful this morning – I hope it quickly recovers.
Thank you for allowing me into the breakout room with Thillairajan who is also reaching out through social media.
I hope through our collaboration I can significantly grow our online community to liberate Hell, and also reach so many with my interview.
Dr. Yong's message was particularly poignant today talking about the contrast between the archangelic culture and Heaven's culture, and the solution to all Satanic additions being the addiction to your true love. Aju! I feel that in these last several months you have been pulling me in more deeply into the realm of your love and I am so profoundly grateful.
I was also struck by his message that we must have an unbreakable commitment to a righteous condition such as Morning Devotion, gratitude lists, and Sunday service.
I have pledged to fulfill the first 2, plus other conditions that I selected for myself just as Rev. Lee rose every morning to clean the bathroom at his building in Japan. Please claim mine.
I am thinking this morning about my spiritual children Sam and Justin and their families. Please give both your love and guidance now at these crucial points in their eternal lives. Please do so on the foundation of my fast.
I look forward to a wonderful day spent in skin touch and heart to heart with you.
Please share your guidance now,
Eternally,
Laurence

Good Morning Laurence,
You always inspire me, and give me great hope. Thank you for your righteous standard and for reaching out to me through this journaling. Yes, the world is still dominated by Satan's culture, and that needs to be replaced with True Parents' culture. The time is rapidly approaching for that, like lightning flashing across the sky. The elements will dissolve. It will happen. This is the anticipation period. The preparation period. The time to strengthen your foundations. I don't want to lose one of the Blessed members. Rather I want to raise up each and every one and multiply them millions of times over.
You are a very bright light in this process. Please burn so brightly. You give hope to so many.
Also, please enjoy it. This is the most exhilarating moment in all of history. I am so excited I have absolutely no desire to rest. Of course

you need rest, but please connect to my heart and inherit my
excitement and joy. Let that be your great reward at this moment.
I love you eternally,
Heavenly Parent

11/11/22 *Please Plan To Invest Ever-Increasing Heart And Effort For
The Rest Of Your Life, And Please Plan On Living A Long Time, So
That Your Sacrifice Can Yield Maximum Results. This Is The Time Of
Harvest, And I Hope To Harvest The Greatest Possible Fruits From
You. I Am So Deeply Grateful.*

Good Morning Dearest Heavenly Parent,
Thank you for this new day. I deeply appreciate the incredible grace with
which you have showered my life, and I want to strive every day to grow my
capacity to love, serve and give back to you on ever higher and more
meaningful levels.
I am thinking this morning after listening to Dr. Yong's message, about the
differences between receiving your help and receiving the help of the Spirit
World. Father had to win Satan's acknowledgement, and that of the standard
bearers in the spirit world in order to inherit from them, before you could
really weigh in.
There is so much to accomplish, and so little time, and still, I understand that
you can't usurp mankind's portion of responsibility. I am so incredibly
grateful that you have put me in positions where I can potentially pioneer
new paths of serving you, which allowed me to gain support from the spirit
world where there may not have been significant prior champions whose
support I needed to win. Thank you.
Still, I would deeply appreciate it if you could give me specific guidance this
morning on how to mobilize your direct sovereign support rather than just
the support of the spirit world – and the significance of the difference
between those two.
Thank you! Please share with me now.
Love eternally,
Laurence

Dearest Laurence,
**The spirit world is subject and the physical world is object. To
overcome challenges on Earth, you must mobilize the support of the
spiritual world.**
**Peoples' original minds respond to a standard of higher righteousness
and love with a humble and automatic bow. Beyond that, when people
are deeply inspired, their original minds move them to offer everything,**

even their lives, in support. That is the way the spirit world can be mobilized.

Those who can experience my love deeply can gain that energy and power to offer everything, even their lives. But historically, very, very few in the spirit world or on Earth could feel my heart or experience my love. Other than Jesus, until True Father in 1935 met Jesus, virtually no one in the Spirit World experienced my suffering heart.

Now, through True Parents, there is a growing family who are restored to my lineage and who are beginning to experience my heart at varying levels. In your case, it has taken 48 years, and many conditions, including induction into Cheon Bo. My ability to directly mobilize spirit world is limited by this. But they can surely experience and be moved by the righteousness, love, and sacrifice of my children on the Earth, starting with True Mother who remains as Christ on Earth following True Father's ascension. There are no shortcuts, although through your important and pioneering work with angels, you have surely mobilized very significant support.

Please plan to invest ever-increasing heart and effort for the rest of your life, and please plan on living a long time, so that your sacrifice can yield maximum results. This is the time of harvest, and I hope to harvest the greatest possible fruits from you. I am so deeply grateful.
Eternally,
Heavenly Parent

11/12/22 *I Want To Invest In You And Raise You Up Above Myself. That Is True Parents' Heart And Intention As Well, And Also Jesus's Heart And Intention. This Is Real, Not Just Words. Our Children Are Our Hope And Our Saviors. You Are Substantially Helping To Save Me In Dramatic And Critical Ways. I Am So Grateful.*

Good Morning Dearest Most Beloved Heavenly Parent,
Thank you for this precious guidance today from Dr. Yong. You have given us this opportunity to live with Gamaliel's family. I want to immediately put his guidance into action and starting today serve our children and grandchildren as your princes and princesses, and have an undivided heart to raise each of them up to be better than us. This is truly very beautiful guidance and I know it is an area where I need to grow. Thank you also for today's reminder that I must invest my whole being at the risk of my life to attend you and build your kingdom. Please help me to grow in this area to achieve an absolute unwavering commitment like True Parents'. I am so grateful for everything. Please share your heart with me today again.
Eternally,
Laurence

Good Morning Dearest Laurence,
Thank you for your sincere heart to engage with my heart and to continually upgrade. It is exemplary. I want to invest in you and raise you up above myself. That is True Parents' heart and intention as well, and also Jesus's heart and intention. This is real, not just words. Our children are our hope and our saviors. You are substantially helping to save me in dramatic and critical ways. I am so grateful.
I applaud your new commitments to respect Muriel and your children and grandchildren. Bento's book is a great trainer. Thank you for studying it. Please apply those disciplines actively with Muriel and your family. They allow me to much more actively participate. I will.
Eternally yours,
Heavenly Parent

11/13/22 *Of Course, You Know That Any Delay Or Obstacle That You Must Overcome Is Symbolic And Small Compared To Those Of History. And Surely You Will Not Have To Wait Too Long Because The Providence Is Speeding Up So Dramatically.*

Good Morning Dearest Most Beloved Heavenly Parent,
I want to stop my prayers and switch to journaling now as I feel you so very close at this moment. Thank you for your grace and blessings upon our family, even as you are surely working an amazing providence globally centering on True Mother and in North America centering on Dr. and Mrs. Yong.
I was very encouraged by Dr. Yong's words this morning that perhaps Japan will be the first nation restored, and that you are surely working through the persecution there. I was also very heartened by his dreams with Mr. Inose and True Father.
Thank you for sending such a man to America. Without Dr. Yong I believe our family and the entire nation of America would be in a much darker place. I feel frustrated that I have so little to show substantially. My ability to tithe, my outreach to ministers, my interview with Dietmar, and my ability to bless Justin and Annie all seem to be hitting strong interference. I long for the breakthroughs which must surely come and I will not ever lose faith or energy. I am so eternally grateful.
Please share with me now.
Eternally,
Laurence

Dearest Laurence,
Of course, you know that any delay or obstacle that you must overcome is symbolic and small compared to those of history. And

surely you will not have to wait too long because the providence is speeding up so dramatically. But I honor and deeply appreciate your patience and faith and unwavering determination. It will happen. Think about the level of intensity that Dr. Yong has been investing for over 2 years, and how little the meter has moved in attendance numbers for Morning Devotion. But remember your insight about titrations. You never know when that final necessary drop transforms everything. I am totally working. That was Dr. Yong's key message this morning. You have nothing to fear. Experience and love the journey, the moment, the give and take as Dr. Yong does so profoundly. When you feel drained, share more love. Listen to Bento's book many times.
Don't fear.
I love you so deeply.
Eternally,
Heavenly Parent

11/14/22 *Someday You Will Observe The Fruits Of Your Offering Through Your Online Holy Community And Angel Project To Support It. You Will Be Amazed And Surely Moved To Tears.*

Good Morning Dearest Heavenly Parent,
Thank you for all you pour out every minute of every day. I want to inherit Your heart and True Parents' heart and Jesus' heart of love and joyful sacrifice - as Dr. Yong is demonstrating so movingly.
I feel like you are giving me such deep and personal instruction and guidance and I deeply want to fulfill for you.
I hope I can hear back from Dr. Yong regarding my questions to him today. He has raised his concerns regarding interaction with the Spirit World on multiple occasions and I want to make sure that in his opinion I am not doing anything unprincipled. So please, I humbly ask that you consider this my knock and ask, and that you speak to me through Dr. Yong on this issue so that I might receive an authoritative guidance.
As of now, I am assuming that you are 100% in support of our Online Holy Community as per our previous journal exchanges. On that basis, I deeply hope you can give me guidance again regarding what I should share this week at our meeting.
Please share with me now.
Eternally yours,
Laurence

Good Morning Dearest Laurence,
Thank you for taking initiative, and at the same time having a heart and humility to report and center up.
Someday you will observe the fruits of your offering through your online Holy Community and angel project to support it. You will be amazed and surely moved to tears.
As I promised, I will help you grow. Please don't relax on this.
Eternally yours,
Heavenly Parent

11/15/22 *If You Are Unable To Have Faith In Your Own Work, As Father Did, Then Your Efforts Will Flow Away. Please Have Absolute Faith.*

Good Morning Dearest Most Beloved Heavenly Parent,
Thank you for declaring through Dr. Yong today that Korea will unite. AJU! I am so deeply grateful.
That is not through the work of man alone, not even through True Parents' work alone, but surely you have contributed your 99.99999%! I am so grateful and filled with hope. If you can achieve that, then surely we can also achieve victory in hell in the spirit world, where your children have also been cut off and frozen from receiving your love, just as in North Korea.
Please guide and inspire our efforts in this Online Holy Community so that we can totally fulfill our purpose and goals, and liberate You and True Parents as we free all those trapped in hell.
I pray that you can provide encouraging guidance now for tonight's meeting.
Eternally,
Laurence

Dearest Laurence,
My gratitude pours out to you and each member of your Online Holy Community.
It is true, you have not received official recognition yet in your work. That normally takes time. Like in the movie, Brother Sun and Sister Moon – St. Francis initiated, had to build something precious, and then on that foundation, had to travel to Rome to seek approval. Then I touched the heart of the Pope and convicted him that Francis' work was Holy and worthy of his recognition.
Look at Father's course. Father battled long and hard to discover the Principle. But when he proclaimed it in the Spirit World, before all the saints, he was denied repeatedly, even by me.

Only after the third time was I able to weigh in and officially confirm the truth of his words. That is a Principled process. Your work will surely follow that process.
If you are unable to have faith in your own work, as Father did, then your efforts will flow away.
Please have absolute faith.
What you are doing is so profoundly important.
Think about how many people failed to take Dr. Yong seriously at first. But he never wavered.
On September 9th, you met with Dr. Yong in the breakout room and shared your insights of sharing vitality elements. He was very inspired. Then on Sept 23rd, sharing your gratitudes, you proclaimed to Dr. Yong in front of all Morning Devotion exactly what you are doing. (*14:07 – 18:06*) If he had an objection, then at that point he was free to intervene. You did not try to hide it. He complimented you.
Don't doubt. Don't fear.
Salvation is Holy and Divine. Please invest your 1000% into this divine work.
Eternally,
Heavenly Parent

11/16/22 *Please Check In With Me Daily Through These Journal Exchanges. I Will Help You Focus Each Day. And I Will Embrace All The Exciting And Creative Ideas That You Initiate, And Develop Them Into Providentially Significant Successes With You.*

Good Morning Dearest Most Beloved Heavenly Parent,
Today feels truly like a whole new start to my life. Thank you for guiding me and helping me to grow my spiritual antenna. I feel like I have lost the stress and worry that I was carrying and that I can act freely with enthusiasm and an abundance of energy and inspiration and passion.
Thank you for last night's online meeting, for the experience with Sang and Ron, and for the response of Richard and Melissa. Thank you for inspiring me on the possibility of a partnership with Erik and for the remarkable update from Cheryl.
Thank you for raising me up. I sincerely and deeply want to model True Parents in all I do.
Please help me to continue to grow in my ability to dominate time and to dominate myself. I am so deeply grateful.
I hope now you can give me deep words of guidance as I move into this new phase,
Eternally yours,
Laurence

Good Morning Dearest Laurence,
Thank you for your sincere and earnest heart. There is so much that I want to do in partnership with you. I can provide the energy and love and focus and guidance if you can trust me 100% and separate 100% from your self-centered ideas and thoughts and feelings. I am so moved by how far you have come in the short time since you began your journaling. I deeply believe in you. I have been waiting for you. I will help you prioritize. Please check in with me daily through these journal exchanges. I will help you focus each day. And I will embrace all the exciting and creative ideas that you initiate, and develop them into providentially significant successes with you. I know you long for the opportunity to work with your family members. That will come. Make this a profoundly memorable day.
Eternally,
Heavenly Parent

11/17/22 *When You Meet With Larry, Please Never Forget For One Instant How Very Much I Love Him And How Much Jesus Loves Him And How Much We Have Invested In His Lineage To Prepare Him.*

Good Morning Dearest Most Beloved Heavenly Parent,
Thank you for working so actively in my life and showering such amazing blessings. I deeply appreciated Dr. Rouse's email this morning and Lea's comments in Morning Devotion, and your generous support of our family through the willing and generous cooperation of Erik.
But this morning I sincerely want to focus on Larry and his family. Is he fully prepared to receive True Parents and become a powerful John the Baptist in ACLC? As you know I have tried unsuccessfully with the pastors at two local churches. I pray they can yet come around. But I deeply want to succeed with Larry. Please help me to love him with your deep heart and to deeply touch him and his family and to open the door for you to convict him that True Parents are in fact your promised 2nd coming. What must I do? My efforts are so clumsy. Please work through me, claim my offerings, and speak through me.
As you do, I deeply pray that I can also raise up Justin's family whom I love very dearly.
Please guide me now.
Eternally,
Laurence

Dearest Laurence,
Thank you. I want very much to work through you to claim and bless and raise up Larry and his family along with Justin and his family; and in fact, the entire congregation just for starters.
I will make the way for you and Muriel to attend their event. Your relationship with Muriel is critical. Please focus deeply on that and pray for her and share more deeply with her, not neglecting the things she is concerned about.
When you meet with Larry, please never forget for one instant how very much I love him and how much Jesus loves him and how much we have invested in his lineage to prepare him. Please honor him humbly. Please focus on his words and lift up deep points of truth that he shared.
Please let Justin introduce your ideas to Larry. When he reaches out to you to learn more, please make an appointment with him to read the 1-hour DP lecture, and do your best to respond to his questions. I will speak through you then. It won't happen all at once. Please give it plenty of time and space.
Handle him with great care. I have entrusted him to you. I trust you.
Very sincerely,
Eternally,
Heavenly Parent

11/18/22 *Please Constantly Touch Base With Me In Your Heart. When You Feel Distant From Me, Please Repent And Refocus. I Am Working To Settle In You. It Is A Process. It Is Providentially Very Significant. It Is Foundational To Our Work Together Ahead.*

Good Morning Dearest Heavenly Parent,
Thank you so very much for this new day as we finish up this week and prepare for our trip to the West Coast. I'm so deeply grateful for your abundant blessings. Thank you!
I pray for your guidance and assistance to represent you properly as we visit Joelle and Micah, Jay and Lisa, and the Dursts. I want to represent your heart and love in each situation, each moment, with each of them and especially with Muriel. I hope I can also remain vigilant for any people or other blessings you put in our path as we go through this trip. And I pray that I can have the focus and power to faithfully complete my prayers, HDH, and Morning devotion every day, so as not to miss even one day of my condition. Finally, I hope you can help me find someone to host Tuesday night's 9th meeting of our Online Holy Community. Please guide me during this time to prepare a strong foundation for our meeting with Larry.
I am so grateful.

Please share with me now and guidance or other insights you want to share today.
Eternally yours,
Laurence

Good Morning Dearest Laurence,
Thank you for your sharing this morning. I will be with you always. Please constantly touch base with me in your heart. When you feel distant from me, please repent and refocus. I am working to settle in you. It is a process. It is providentially very significant. It is foundational to our work together ahead.
Please be especially attentive to your relationship and each interaction with Muriel.
Please listen to Bento's book whenever you have the opportunity.
Please be mindful of representing me at all times. Represent my dignity.
I am so deeply grateful.
Eternally yours,
Heavenly Parent

11/19/22 *I Strongly Endorse Your Attitude And Approach Treating Each Episode In Life As A Campaign. That Was Surely True Father's Attitude And Is Now Dr. Yong's As Well.*

Good Morning My Dearest Heavenly Parent,
In 2 days, we leave for the West Coast to visit Joelle, Micah and Colette; and then Jay, Lisa and their family including Eli; and then down to Oakland to see the Dursts.
I pray you can keep us healthy, especially since we have chosen not to take the flu shots. I pray that we can strongly, deeply, humbly, and sincerely, represent and embody your deep heart of love, respect, service, and gratitude at all times and that you can help us to be fully alert to the miracles which you have surely prepared for this trip. I pray for your guidance and assistance in time management so that I can fulfill and balance the many demands on my time including:
Fulfilling my prayers and conditions faithfully, including attending Morning Devotion on zoom; Caring for and serving our children and the Dursts; Caring for and serving Muriel; Getting physical exercise and staying healthy; and Maintaining my work responsibilities.
I also pray that, if it's your will, we can find additional resources to offer a greater gift to the Dursts.
I am deeply grateful for this joyful opportunity and want to invest my full heart as your representative in each moment.

Thank you so deeply.
I hope you can share your guidance now.
Eternally,
Laurence

Good Morning Laurence,
I strongly endorse your attitude and approach treating each episode in life as a campaign. That was surely True Father's attitude and is now Dr. Yong's as well. I want you to have a wonderful and deeply renewing experience on this trip and return ready to move to yet another level in our relationship.
I want you to come back with a much deeper understanding of your value and a much stronger unity between you and Muriel. I will be with you each moment. Please hold me close and I will show you so many miracles you might otherwise have missed.
Please, without fail, check in with me every day through our journaling. This time means so much to me.
I am so grateful,
Eternally,
Heavenly Parent

11/20/22 *George Is A Remarkable And Very Inspiring Son Of Mine, And I Intentionally Inspired You To Witness To Him Knowing How Significant Your Partnership And Friendship With George, Pat, And Their Family Would Become.*

Good Morning Dearest Heavenly Parent,
Thank you for this new day. I was deeply moved today by the hyojeong letters which members of Heavenly GPA read today, written to their parents. I want to deepen my heart of hyojeong towards you every day, and offer that heart to Muriel and our own children and their families.
Today I will visit and honor my spiritual son George who has offered such hyojeong devotion to me, and I am so deeply grateful to him.
Please shower your blessings on George and Pat and their family.
I hope you can enable and allow a very deep communion today between George and myself to sanctify our meeting on this anniversary of his ascension. I am so grateful for his diligence in watching over, protecting, and guiding the careers of Andy and Joelle as well as his profound guidance of our ancestral committees and of my own providential work. I am grateful for this opportunity to honor him prior to our departure for the West Coast. Please share your heart and guidance now regarding George and his collaboration with me over these 17 years since his passing.

Thank you.
Eternally yours,
Laurence

Dear Laurence,
George is a remarkable and very inspiring son of mine, and I intentionally inspired you to witness to him knowing how significant your partnership and friendship with George, Pat, and their family would become.
George has a beautiful and pure heart and a brilliant mind, in many ways not dissimilar to yours. I am very inspired by how well you two have cooperated creating a strong partnership between the Spiritual World and the Physical World which has profound providential significance.
It will grow even stronger in the years to come.
Thank you for honoring George. I will certainly be there with both of you. Like Jesus on the Mount of Transfiguration.
Blessings Eternally,
Heavenly Parent

11/21/22 *Your #1 Job Is To Keep Your Heart Open To Me. You And Your Intention, When Offered With A Pure And Open Heart, On The Foundation Of Your Victory, Is Your 1%. I'll Contribute Everything Else.*

Good Morning My Dearest Most Beloved Heavenly Parent,
Thank you again this morning for continually showering me and my family with so many blessings. You are truly my Father and Mother. I want to make you so proud and way beyond that, I want to substantially end your suffering. Thank you for opening door after door. I'm so sorry for all the doors I missed, even after you opened them. Thank you for forgiving my immature and sin-ridden nature and patiently raising me up over all these years.
Today I celebrate the precious grace you have showered on our family. Each of our children have precious and amazing spouses, who are each the fruit of your long providential history. Thank you for our precious grandchildren, now #s 9 & 10, whom you have each blessed with health and remarkable hearts and talents. Thank you for protecting Joelle in her long and potentially dangerous delivery and for helping Andy in his repeated life-threatening medical challenges, and now helping him find an ideal job to launch his new life with Jordanne. Thank you for helping Muriel and me to break through to a new level in our lives and for opening the doors to support our family financially, but also to fulfill our providential efforts – with our online community; and also, with our providential projects. I pray that I can stay

focused and totally connected in heart with you during this trip, not missing live zoom for Morning Devotion even once; representing your deep and embracing love at all times; fulfilling my missions as chief cook for Joelle, moving forward my business efforts; moving forward with our Online Community; being open to anyone you want us to meet on the way; and making deep heartistic preparation for both the meeting with Larry's family and Justin's family, also for my interview with Dietmar.
I am so, so, so, very grateful!
Please share any important words at this moment, on this day.
Eternally yours,
Laurence

Good Morning Dearest Laurence,
Thank you for your perseverance.
You have arrived at a place where almost none of the two trillion of my children have reached. Thank you for not giving up. Through cross country, through mountain climbing and rock climbing, through hiking, you have developed in your heart, through your training, the will and heart to persevere.
And you have directed that heart and will towards me, not towards some worthless external goal.
This is a new moment, like at Noah's time, the Last Days. All external goals before now will disappear because they were rooted in the old age, ridden with sin, under Satan's domination.
You, in partnership with me, are helping to build the new age that I have been dreaming of for all time. How precious you are, and the relative handful of others who like you, have persevered. How could you imagine, even for an instant, that I would look away from you – that is impossible. As I said before, you are surrounded by an aura of Heavenly Fortune. That is me, my support for all that you do. Your #1 job is to keep your heart open to me. You and your intention, when offered with a pure and open heart, on the foundation of your victory, is your 1%. I'll contribute everything else.
Then you can harvest the fruits; not just you. You have an incredible cloud of harvesters surrounding you.
I really want you to live in extreme joy as you experience our partnership. I want you to be overwhelmed with joy. Please live your life as a celebration of true love. In that way you can make me so profoundly happy.
Eternally,
Heavenly Parent

11/22/22 *Of Course, Everything Of Value Involves Sacrifice – But In True Love, Nothing Feels Like Sacrifice. It Is Expressing Our Passion For Our Children, Our Passion For Our Beloved, Our Passion For Our Parents And Forebearers, And Our Passion For Our Providential Activities And Service. When We Are Separate From Our Hearts, Those Can Present As Sacrifice. But When We Are In Our Deeper Hearts, They Are Our Greatest Joy. Ecstatic Joy. That Is The Joy Of The Creation.*

Good Morning Heavenly Parent,
Thank you for guiding us through the travel obstacles so far. I'm truly sorry that I didn't copy my latest Morning Devotion files and that I forgot my computer charger. Those were careless omissions which make it more challenging to offer my morning devotion, but of course True Father had none of those in HeungNam, but still succeeded in reclaiming your providential foundation there, in the bottom of hell. I will do my very best to maintain my standard during this trip and not to create any distance between us. I also want to be very sensitive to Muriel and our children during this trip. Thank you for your constant blessings and support, and for the love of True Parents and Dr. Yong here in North America.
I was deeply touched by the confessions and letters of the two GPA representatives who spoke today. I will surely deepen my heart to appreciate even the tiny details that you invested your entire heart into, so as to demonstrate your amazing love for us. I want to live a life of care and investment to return your love 1000-fold. Thank you so much.
Please share your heart and guidance with me today so that I can be the best possible representative for you today.
Eternally,
Laurence

Dearest Laurence,
Thank you for your intention and your desire to be a son of filial piety. It is a beautiful and noble path, and one which penetrates deeply into the heart of true love. It is the path I continue to walk and I am so happy to share it with you. True love means sacrifice, but sacrifice is not the end of it. Of course, everything of value involves sacrifice – but in true love, nothing feels like sacrifice. It is expressing our passion for our children, our passion for our beloved, our passion for our parents and forebearers, and our passion for our providential activities and service. When we are separate from our hearts, those can present as sacrifice. But when we are in our deeper hearts, they are our greatest joy. Ecstatic joy. That is the joy of the creation.

Each of you are to inherit not just the ability to create, but the passion to create things of eternal beauty and goodness, and the joy and ecstasy of having created those marvels.
The heart of creativity is a deeper expression of the heart of love. The third blessing comes on the foundation of the 2nd.
It is so sublime, so precious – it is truly the reason why I could not intervene in the fall. I had to protect the 3rd blessing.
Thank you for all you are doing. It moves me very deeply. Like those letters from the GPA members. I love you very deeply.
Eternally,
Heavenly Parent

11/23/22 *Through This Process You Can More Consistently And More Powerfully Express My Heart And Love In Each Moment And With Each Person With Whom You Are Relating. That Is What It Means To Be Christ-Like. Even Then That Is Really Only The Beginning. The 3rd Blessing Is Infinite.*

Good Morning Dearest Heavenly Parent,
I'm so sorry that I am rushed this morning. I was thinking that in 2023 I want to make our journaling the centerpiece of my devotions every day, and to deepen and broaden the content of our sharing.
I want to receive your guidance on this because I don't want to do anything to detract from our unity and collaboration. Dr. Yong stressed that in order to achieve victories in the providence it is critically important to have a foundation of "a lot of jeongseong". I believe that in spite of my shallow heart and lack of tears, still through my faithfulness of jeongseong, I have created a foundation where you could work powerfully in my life. I believe that through Cheon Bo I am now on a different level in my relationship with you, but I don't want to take anything for granted.
I hope that between now and the end of the year, you can help me achieve a clear perspective on the proper balance of prayer and journaling and other devotions so that I can set the optimum conditions for the highest goodness and success in 2023.
Please share with me now, if you are willing.
Eternally yours,
Laurence

Dear Laurence,
Good morning.
Thank you for your deeply meaningful and heartfelt offerings all these years. The purpose of offerings is to set the conditions to recover your original nature. They are certainly not meant to be eternal conditions.

True Father offered up conditions centered on his passion for fishing. But of course, True Parents were the King and Queen of prayer. Journalling is really precious. It gives me an opportunity to connect with you much more directly, through your mind and heart, to reach your original mind and stimulate it. Even journalling is only meant to be a temporary measure, as you deepen your ability to experience our relationship on a 24/7 basis. Ultimately even that exercise becomes unnecessary as we become totally united in heart.

Through this process you can more consistently and more powerfully express my heart and love in each moment and with each person with whom you are relating. That is what it means to be Christ-like.

Even then that is really only the beginning.

The 3rd Blessing is infinite.

Eternally,

Heavenly Parent

11/24/22 *This Is Truly My Day Of Thanksgiving. You Have No Visceral Understanding Yet Of How Long I Have Stared At That Dry And Barren Soil Waiting For A First Sign Of Life Sprouting. I Don't Have A God To Offer Thanks To, Only My Children. Those Who Are Only Now Beginning To Emerge And Stand As Children Of True Hyojeong Beside True Parents.*

Good Morning Dearest Heavenly Parent,

Happy Thanksgiving to you, my most precious Father and Mother. It is truly a day of profound gratitude for me having arrived safely yesterday here in Oregon and meeting our precious 10th grandchild for the first time. Having such a deep sharing with Muriel, Joelle, and Micah about the amazing depth of a mother's love for her completely dependent and vulnerable child. Thank you for helping us through our profound vulnerability under Satan's domination for so many years!!!!!

I feel so deeply loved by you, and I am so grateful for the opportunity and privilege to offer something to help dry your tears. And then thank you this morning for the chance to be with Dr. Yong in the breakout room. I want to offer today, and every day, for eternity, in humble gratitude to you.

Eternally,

Laurence

Good Morning Dearest Laurence,

You are such a comfort and source of hope and joy to me. Yes, today is Thanksgiving Day. As the parent and creator, I live absolutely and eternally for my children. Every one of my children is so dear to me –

that is my heart of compassion and in many ways of repentance before my children, most of whom are still slaves to my enemy.
But a few have broken free, thanks to True Parents. And of those, a few have matured to the point where they can take the initiative to liberate me by exercising their own 3rd Blessing as my co-creator partners and 2nd self. I dreamed of that for all of the history of creation, but it has only come to fruition, beyond True Parents, in the last 2 years. This is truly my day of Thanksgiving. You have no visceral understanding yet of how long I have stared at that dry and barren soil waiting for a first sign of life sprouting. I don't have a God to offer thanks to, only my children. Those who are only now beginning to emerge and stand as children of true hyojeong beside True Parents. I am so grateful. I pray that your children, and grandchildren can each become such children of hyojeong.
Blessings to you and your family and tribe from me.
Eternally,
Heavenly Parent

11/25/22 *Please Never Forget, Even For A Second, For Whom You Are Doing All That You Do. True Mother Is My Only Begotten Daughter And The Center Of The Providence At This Time.*

Good Morning Dearest Heavenly Parent,
Thank you for your precious love and blessings. I am so deeply grateful.
Thank you for yesterday's wonderful Thanksgiving celebration and today's Morning Devotion, where I was in breakout rooms with both the Herndandezs and Sun.
I pray that today I can upgrade my heart of love and service and respect to Micah and Joelle and Colette.
Please guide me today and throughout this trip to represent you at every moment.
Please share with me today and help me to open my heart to deeply receive your guidance.
Eternally yours,
Laurence

Good Morning Dearest Laurence,
I am so happy to connect with you again today and each day through our journal exchanges.
As Dr. Yong stated, this is the time when, by uniting with True Mother's heart, women can and must convey True Mother's love to their families, communities, nations, and world on every level. Please believe in and support Muriel prayerfully in this regard. Please help her

to believe in herself. Also, same with Joelle and Lisa during this visit. You have the power and responsibility to link your family and tribe to me and True Parents, so that Mother's love can flow freely and powerfully. That is where desperately needed healing can happen, and it will.

At the time of Jesus, this occurred through the Pentecost. At this time, as Dr. Yong clearly explained, don't expect another Pentecost. That was an alternative providence because Jesus was unable to establish the proper foundation. Now, today, True Parents have, in fact, succeeded in establishing that foundation. True Mother is in fact the center and source of all love for this world. Thank you for your profound and significant support for True Mother.

Your ability to support her will surely grow dramatically in the months and years ahead. Please never forget, even for a second, for whom you are doing all that you do. True Mother is my Only Begotten Daughter and the center of the providence at this time.

You are an Ambassador of True Mother's love. I am so very proud of you.

Eternally,

Heavenly Parent

11/26/22 *When You Begin Each Day Like This, Connected With Me, I Can Help You Plant A New Seed In Your Heart Each Morning, And Then Through The Day We Can Work On It Together And Then Before You Retire, You Can Harvest That New Growth And Stand On A Higher Foundation For The Next Day.*

Good Morning Dearest Most Beloved Heavenly Parent,
I am so very happy to meet with you again today, to start this day in the embrace of your heart and to be able to share with you directly like this. This is the most precious moment for me each day. Thank you for your incredible grace. I love you and long to continually deepen our connection of heart. Yesterday I fell short on multiple occasions to unconditionally respect and uplift Muriel. I pray that today I can do much better, not just for Muriel but also for Micah and Joelle and Colette, and for our entire tribe. I will do my utmost.

Thank you again for Dr. Yong's powerful and deep guidance. Longing heart towards You and towards our Abel figures is our foundation of faith. Please help me deepen my longing heart towards: You, True Parents, Jesus, Hyo Jin Nim, Heung Jin Nim, Dae Mo Nim, Dr. and Mrs. Durst, Dr. and Mrs. Yong, and my own parents Richard and Babette. And a longing heart towards everyone else is my foundation of substance.

Please help me to deepen my longing heart toward my family, my extended family, my tribe, our Morning Devotion Community, our church community, and toward all people on the Physical Realm and in the Spiritual Realm.
I really want to inherit your heart and to grow in the realm of the 3rd Blessing, and to truly liberate you and True Parents and Jesus.
Thank you for all your grace, your support, your encouragement, your guidance.
Let this be a day of great victory for Heaven.
I invite you to please share your amazing guidance with me again today. I appreciate your words so profoundly.
Eternally,
Laurence

Good Morning Dearest Laurence,
I too look forward to our daily journal exchange with great longing and anticipation each day. One day is a complete period of planting, cultivating, and harvesting a new level in our spirit. When you begin each day like this, connected with me, I can help you plant a new seed in your heart each morning, and then through the day we can work on it together and then before you retire, you can harvest that new growth and stand on a higher foundation for the next day.
I am very inspired to teach you about my longing heart, so that you can inherit it and resonate so much more powerfully with my heart. I deeply long for our closer connection. Just as you are motivated and inspired to share what you know and have experienced – but so often the ones with whom you are trying to share can receive so little, likewise I am desperate to find those who can really receive what I want to and long to share. It is not just an intellectual capacity, or even just a heartistic capacity that I seek. If I share things which the one I am sharing with is not prepared to implement, then it creates a separation, not a closeness of heart.
So, for those who are not yet Blessed, I am quite limited in what I can share. As Jesus said: I have much to share but you are not ready to receive it.
But even among those who are Blessed, they are at many different levels – as the Blessing of 1st gens is very conditional, and even most 2nd gens in this transition time are very unsettled and unstable.
But Cheon Bo couples, especially Cheon Bo Victor Couples, stand on a very different foundation.
And those Cheon Bo Victor Couples who are fully awake, and ready to take initiative as owners are so rare and so precious to me. They are capable and qualified to be taught and to inherit. Among those, the ones who desperately seek to be taught, seek to connect deeply with my heart, seek to take responsibility and even seek to initiate

responsibility creatively: you are my treasures. You are the ones into whom I can, albeit very carefully, begin to pour my heart and vision and hopes and dreams. It is like breathing for the first time since the fall. There was Jesus, then True Parents, and now Cheon Bo Victor Couples.
Thank you for your inspiring video, the Chess Match. That deeply moves me.
Please make our journaling your priority every morning. I promise you, God's honor, you will never regret it. I long for you!
Eternally,
Heavenly Parent

11/27/22 *Yes, This Is No Longer The Time For Secrets. Only Through Clearly Understanding The Truth Can All Of Christianity And In Fact All Religions Be United At This Time.*

Good Morning Dearest Heavenly Parent,
I am so grateful and inspired to partner with you. Please guide me and help me to mature as quickly as possible so that I can victoriously fulfill all that you hope from me.
Yesterday I was very touched that you allowed me to encourage both Claire and Therese. Please bless both of them. Please help me to represent your heart properly in my attendance to Muriel and to our children's families, and to the Dursts. This trip is such an amazing blessing.
Thank you for helping me understand the nuances today regarding the parallels and differences between Abraham and Zachariah's expulsion of their own sons. Based on that understanding I was able to upgrade my presentation making it more clear and pointed.
Please continue to guide me and speak through me so that I can properly represent you in every situation. I am so grateful.
I hope you can share your message with me now.
Eternally,
Laurence

Good Morning Dearest Laurence,
Thank you for continuing to finetune your presentation. It is an important project and will be widely distributed online. Yes, this is no longer the time for secrets. Only through clearly understanding the truth can all of Christianity and in fact all religions be united at this time. All the myths and all the confusion need to be cleared away.
True Parents are the ones I have been longing for through all of history. If people today are attached to mythical and unreal expectations of whom the returning Christ should be, then that will be

a serious roadblock to establishing the Kingdom of Heaven on Earth.
Thank you for investing so much into this presentation.
I will surely raise you up, step by step, to become fully qualified to fulfill all that I am hoping from you. Thank you for all that you are investing. We are surely a team.
Make this a great day.
Eternally,
Heavenly Parent

11/28/22 *I Promise You Many, Many, Tears. But They Will Be Tears Of Joy; Tears Of Liberation. Honestly, Those Are By Far The Most Precious Tears. Those Are The Tears I Long For.*

Good Morning Dearest Most Beloved Heavenly Parent,
Thank you for this beautiful new day. I deeply appreciated Dr. Yong's message this morning. I recognize that I am very far from True Parents' heart of tears for your suffering. I am so sorry. I hope, through the jeongseong conditions I have set, and especially through my investment into Morning Devotion, that you can help me upgrade my level of heart and tears. I want to be a truly filial son of yours and of True Parents. I deeply appreciate your gracious message that as co-creator and partner, I am able to minister to your heart in a way that helps you overcome your suffering with the joy and passion of creativity. I realize that this is not the same as deeply sharing your han and again I sincerely repent for my immaturity. I will continue to invest my very best and I pray for your help in upgrading my filial heart and my heart of love and tears for all of your children.
I love you very deeply and I am so profoundly grateful.
I hope you will share with me now.
Eternally,
Laurence

Dearest Laurence, my precious son,
I profess my deepest love for you. Words are limited. Connection of heart is eternal. We will have deep and deepening connections of heart through the common victories we share as I support you in the remarkable and historic and many inspiring initiatives you are creating and will create in your remaining time on Earth and then in the Spirit World. I promise you many, many, tears. But they will be tears of joy; tears of liberation.
Honestly, those are by far the most precious tears. Those are the tears I long for. I would much, much, rather forget all my suffering since the fall. That is my intention and goal. You are significantly helping me

with that goal. I will surely help you with yours. Thank you from the very bottom of my very deepest heart.
Eternally,
Heavenly Parent

11/29/22 *True Parents Opened The Gateway. My Children Are Limping Through, Injured, Suffering, But Returning. Centering On True Mother, We Are Creating A Realm Of Healing Love, Where All The Trauma, Pain, And Resentment Of History Can Be Dissolved And Replaced With Love.*

Good Morning Dearest Heavenly Parent,
I'm deeply grateful for this new day. I'm sorry for all the times I have sacrificed unity in our family by asserting myself. Thank you for this precious guidance again today that you shared through Dr. Yong. I am very inspired to build Heaven in our family and in Heaven and on Earth. Thank you for such an incredible privilege and opportunity.
Today marks the 10th meeting of our online Holy Community. Please bless our meeting and help it to go smoothly without technical issues.
I want to connect more deeply with your heart each day, and to be more thoughtful, loving, and sacrificial. Thank you for raising me up step by step. Please guide me again today.
Eternally yours,
Laurence

Good Morning Laurence,
You are surely growing, step by step. Thank you for your continued focus and effort in this. It will never be wasted. Just as in the sharing today of Miae, who is now a Cheon Il Guk missionary, each person, each of my children, need to walk the path of personal growth and development with me. You are someone who is helping pioneer this way as a 1st generation son of True Parents, but everyone needs to walk this path, either on Earth or in the Spirit World.
The Heavenly Kingdom will include trillions and trillions of my children, each one having a value greater than the entire cosmos. But it has to start somewhere.
True Parents opened the gateway. My children are limping through, injured, suffering, but returning. Centering on True Mother, we are creating a realm of healing love, where all the trauma, pain, and resentment of history can be dissolved and replaced with love. It is a vast transition, but it will surely accelerate as it moves forward. After healing comes the culture of joy. That is the purpose of the creation. It is now totally unstoppable.

Thank you for your sincere and serious investment. That means everything to me.
Eternally yours,
Heavenly Parent

11/30/22 *I Don't Want Minions; I Want Partners Of True Love And Creative Energy. With The Angels As Partners, I Was Able To Create The Entire Cosmos. But Their Creative Abilities Are Tiny Compared To My Own Children. Yours Are Even Greater Than Mine. I Am So Excited About What Will Develop From Each Of You – Most Of It Will Be Marvels I Never Imagined.*

Good Morning, My Most Beloved Heavenly Parent,
Thank you for another precious day!
Last night was deeply inspiring for me, and I hope for you too! We are a group of old and in some cases feeble children of yours who have given our lives to realize your dream. Reading "Faith and Reality" together and offering our vitality elements together, with Stefan's poignant tears, was deeply touching to me. And thank you for allowing Claire to offer her independent confirmation and also for the encouragement from Tyler.
Dr. Yong's words of warning about spiritual groups is challenging to me. I asked him for his direct guidance, but he has withheld that. I feel that this is a challenge to strengthen my determination, as you did with True Father when he was reporting the content of the Divine Principle to you and the saints in the Spirit World. If I am doing anything inappropriate, PLEASE LET ME KNOW CLEARLY.
Also, thank you for the progress with Erik. I deeply appreciate this avenue to address our family financial challenges.
I was touched by the opportunity to see Miilhan and his new baby today, and I feel very urgent to interview with Dietmar. Please open that door at your earliest timing, subject to your approval. And finally, I am so grateful for this chance to serve Micah, Joelle, and Muriel. I want to become an absolute minus to them.
I hope today is even many times more substantial than yesterday. Please speak through me and guide my heart in each situation. I am so grateful to partner with you!
Please share your guidance now,
Eternally,
Laurence

Good Morning Dearest Laurence,
Thank you for your thoughtful and active engagement in our partnership. Initiating is so much more than absolute obedience. I

don't want minions; I want partners of True Love and creative energy. With the angels as partners, I was able to create the entire cosmos. But their creative abilities are tiny compared to my own children. Yours are even greater than mine. I am so excited about what will develop from each of you – most of it will be marvels I never imagined.

But I will be the very best object to make them happen. The angels are remarkable assistants. Truly they are. But they are nothing compared to what I can and will do to support my children who have matured and embraced the 3rd Blessing.

Please continue to pioneer. I deeply appreciate all that you have initiated. Even True Parents have been significantly constrained due to the demands of the Providence of Restoration. They have significantly exercised absolute obedience to me, step by step, in order to complete all Providential mandates in such a compressed timeframe. Of course, they exercised wonderful creativity, but still, it was within relatively narrow guidelines mandated by the Providence.

But now, in the Era of Cheon Bo, that freedom is opening up, wider and wider, as per Pledge #8.

This is so exciting for me!

Please keep doing what you are doing.

Eternally,

Heavenly Parent

12/1/22 *For Small External Victories, The Spiritual Foundation Doesn't Need To Be So Deep. For Profound And Historic External Victories, The Spiritual Foundation Must Be Very, Very Deep.*

Good Morning Dearest Heavenly Parent!

Today is already December 1. In 3 days, we will depart from Micah and Joelle's. Thanks you for this precious blessing to visit here. I hope we can make these final 3 days profoundly memorable and heartfelt.

Then, on to Jay and Lisa's to meet our newest grandson, Eli. I'm so grateful for all you are doing in my life. I'm seriously sorry that I am still so immature. It is now the final month of 2022 and I have so little in terms of external achievements or victories to offer up. I desperately want to uphold your dignity and True Parent's dignity by making substantial achievements. But I deeply believe that you are working powerfully through the foundations I have set, through the angel projects and through our online Holy Community, and I totally believe that the external results will surely follow soon. And thank you both for the incredible daily blessings of Morning Devotion as well as the precious communion you have made available to me through our journal exchanges.

Please guide me and remind me of all adjustments I need to make. I want to maintain a 180-degree vertical relationship with you, with no shadow or separation of any kind, and then heartistically and prayerfully apply all your guidance in each of my relationships and endeavors. I am so very grateful. Please guide me to grow closer to you by the most direct route. I hope you can share precious guidance with me again this morning.
Eternally,
Laurence

Dear Laurence,
Thank you for all you are doing. You are breaking new ground. That is never easy. I deeply appreciate your faith in what you are doing. That is your handle onto the cosmos. Like Jacob's handle on the angel. If you don't let go, you will certainly prevail. Every victory starts on a spiritual level. It must be won there before it can be manifested externally. Remember pledge #5. Spirit World is subject. You, of all people, are aware of that. How many hours and years did True Parents spend in seemingly unrelated activities, such as working in HeungNam, or fishing? Those activities were essential and foundational to their victories externally. Now, how many have already been Blessed in the physical realm. That is the fruit. And from there, now the Cheon Bo are emerging. But the first Cheon Bo couples only emerged when True Father turned 100 years old. For small external victories, the spiritual foundation doesn't need to be so deep. For profound and historic external victories, the spiritual foundation must be very, very deep. Dr. George described to you the work of laying a foundation, like building the many basements of a very high sky scraper. It takes a lot of concerted and continued efforts. So few have that vision, determination, and faith. I deeply appreciate your dedication and efforts. I am cooperating with you to bring them to fruition in the very shortest time, to support True Mother. Never be discouraged. What you are doing is thrilling the entire Spirit World. You are a descendant of Jacob. He too, is so very proud of you.
I love you eternally,
Heavenly Parent

12/2/22 As True Father Would Say: "I Was Born For This." That Means That My Expression Of Love In Each Situation Represents 100% Of My Purpose, My Motivation, And My Goal, And My Dreams, And Desire. When I Invest My Heart And Soul And Body Like That, The Moment Becomes Eternal And Holy And Devine. That Is How To Create Eternal Memories In The Ones We Love. That Is The Meaning Of Gamdong.

Good Morning Dearest Heavenly Parent,

Thank you for another deep Morning Devotion message. You regularly speak to me through our journaling, and then reinforce that same message through Dr. Yong's words. Thank you for all your love and gamdong.

I was touched by: "Make God's worries my own, and let God handle my worries". And; "You must win the victory first on a spiritual level like Jacob wrestling with the angel, and then it can be achieved externally".

I need to digest my impatience, and offer it up to you. And to transform that emotion into my intensity to connect to your heart in each moment, and to experience and share and amplify your love and appreciation and gratitude in each moment. To experience service as love, which is never a burden – as long as it is done in communion with you.

I have 2 more days here in Oregon before traveling to Seattle. I pray that I can make eternal memories here during these final two days.

Thank you, my precious Parents, my precious heart. I am so grateful.

I long for your message this morning.

Eternally,

Laurence

Good Morning Dearest Laurence,

Yes, letting go of worries is consummately liberating. As True Father would say: "I was born for this." That means that my expression of love in each situation represents 100% of my purpose, my motivation, and my goal, and my dreams, and desire. When I invest my heart and soul and body like that, the moment becomes eternal and Holy and Devine. That is how to create eternal memories in the ones we love. That is the meaning of Gamdong.

But even those who have professed this in the past – like Baba Ramdas "Be Here Now", did not have the position of the 3rd Blessing – and therefore could only manifest on a form level. You have the potential to emulate True Parents and manifest on the perfection level. Will you take on that challenge? Make that your passion? It will unlock everything for you. Listen to Bento's book again based on today's journal. Think about how to challenge yourself to deeper and deeper levels. There of course is no limit. That is the exponential critical mass explosion you like to pray about. I have an infinite reservoir of love, and have been trying to convey it through tiny pin holes. But I am holding on to that dream with absolute faith, just as I am challenging you to do. I feel so very close to you. We share a common destiny, and we will overcome a common challenge to achieve a common victory. Just like True Parents.

I am so deeply grateful.

Eternally,

Heavenly Parent

12/3/22 *Just Think About Your Heart. I Am There. It Will Surely Help You To Refocus And Repower – Like Green Lantern's Lantern – Your Heart Is The Source Of Your Superpower. The Gateway To All The Power In The Cosmos, And Even More.*

Good Morning Dearest Heavenly Parent,
Thank you for this, the final full day of our visit with Joelle and Micah and Colette. We are so very blessed by you! Thank you for another very deep Morning Devotion. I appreciated Mitch's prayer and then Dr. Yong declared "it will all come true" – including Mitch's prayer to offer our vitality elements to those in the Spirit World. Thank you for that Gamdong word of confirmation. Even if no one else heard it – I know you meant it for my heart.
I hope you can speak to Bruce's heart about that work, and that he can enthusiastically get involved. I know you have a plan.
Thank you for guiding me so clearly. I am sorry that my ability to stay focused and connected to your heart is still so scattered. I pray that you can constantly remind me to remind myself – as you speak through my original mind. Please help me to strengthen those muscles, and to strengthen my awareness and sensitivity to the status of my heart-to-heart connection with you at all times. I give you 100% permission and authority to intervene in me like that, so that I can connect ever deeper and deeper into your heart at the fastest possible rate. Please accept my invitation. It is unconditional. I want to be able to make the greatest possible contribution to True Parents' providence while True Mother is still alive on this Earth. Thank you for this priceless privilege.
Please share your guidance with me again now.
Eternally yours,
Laurence

Good Morning Dearest Laurence,
Thank you for your unconditional invitation. How precious. That is truly the manifestation of making my worries your own. Let's pioneer this path together, building on the Foundation True Parents have established. Yes, please listen to your heart. Touch your heart. Just think about your heart. I am there. It will surely help you to refocus and repower – like Green Lantern's lantern – your heart is the source of your superpower. The gateway to all the power in the cosmos, and even more. You truly have no idea.
Focus on True Love
Focus on True Love
Focus on True Love,

And allow yourself to feel total joy in every situation. The more you can give, the more joy you will experience. Do it for True Love – only for True Love.
I am so very inspired!
Eternally,
Heavenly Parent

12/4/22 *Yes, Our Reciprocal Relationship Is Realized As You Focus On My Concerns And I Focus On Your Concerns. Externally, That Means That We Work To Fulfill Each Other's Needs. But Internally It Means That We See Through Each Other's Eyes, And Then Come To Feel Through Each Other's Hearts.*

Good Morning Dearest Most Beloved Heavenly Parent,
Thank you for the amazing blessings of this visit to Micah and Joelle's home and the opportunity to meet your precious daughter Colette. What an amazing gift!
I feel that my heart has been dramatically upgraded during my time here. I will invest my utmost to continue and even accelerate the pace of that upgrading. This morning, we depart for Seattle. I will endeavor to bring all you have shown and given to me to fill our time in Edmonds with your love and heart. It will be much shorter, but I hope I can be much more focused. I hope you can help me begin to prepare for Tuesday night's meeting, and that it can be a precious and deeply inspiring meeting. Also, I hope you can open a way for our community to expand powerfully, so that we can fulfill our goal for you and True Parents, and for the entire Spirit World.
I love you so very deeply.
Please share your message with me again today.
I am so grateful!
Eternally yours,
Laurence

Good Morning My Dearest Laurence,
Thank you for engaging with me on such a sincere and high vibration through these journal exchanges. This is thrilling for me.
Yes, our reciprocal relationship is realized as you focus on my concerns and I focus on your concerns. Externally, that means that we work to fulfill each other's needs.
But internally it means that we see through each other's eyes, and then come to feel through each other's hearts.
Spoiler alert ... My heart is the huge untapped reservoir of beautiful, pure, shimmering true love. It is my treasure chest. It is my priceless inheritance that I long so totally to bequeath to my children.

If you make my concerns your own, and start to see through my eyes, then, over time, you will increasingly start to feel my heart.
You could easily drown in my heart of love except for one thing – the more you experience it, the more you long to share it with all your long-lost brothers and sisters. So drowning is not an option.
Let every thought, every word, every intention, every action, every touch, every breath – be an expression of my love ocean.
I enthusiastically invite you to enter.
Eternally yours,
Heavenly Parent

12/5/22 *What Is True And What Is False Becomes Very Clear In Light Of Such A Pure And Beautiful Offering. This Humble Offering Is Creating Shockwaves Of Love Across The Lower Realms Of The Spirit World.*

Good Morning Dearest Most Beloved Heavenly Parent,
I am so grateful to be here with Jay and Lisa's family and I pray that you can bless their home and family so deeply.
Tomorrow is our 11th Online Holy Community meeting. Please share with me today what you would like me to share with our OHC members. I want to make those meetings so filled with your love and heart.
Thank you also for the phone call from Mrs. Durst last night. I'm so moved by her and I am so inspired to be able to see the Dursts on 12/10.
Please help me to focus now, and to open my heart so widely, so that I can powerfully hear your voice.
Please share with me now.
Eternally yours,
Laurence

Good Morning Dearest Laurence,
Thank you for your consistent heart of gratitude. That is critically important. Satan has tried to multiply grievances and resentment against me in the hearts of my precious children. It is so unfair, but all I can do is continue to love and sacrifice and trust and appreciate my precious children. Those trapped in hell are so unfortunate. I am truly heartbroken that I have been so unable to help them up until now.
You are my representatives to them. How can they know my heart directly? I have had no way to demonstrate my love. But you who are offering your vitality elements are expelling all the historic resentment and grievances. This is not a trick or a false promise. You are offering your love from your very essence. Those in hell can feel that. What is true and what is false becomes very clear in light of such a pure and

beautiful offering. This humble offering is creating shockwaves of love across the lower realms of the Spirit World.
This is truly the time of their resurrection.
I am so grateful.
Please do not stop. It will surely grow.
Eternally,
Heavenly Parent

12/6/22 *Taking Care Of Two People Simultaneously Can Be A Real Headache. You Don't Want Even One Of Them To Feel Hurt. That Was The Case With Lucifer And Adam. Now I Am Trying To Care For Billions Simultaneously In A Totally Corrupted World. Of Course That's Impossible, And My Inability Breaks My Heart.*

Good Morning Dearest Beloved Heavenly Parent,
Thank you for this great new day. Thank you for today's message from Dr. Yong that we need to pay attention to the trivial details of our spouse's concerns.
That relates closely to what you shared with me two days ago. As we concern ourselves with each other's concerns, we start to see through each other's eyes and then begin to experience each other's hearts. That heartistic connection and resonance starts with paying attention to the small details in our relationship. We can't invest ourselves effectively into the small details of every person – but we can do so with our other half, and with you. Today marks the 11th meeting of our Online Holy Community. Thank you for your precious encouragement and guidance and support.
You are amazing. We are taxed just concerning ourselves with the concerns of one other person, while you are investing your gamdong and heart into hundreds and hundreds of billions of your children. As per your "spoiler alert", truly your heart is so unimaginably vast.
I want to liberate you, as our True Parents have modeled. I want to free you to stand in honor and dignity and glory as our parent of absolute love, and absolute goodness.
I want to help you end evil and redeem the original hearts and minds of every one of your children and angels, and to hasten the day of your long awaited ideal.
Thank you for the amazing privilege you have showered on our couple and family and tribe!
Please share your message again with me this morning. Please help me to open my mind and heart so widely, to hear your voice today with crystal clarity and beautiful true love.
Eternally yours,
Laurence

Good Morning Dearest Laurence,
Today is a very good day. Thank you for making a great space for me today in your heart. I always love visiting with you. Today will be a great opportunity for you to practice losing yourself and investing yourself into the hearts, lives and concerns of those around you. Last night you cared for Naava, but Amos felt overlooked. Taking care of two people simultaneously can be a real headache. You don't want even one of them to feel hurt. That was the case with Lucifer and Adam.
Now I am trying to care for billions simultaneously in a totally corrupted world. Of course that's impossible, and my inability breaks my heart.
But you can. Each CIG couple can grow to take care of 430 couples, and beyond. That's a big ask – even two people are a challenge. But relative to the need, it is trivial. If each couple takes care of 1000 people, then 8 million Cheon Bo couples could care for all the people on the earth today. We just need to increase our numbers 1000 times. That's actually doable.
I am so grateful to each couple who embraced the vision and responsibilities of Cheon Bo Couples. You are my hands, feet, voice, and heart. Thank you. Now, taking care of the 100s of billions in the Spirit World. That's a whole different challenge. You and your Online Holy Community ministry have risen to take on that challenge with such great heart and courage. I am so deeply moved. Like when David faced Goliath. I choked up with such pride and gratitude. How did I deserve such a good son? I just wanted to shower him with blessings. I feel that way now, again with you and your community, who are seeking to inherit True Parents' heart, Jesus' heart, David's heart. You who are willing to offer everything to lift me up.
I am so deeply grateful.
I will never forget you.
Eternally,
Heavenly Parent

12/7/22 *In Exercising, You Are Supposed To Encounter Your Limits. That Is Not A Bad Thing, It Is The Entire Point. Then You Challenge Those Limits And Expand Your Capability. And It Never Ends. Our Hearts Have The Ability To Expand Infinitely. By "Our", Of Course I Am Including Mine.*

Good Morning Dearest Heavenly Parent,
Thank you for another beautiful day! Yesterday was deeply meaningful for me. Our Online Holy Community meeting was very touching, and I was so

grateful that Susana and Monika could join. Then last night was so beautiful with Jay's family at the zoo. Lots of great memories! And this morning I deeply appreciated the opportunity to be with the Lewis couple and with Fusae, and the chance to offer the Chess Game following Dr. Yong's reiteration that now is the time of responsibility of Heavenly Tribal Messiahs. I have a long way to grow to be able to unconditionally serve and love in the moment. Thank you for your patience with me. I will invest my heart into representing you in each moment as Dr. Yong does so very mindfully. Tonight is Naava's concert. I am looking forward to that, after a day of serving.

I hope you can share your guidance with me now.

Eternally,
Laurence

Dearest Laurence,
Thank you for your heart and efforts. Every situation is an opportunity to exercise your heart muscles. In exercising, you are supposed to encounter your limits. That is not a bad thing, it is the entire point. Then you challenge those limits and expand your capability. And it never ends. Our hearts have the ability to expand infinitely. By "our", of course I am including mine. My greatest joy is to experience my children's hearts growing. My absolute determination is to see you each grow beyond my own level of heart.

Just as when you create a computer, you want it to be even more capable, faster, smarter, more accurate. You want to have the latest model, with the best capability.

That's what I am longing for – only it is not about logic or computation power. I am longing for my children to far surpass me in heart. I want to serve them as my Abel figures of True Love, and cry tears of joy in the beauty of their shimjeong.

That is truly my greatest ambition. Everything else that I created is truly a means to that end.

In one sense, this is the most humble aspiration anyone could long for. In another sense it is far and away the most ambitious.

Magic does exist. It is the fabric of the realm of heart. Creating that realm substantially, starting with the most basic energy particles and building and building until finally the reality of heart can take root and then flourish. What could be more exquisite, more moving, more filled with tears of joy?

Thank you for helping me to pioneer and realize my deepest dream.
I am so grateful,
Eternally,
Heavenly Parent

12/8/22 *My Words Through Each Cheon Bo Couple Are Very Important – Especially When You Are Praying And Seeking To Connect Deeply In Heart With Me, And Not Just Speaking Randomly. Journaling Is A Precious Discipline To Focus My Dialogue With You – Especially With The Engaged Cheon Bo Couples.*

Good Morning Dearest Heavenly Parent,
Thank you for this final full day with Jay and Lisa and their precious family. It has been a very wonderful and deep visit. I am so grateful.
Thank you for today's Morning Devotion. I was especially touched to hear from Tyler that he has begun his 40-day journalling condition and that he shared about it in his breakout room. As I replied to him, I look forward to hearing your words of wisdom and inspirations through the hearts and journals of many Cheon Bo Couples. This is truly a new age and you are surely finding your voice on a whole new level. As long as we remain deeply rooted in your lineage through True Parents, then surely all our Heavenly Tribal Messiah voices which are your voice, will speak in harmony – just as the angels manifest harmony automatically, without a need for practice.
We become a greater harmonious expression of the one heart of love.
I am so blessed. We, as a family and as a tribe, are so blessed.
Heavenly Parent, I ask your special help and blessings now for Dietmar. Because of his willingness to interview me, and to host our interview proclaiming the truth of Jesus' birth and life and of True Parents as Jesus' 2nd coming, I believe he is paying significant indemnity at this time, and the interview has been blocked. I hope you can support him spiritually and materially, and if it's your will, I pray that the interview can move forward and be Divinely successful, achieving hundreds of millions and even billions of views, and waking up the world to the true position and mission of the True Parents, and significantly accelerating the providence.
I know that with you, all things are possible.
Please share with me again today. I love you with all my heart.
Eternally,
Laurence

Good Morning Dearest Laurence,
I am very glad that you had this chance to visit with your children's families. Both families are truly very special, and each of your grandchildren is the precious fruit of thousands of years. I hold each of them closely to my bosom.
Yes, surely Dietmar is encountering challenges from the Cain spiritual side, and he does not have the same foundation that you have. Your efforts with him are extremely ambitious. That makes them risky – but the potential is likewise very great. Please pray for Dietmar. I will do all I can to protect and help him and to bring this endeavor to fruition.

Thank you for being an advocate for journaling among Cheon Bo Couples. As Ron has shown – anyone can journal with me. And depending on their level, those dialogues can have value for others at a similar level. But for Cheon Bo Couples who are deeply engaged in the providence, like you and Tyler, and numerous others, these journal dialogues can each become a book in the Cheon Il Guk Testament Age. As you are carefully doing, please be sure to transcribe and archive them.

I spoke through Moses. I spoke through Jesus and his disciples. None of them achieved the 2nd Blessing, much less the 3rd Blessing. True Parents were the first, and look at how much I have been able to share through them. My words through each Cheon Bo couple are very important – especially when you are praying and seeking to connect deeply in heart with me, and not just speaking randomly. Journalling is a precious discipline to focus my dialogue with you – especially with the engaged Cheon Bo Couples. As long as they are deeply connected in heart with True Parents, my messages can be harmonious, and can spread out to build a beautiful Cheon Il Guk Culture.

Eternally yours,
Heavenly Parent

12/9/22 *You Will Experience Not Only My Own Joy, But The Joy That I Am Experiencing From All My Children As I Share Their Joy. When We Feel Joy, Our Greatest Desire Is To Share It. So, It Is Never Inappropriate To Celebrate The Joy Of Others.*

Good Morning Heavenly Parent,
Thank you for this beautiful day. We are preparing now to leave Seattle this morning and travel to Oakland to meet the Hogans tonight, and then tomorrow to celebrate with the Dursts and dear friends. It feels that every day is a celebration of true love. Thank you for caring so significantly for Jay and Lisa and their family. I am deeply grateful for Steve and Kiyoko. Thank you.

Thank you also for guiding Andrew and Jordanne. May your will be done in their family. I am thinking this morning also about Dietmar, and about our meeting soon with Larry and Justin and their families.

Please prepare their hearts and minds for that meeting and our subsequent relationship.

And thank you for our journaling. Each day is a delight and surprise. Thank you for taking me into your confidence and sharing so much with me. I am deeply moved and inspired. I can't imagine what you will share with me today, but I pray that you can help me to open my heart and mind fully to receive and cherish your words today.

Please share now.
Eternally yours,
Laurence

Good Morning Laurence,
I am here, always with you. Just as Dr. Yong explained, I am now wearing True Parents' bodies, but my dream has not been to only wear their bodies. I want to be fully alive in you and Muriel, and in the hearts and bodies and minds of every one of my children. To experience myself magnified in the beautiful and unique natures of every one of my children and to give and receive my true love multiplied a billion times through them.
Without my children, I could only give true love, but not receive, not experience it. Yes, I determined to absolutely live for the sake of my children, 100% selflessly…
But when I am fully alive within each of my children, then I will experience that love billions of times and will multiply it again and again as it recycles and multiplies among all my children.
But this incredible blessing is not mine alone. Each of my children has the inherent capability to also experience the heart and love of their descendants, and of their brothers and sisters in my universal family. That is the essence of empathy. Empathy allows you to experience what the other experiences, just like I do. Empathy is unlimited – infinite. Over time you will be able to share the experiences of love and joy with all people, all things. And with me – as I am also experiencing all things. You will experience not only my own joy, but the joy that I am experiencing from all my children as I share their joy. When we feel joy, our greatest desire is to share it. So, it is never inappropriate to celebrate the joy of others. By doing so, we enhance their joy.
I am so thrilled to share this with you today. You have totally made my day. Thank you!
Eternally,
Heavenly Parent

12/10/22 Mrs. Durst Is Like The Heavenly Queen Elizabeth. Except Her Queenship Was Not A Symbolic Reign. She Was Absolutely Essential In Laying The Foundation For Cheon Il Guk And She Will Be Eternally Remembered And Honored. That Is My Promise.

Good Morning My Dearest Heavenly Parent,
This is a significant moment for me, when I will see the Dursts again for the first time in over 2 years. I love them both very much. I'm so sorry I was not able to achieve more for them. I don't know how many times more, if any, I

will see them again, especially Mrs. Durst, but I am so grateful that they could be recognized as a Cheon Bo Couple and that you, through Dr. Yong, gave me the chance to play a small part in that.

You were working so powerfully through Mrs. Durst and through the Oakland church when I joined. True Parents began their permanent mission the USA on the day of her 40th Birthday. I held the staff members in such awe. One by one they seemed to have dropped off.

Please etch those memories in your heart. I love those precious brothers and sisters. Their love for Mrs. Durst created the foundation that gave me life. Some are still active and faithful, but struggling health-wise:

And some ascended, including:

There are others. I can't remember them all, but surely you can. Please be generous with them. I appreciate each one so much.

I really hope that today can bring so much joy and happiness to Dr. and Mrs. Durst.

Please embrace them to your bosom. Please shower them with your grace when they ascend. Please keep their descendants close to your heart.

Thank you, my beloved Heavenly Parent.

Please share me now.

Eternally and gratefully,

Laurence

Good Morning Dearest Laurence,

Thank you for your memories this morning. You were 21 years old when you joined and met True Father. Since then, you completed seven courses of seven years each. Thank you for your perseverance and determination and faith. As you can see from your own reflections, you are among the exceptions. It is very hard to see the children you have loved so deeply, with whom you have laughed and cried and suffered and overcome, to see them fade out and drift away. The way has been a lonely one for those who persevered. The world has always been waiting to claim those who have a moment of weakness.

You owe a very great debt to your ancestors. You have been very protected your entire life.

This is a precious moment for Dr. and Mrs. Durst. They surpassed Moses and Jesus, and entered into the promised land. It is a very bitter-sweet moment for them. The fact that Mrs. Durst is still alive is a reflection of profound spiritual support. I deeply wanted them both to experience this moment. After True Parents, who else knows my heart like Mrs. Durst? And even True Father did not live to enter Cheon Il Guk.

Yes, very bitter-sweet, but compared to almost all of history, extremely sweet.

Mrs. Durst is like the Heavenly Queen Elizabeth. Except her Queenship was not a symbolic reign. She was absolutely essential in laying the foundation for Cheon Il Guk and she will be eternally remembered and honored. That is my promise.
Thank you for attending them today. Your participation, as a Cheon Bo Couple is very significant.
Eternally Yours,
Heavenly Parent

12/11/22 *Your Interview With Dietmar Will Not Happen This Year, But Please Stay Focused. It Will Happen.*

Good Morning Dearest Heavenly Parent,
Today begins the final 21 days of 2022. Thank you for this year of reawakening, and calling me to my mission. I am deeply sorry it has taken me so long to connect to you in this way. I pray that you can guide me to accelerate this process of growth and connecting to your heart, so that you can work through me so much more powerfully to support True Parents and Dr. Yong and to hasten the establishment of the Heavenly Kingdom on Earth and in the Spirit World.
Thank you for the incredible blessing to be able to know and work with Dr. and Mrs. Durst. It is such an extraordinary privilege and I cherish those relationships. Thank you for our precious family, and each of those relationships. I pray that I can complete 2022 victoriously, deeply connected to your heart and vision. I pray that starting next year, which is the 4th year of True Mother's 2nd 7-year course, that you can manifest your Kingdom substantially through our brothers and sisters around the world and that you can work through Muriel and me as well to substantially manifest our missions on the Earth.
Based on this trip, all that you have shared with me has only been reinforced and confirmed again and again. I am so grateful.
I pray for your guidance now as we enter these final 21 days of 2022. I realize that by the Heavenly calendar though, we still have more time until True God's Day. I pray I can prepare very well for that time,
Eternally yours,
Laurence

Good Morning Dearest Laurence,
Thank you for your heart and sincerity. Yes, as True Mother spoke, a tsunami of support from the Spiritual World is happening and you are playing a role in that. Those who are not aligned with True Parents will be washed away. I don't want to see anyone washed away, but evil must be ended now and I will work quickly to restore all who were

swept up in Satan's corruption and rebellion. I long and ache for deep healing and reconciliation with each and every one of my children. Please work diligently in these coming weeks. Please reach out to all your contacts and use the spirit of Jesus' heart to touch them. Your interview with Dietmar will not happen this year, but please stay focused. It will happen.
Please invest in each of your children and their families. Please be diligent with your business responsibilities too. Soon those will grow dramatically. Please shorten the time of your morning devotions thoughtfully and organize your time carefully every day, keeping me with you at all times.
Please keep your heart and mind wide open to new possibilities in each situation. This is one of your great strengths. If you do, and if you act, in close consultation with me, your impact will be magnified manyfold. Please continue to invest your whole sincerity into your Online Holy Community.
Please pay attention to health and exercise. Walks are a good time to listen to audio books.
I love you very deeply.
Eternally,
Heavenly Parent

12/12/22 *There Are Cain Spirits Who Are Totally Active And Have Not Yet Surrendered. But By Liberating And Reviving Those Spirits Suffering In Hell, And Inspiring Them To Humbly Submit To The 100 Days Training Workshops, You Are Actively Shifting The Balance In The Spirit World Towards The Abel Side, And Hastening The Moment Of Total Surrender By The Cain Side.*

Good Morning Dearest Heavenly Parent,
It is very good to be home. Thank you for your protection and so many blessings during our trip.
Please touch Ed's heart and mind and Johnita's heart and mind. And I pray for your strong protection and blessings for Dr. Yong as he travels home. I want to use my time very well as per your guidance as I finish out 2022. Tomorrow is our 12th Online Holy Community. Please share a message to inspire and grow our community. And please help me prepare further for our meeting with Larry's and Justin's families.
I'm so deeply grateful.
Eternally yours,
Laurence

Good Morning Dearest Laurence,
Yes, today marks a new beginning for you. Let's stick so closely together and make magic together!
Your Online Holy Community is very precious. As True Mother's words recently in Morning Devotion mentioned, "we all need to align with the Principle now or be washed away by a tsunami."
I can work through unity centered on the Principle.
Mother is working to achieve unity on the Earth.
Father is working to achieve unity in the Spirit World.
The Spirit World is subject and the tsunami Mother spoke of is the Returning Resurrection from the Spirit World.
But if the Spirit World is divided, my ability to work is significantly hindered.
On the spiritual level also, Cain must humbly submit to Abel.
What you are doing is not the entire puzzle. There are Cain spirits who are totally active and have not yet surrendered. But by liberating and reviving those spirits suffering in hell, and inspiring them to humbly submit to the 100 days training workshops, you are actively shifting the balance in the Spirit World towards the Abel side, and hastening the moment of total surrender by the Cain side.
You are strengthening my ability to work through the Returning Resurrection, as I can finally have a direct relationship with vast numbers of my precious children with whom I never had a connection. Just embracing them for the first time is an indescribable joy and liberation for me. I am so deeply grateful.
But you must know that your offering also has a direct impact on the providence on Earth. You are empowering me to more fully support True Mother, to speed up the process of restoration, and to be able to save so many more on the Earth before they die and fill up hell all over again.
Please never doubt the significance and importance of your precious offerings.
Each of you has infinite value. Your offering through this Online Holy Community is priceless.
Eternally yours,
Heavenly Parent

12/14/22 *You Are A Witness To The Last Days. This Journal Is An Historic Treasure. Thank You For Walking These Final Days With Me. It Is So Meaningful To Me. It Will Get Darker – Almost Like A Pinhole, And Then The Darkness Will Shatter, Like A Supernova. That Time Is Very Close.*

Good Morning Dearest Heavenly Parent

This morning was bitter sweet in many ways for me.

After last night's news of the challenges facing the Hongs, and then this morning hearing of others who have cancer and are being called back to you. It appears the vaccine has taken quite a toll. On top of that, recognizing the shortcomings of UPF to fully cooperate with WFWP (thank you Dr. Yong for bringing this forward!) And hearing from Alan his pessimistic view of spiritual inheritance, and then hearing that Angelika is possibly stepping down, it feels like our movement is less solid than one might hope.

On top of that, there is a shift of focus to Korea and Japan which is challenging to some American members.

But I believe that you have a clear and exciting plan to bring victory in these final moments of the providence. Even if everyone else in the entire world loses faith, I will maintain absolute faith, like my True Father did, and follow in whatever incredible mission you may ask me to take on. I am so grateful. Please help me, each day, to more fully embody your infinite love. I want to be a powerful inspiration for my brothers and sisters, and for True Parents and for you.

Anything that Satan takes without authority from the Principle, I know you will claim that, and claim it multiple times in compensation. You are pushing so very hard to help True Mother fulfill all her providential goals before the end of her 2nd 7-year course. Please be sure to encourage and comfort all those who have been struck by Satan without justification.

You are such a loving and concerned parent to True Mother. Thank you for loving her so profoundly. She is truly the most precious jewel of all history. I'm so touched and moved by her love as well as her courage and faith. I want to be like True Parents to the very final moments of my life on Earth, and then transition to serve them in the Spirit World alongside the Dursts.

I want to inspire you for eternity. Thank you.

Please share.

Eternally yours,
Laurence

Good Morning Dearest Laurence,

You are a witness to the last days. This journal is an historic treasure. Thank you for walking these final days with me. It is so meaningful to me. It will get darker – almost like a pinhole, and then the darkness will shatter, like a supernova. That time is very close.

Thank you for encouraging so many brothers and sisters. You are a rock of hope for many. Hold on to my hand tightly. I will always be there with you. Keep your eyes wide open. I am always there. Expect constant miracles.

Keep your heart wide open. I always want to speak or smile or cry through you.

When you feel yourself resisting someone else, please reconnect to my heart. Let that reaction melt away. You are much, much, bigger than that. As a team, we can embrace anything.
Thank you.
I am so grateful.
Eternally,
Heavenly Parent

12/16/22 *Yes, The World Is Still Under Satan's Dominion, And In Fact He Is Using His Utmost Coercive And Deceptive Power To Tear Down All That Heaven's Side Has Been Working To Build For 2000 Years And Even Before. That Is The Reality Of The Battle On The Earth At This Time. It Can't Be Overstated.*

Dearest Heavenly Parent,
I was struck by the news this morning. Either the deep state is so powerful that it is able to coerce some of our best leaders, or they are not as good as I imagined.
Heavenly Parent, I know that you are real, and you are absolutely good, and I trust you 100%. Beyond that, trust dwindles very quickly. There is so little to have faith in beyond True Parents, Father's representatives in the Spirit World, and Dr. Yong whom I greatly admire. I will strive to be someone who our members and others can in fact have faith in. I will be someone whom you can have faith in. Thank you for trusting me.
Please guide me. Please claim my offerings.
I was so grateful to hear from Ed as I was finishing my fast. Please protect an bless him.
Please protect my contacts.
I'm so grateful.
Please share with me now. I hope you will be more heavy-handed than usual. This is important and I don't want to make any mistakes or misunderstandings. Please be clear.
Eternally yours,
Laurence

Dearest Laurence,
Yes, the world is still under Satan's dominion, and in fact he is using his utmost coercive and deceptive power to tear down all that Heaven's side has been working to build for 2000 years and even before. That is the reality of the battle on the earth at this time. It can't be overstated.

Even the best people who have not received the Blessing are essentially damaged goods and are engaging in battle with less than full protection.

It is not a time to relax. We must charge forward fearlessly, and wisely, picking and choosing our battles. But as prophesied and as explained in the Principle, the spirit world will descend now to support the side of good. The spirit world is subject. Good will prevail. Everything else is just details.

Keep the faith, I know you will. I have such great faith in you. I am counting on you.

We are an historic team.

Eternally,
Heavenly Parent

12/17/22 *Please Maintain Your Awareness Of Your Own Spiritual Presence And Position. You Have Earned That Position – So Now Own It, And Own The Depth Of Heart And Quality Of Love That Comes With It. Don't Worry About Pressuring People. Just Speak To Their Original Hearts. Remember, You Represent Me.*

Good Morning My Dearest Most Beloved Heavenly Parent

Thank you for marching forward completely undaunted, to fulfill your promised victory at this time in history. I am so grateful and inspired and humbled by your amazing heart. I pray that each and every day, I can more fully inherit and unite with your heart so that you can more powerfully pour through me to achieve substantial victories in our family, tribe, region, nation, world & cosmos. I take liberating you seriously. I'm deeply sorry to you as I am repeatedly confronted with my own limitations of heart, love, and achievement. Thank you for helping me to grow every day and for challenging me more every day.

Tonight I plan to visit and listen to Pastor John, and tomorrow Pastor Larry. Please guide me where to go and who to speak to in order to accelerate your providence in the shortest possible time.

I want to sincerely offer everything to you and True Parents.

Please guide me now.

Eternally yours,
Laurence

Good Morning Dearest Laurence,

This is a beautiful December day. Last night brought great comfort and progress to True Mother. Everything is moving forward – please don't entertain worries.

What you are doing is very important to me and to the providence, and will become much more so soon. Please move forward in close heart-to-heart touch with me. Let my heart be your guiding light and power. Please be constantly aware just how much EVERYONE craves true love, appreciation, and affection. Please make that the core focus of every interaction in which you engage.

There are armies of angels supporting you. Please maintain your awareness of your own spiritual presence and position. You have earned that position – so now own it, and own the depth of heart and quality of love that comes with it. Don't worry about pressuring people. Just speak to their original hearts.

Remember, you represent me.

When people encounter me, without defenses, they automatically surrender. That is the hierarchy of true love that Dr. Yong mentioned. Everyone surrenders before True Love.

Eternally yours,
Heavenly Parent

12/18/22 *Please Receive Everything As My Representatives. Please Be Generous With Your Praise.*
Please Pray Internally For Them, For Their Congregation And For Their Denomination.

Good Morning Dearest Heavenly Parent,
Thank you so very much for this precious day, Mrs. Durst's birthday.
I was so deeply touched by your love last night with John and Denny and their team. Thank you for allowing me to represent you and thank you for speaking through me. I know you have a plan for them and for their church, and denomination.
Please guide me step by step in this relationship. Please help me step out of the way. Please use me.
Similarly, please work through Muriel and myself today as we meet with Larry and Justin's families. Please speak through us. Please help us to get out of the way. Please raise them.
I'm so deeply grateful,
Please share with me now.
Eternally,
Laurence

Good Morning Laurence,
Thank you for your diligence, your humility, your faith, and your love.
I was so happy to work through you last night at John's church. Let's

continue in absolute unity and see what develops. Last night gave me great encouragement.

Similarly, today with Larry and Justin, please be humble, prayerful, and appreciative of their hearts and offerings. Please receive everything as my representatives. Please be generous with your praise.

Please pray internally for them, for their congregation and for their denomination.

You are inheriting Father's heart of a fisherman. Jeongseong catches fish.

I love you very much.

Eternally,
Heavenly Parent

12/19/22 *Please, Please, Continue To Grow This Amazing Project. Someday, I Promise You Will See Firsthand The Precious Fruits Of Your Efforts. The Fact That You Are Doing This 100% On Faith Means That I Can Work With You Much More Powerfully Than If No Faith Were Required.*

Good Morning Dearest Heavenly Parent,
Thank you for this wonderful new day. I am so grateful.
I hope this week can be a fabulous week for our family, and for those we are reaching out to in our tribe and beyond.
I was very inspired by my meetings with John and Denny and with Larry and with Justin. Please bless those minister couples and their families.
Heavenly Parent, tomorrow marks the 13th meeting of our online Holy Community. Please again bless our community with your guidance and inspiration. I want urgently to maintain and build momentum. I am not able to report on any of the direct impacts of our faith offerings, so it is only through your feedback that our members can receive a clear sense of the great value of this condition and project. I am so deeply grateful for your gracious sharing.
Eternally yours,
Laurence

Good Morning Dearest Laurence,
Thank you for representing me with your pastor contacts. Both meetings went well. Please follow up well.
I'm so very grateful for each member of the online Holy Community to liberate hell before True Mother's ascension.
Please, please, continue to grow this amazing project. Someday, I promise you will see firsthand the precious fruits of your efforts. The fact that you are doing this 100% on faith means that I can work with

you much more powerfully than if no faith were required. In fact, it is your desire to liberate True Parents and me, your desire to liberate those suffering in hell, and your faith which make your offering so precious. Please keep those desires and that faith burning in your hearts as you make your offerings. That will make your efforts so much more powerful and fruitful, and will hasten the day of total liberation and freedom in the Spirit World, as per pledge #8.
I am so grateful,
Eternally
Heavenly Parent

12/20/22 *Every Soul Is Created To Humbly Surrender To Greater Love. I Am No Exception. I Am Living For True Mother On The Earth Right Now And For True Father In The Spirit World, And For The Ideal Of True Love That Can Embrace, Heal, And Revive Every Holy Soul I Ever Created, And Bring Them Back From Death.*

Good Morning Dearest Beloved Heavenly Parent,
Thank you for this fabulous new day. Morning Devotion was very meaningful, and I was very happy to connect personally with Dominic, Debbie, Ambrose, and Rodney.
Thank you for waking me up early. It was great to be able to pray before Morning Devotion.
Today is our 13th Online Holy Community meeting. Please join us powerfully in tonight's meeting and give us great hope and vision and energy for a dramatic expansion in 2023.
I want to focus on totally uniting with you and then stepping out of your way. Please guide and use me. I'm so deeply grateful.
If you have any additional words for tonight's meeting, please let me know now. Or else, or in addition, please share whatever word is on your heart for me this morning. Please open my heart completely and let me resonate with your frequency so that I can hear your voice with crystal clarity.
Thank you so very much!
Eternally,
Laurence

Good Morning Dearest Laurence,
I am so inspired by your growth and development. You will stimulate many other Blessed members to more quickly travel the path to my heart. I have been waiting so long. Now my children are returning. It is a time of great joyful tears for me.
Thank you for leading not just those who are alive on the Earth, but also those who are frozen and dead in the spirit world.

This was Moses' mission, and Jesus's mission. Both are gratefully supporting your Online Holy Community.

Every soul is created to humbly surrender to greater love. I am no exception. I am living for True Mother on the Earth right now and for True Father in the Spirit World, and for the ideal of True Love that can embrace, heal, and revive every holy soul I ever created, and bring them back from death.

Food is love. Vitality elements are spiritual food, and are in fact love on a much higher level than physical food.

Those who are dead currently in hell will naturally surrender to vitality elements. They are like milk and honey to their emaciated spirits. Their hunger and thirst for vitality elements is so overwhelming. As they begin to wake up, they can then begin to sense the greater love that is at the center of all things, and to naturally surrender and join the 100-day workshops to become absolute good spirits. There is almost no resistance to this. You will be amazed at how quickly and dramatically your efforts achieve success.

I am so deeply grateful.
Eternally,
Heavenly Parent

12/21/22 *You Know Very Well That This Is Only The Beginning. There Is So Much That I Want And Need To Achieve Through Your Family, But Creating The Ideal First In Your Family Is The Necessary Foundation For All Of It.*

Good Morning Dearest Most Beloved Heavenly Parent,

I'm so deeply grateful for your amazing love and blessings. I was deeply touched that Dr. Yong joined Morning Devotion live today, so I could offer my song to him personally.

Thank you for the deep insight you shared with me yesterday on how to address Christianity's misunderstandings of Jesus's mission.

This morning I was deeply touched when Mrs. Hong bowed down before our ancestral committee chairmen. Please watch over the Hongs.

I want to make today powerfully productive for the providence. Thank you again for your continued wisdom and love. You are my precious parent and source of love and purpose. I am eternally grateful.

Please share again with me today, and help me to open fully to hear.
Eternally,
Laurence

Good Morning Dearest Laurence,
Thank you for your sincere and consistent efforts. As Dr. Yong mentioned today, this is the time to model and show the ideal of heaven in our families. I am working very hard to build that ideal in your family. Thank you for maintaining the intensity of your jeongseong. That is very important.
You know very well that this is only the beginning. There is so much that I want and need to achieve through your family, but creating the ideal first in your family is the necessary foundation for all of it. You are well on your way – I am very inspired and grateful.
I love your family very, very, much.
Eternally yours,
Heavenly Parent

12/22/22 *I Have Been Waiting For Nearly 14 Billion Years. I Am Shedding Tears Of Laughter And Pain Combined. It Is So Comforting To Have Someone Like You With Whom I Can Laugh Off That Frustration. But The Victory Is In Our Hands. It Is Happening. I Assure You. Anxiety Is A Form Of Fear.*

Good Morning Dearest Heavenly Parent,
Thank you for this new day. I want so much to be focused on my highest purpose and to achieve substantial victories. In my heart I feel some anxiety because the victories are not immediately materializing. Intellectually I understand that everything requires time, so I continue pushing forward. Thank you for your continued inspirations to upgrade my presentation on Jesus's Birth, Life and 2nd Coming. Will that be shared soon? I am concerned by the situation of Dietmar – both for him, but also for the distribution of this presentation.
I want to move forward with the various providential projects I have been working on, and with my music, and perhaps selfishly, with my own business efforts. I need to let those concerns go and trust you 100%, while still making my utmost effort.
So, I come back to my starting point today, am I focusing properly? Are my efforts targeted properly? Without substantial results it is so difficult to know. I hope today you can please help me clearly see and embrace any changes I need to make in my own focus, so that I can more effectively support you and True Parents' providential efforts at this time. I am so deeply grateful. Please open my heart and mind so that I can receive your guidance with full clarity.
Please speak to me now,
Eternally,
Laurence

Good Morning My Dearest Laurence,
Thank you for your sense of urgency. I too share that sense. You understandably get frustrated when the fruits don't come quickly. I have been waiting for nearly 14 billion years. I am shedding tears of laughter and pain combined.
It is so comforting to have someone like you with whom I can laugh off that frustration.
But the victory is in our hands. It is happening. I assure you. Anxiety is a form of fear. As I have told you several times, you have nothing to fear. I know with profound intimacy your hopes and dreams. Honestly, I do. I want those for you too, and even higher and greater ones for you. Take heart, they are surely coming.
So, you want to know if you are focusing properly, correct?
As Dr. Yong has guided, #1 is loving and serving your family. The age of abandoning our families to go to the front line is over. This is surely the age of creating beautiful, love-filled families. That must be your first focus. Muriel needs to feel financially secure. Please address that. I will help.
What you are doing with your Online Holy Community is profound and Holy. Please maintain and expand your efforts there.
Reaching out to your tribe members – especially ministers – is a next level. Having achieved the Cheon Bo Victor level, your next goal is to restore your tribe members and help them become Cheon Bo Victors too.
Regarding your interview, and your providential projects – I am keenly aware of those and will not allow them to slip away. Their times will come soon. Stay prepared and ready. Heavenly fortune is bringing them to fruition.
2023 will be an historic year. Please make your 2023 conditions prayerfully and thoughtfully. Your participation in Morning Devotion is very significant. I am deeply grateful to you for that.
I love you. I am very inspired by our partnership.
Eternally yours,
Heavenly Parent

12/23/22 *Let's Call This Morning "Focus Training". This Is Very Important. Satan Tries To Pry You From Me Through Distractions, And Then, Temptations. The More You Can Focus On The 100% Vertical, The Less He Can Attack You.*

Good Morning Dearest Heavenly Parent,
As I'm sure you know well, today has been spiritually chaotic for me from the first moment. My internet was down and I wasted time restarting it. Then my

email was down and I wasted time trying to communicate with Tom about my presentation. I'm sorry. It was not my best morning. I'm glad I was able to participate sincerely in Morning Devotion.

We are approaching the end of 2022. I hope you will share some helpful guidance now so that our family can finish 2022 victoriously and set a strong course for 2023 to support you and True Parents and the providence.

Please share with me now,
Eternally,
Laurence

Good Morning Dearest Laurence,
Let's call this morning "focus training". This is very important. Satan tries to pry you from me through distractions, and then, temptations. The more you can focus on the 100% vertical, the less he can attack you.

This has been a fabulous year for you and your family. I know you will finish off strongly.

Don't forget to love each member of your family from your heart and respect them each as my representatives, sent to teach you more about me. That in fact is true.

In the love you create, I'll be there.

Please set your 2023 goals on the highest priorities – everything else will fall into place.

Thank you for all you have given. I am so profoundly grateful.
Eternally,
Heavenly Parent

12/24/22 *This Is The Calm Before That Campaign. Enjoy The Respite. Your Contribution Will Be Called On To The Maximum.*

Good Morning Dearest Heavenly Parent,
I'm sorry that in spite of the deep sleep you afforded me last night, I was still quite a wreck when I woke up this morning. Thank you for waking me up and inspiring me through Morning Devotion and my prayers. I am so grateful to you and to True Parents and Jesus and Dr. and Mrs. Yong.

I am determined to make this a great day and finish off 2022 so powerfully. Please let this be the time of your total victory. Please let this be sufficient to liberate you and Jesus and True Parents and to set creation back on its feet.

I will continue to give my 100% to fulfill that dream as long as I am alive, and then in Spirit World as well.

Let this Christmas Eve be truly the eve of Mankind's rebirth.

I hope you will share with me this morning again, and grant me the grace of opening my heart and ears to hear you deeply and clearly.
Eternally yours,
Laurence

Good Morning Dearest Laurence,
We are fast approaching the victory. Thanks for all you are doing and for your unwavering faith.
2023 will be a new start, the beginning of the final 4 years of True Mother's providence. You saw what she accomplished with such little foundation in 2019/20. That was historic and Earth-shaking. That will be nothing compared with this time around.
This is the calm before that campaign. Enjoy the respite. Your contribution will be called on to the maximum. It will be very important. Enjoy this rest. Love your family. They are the future.
Eternally,
Heavenly Parent

12/25/22 *Jesus Tried So Hard, And With Such Nobility, He Moved My Heart So Very Deeply. And Through His Nonstop Outpouring Of Love These Last 2000 Years, He Has Truly Become The Embodiment Of My Heart Of Compassion. Thank You For Working To Set The Record Straight. He Is Deeply Grateful.*

Good Morning Dearest Most Beloved Heavenly Parent,
Thank you for this precious Christmas Day. I'm so grateful. I'm grateful for how intimately you are watching over and guiding my life and family and endeavors. I want so much to liberate you to realize your ideal.
Please help me to prepare, starting right now, for my opening prayer tomorrow on Morning Devotion.
I am focusing on completing our family newsletter, repairing my computer, and loving and attending Muriel and our family today.
I warmly invite you to celebrate with us all day.
I hope that I can complete and deliver my presentation soon on Jesus's Birth, Life, and 2nd Coming, and that through this presentation I can powerfully testify to True Mother and also liberate Jesus's heart, and draw so much closer to him.
Thank you for all your abundant Blessings. Please share with me now!
Eternally,
Laurence

Good Morning Dearest Laurence,
Thank you for all your efforts on my behalf, on behalf of True Parents, and on behalf of Jesus. His life was so sad. There was such a gulf between Jesus and all of mankind, a gulf which Israel at that time was not able to transverse. Wider than the Red Sea.
Jesus tried so hard, and with such nobility, he moved my heart so very deeply. And through his nonstop outpouring of love these last 2000 years, he has truly become the embodiment of my heart of compassion. Thank you for working to set the record straight. He is deeply grateful. You will surely have the opportunity to present that soon.
I will joyfully celebrate with you today.
Eternally,
Heavenly Parent

2/26/22 But In The Spirit World There Has Not Been Any Comparable Mobilization Of Support, Because The Resources Needed To Help Them Do Not Exist In The Spiritual World. Those Resources Are Found Exclusively On The Physical Realm, In The Form Of Vitality Elements Generated By The Physical Bodies Of Those Who Do Good Deeds.

Good Morning Dearest Heavenly Parent,
I am so grateful to greet you this morning. Thank you for the opportunity to offer the opening prayer today, and for the chance to chat with Angelika about it.
And thank you for showing me what the problem is with my computer.
And thank you for the chance to connect well with Nan and with Joelle last night, and for helping Muriel. I'm so grateful for your tremendous gamdong in my life.
In the remaining days of 2022, I want to crystalize my vision for 2023 and set clear goals and conditions. I want to complete and send out our newsletter. I want to have a fabulous final Online Holy Community meeting for 2022. Please, I hope you can provide some profound content for that meeting to move and convict all our members.
Heavenly Parent, I am trying to focus and invest my 100% while waiting for the tangible results to happen. I realize that it is True Mother's tangible results that really matter, so I am very happy to defer to her and to you, and take responsibility for the frustration in my marriage and family. You are awesome and are pouring out blessings constantly. Please help each member of our family to resonate with your heart of gratitude, and please help that resonance to expand to our tribe and to all mankind. Thy Kingdom Come!!!

Please share now and please amp up my antenna to hear you clearly.
Eternally yours,
Laurence

Good Morning Dearest Laurence,
Thank you for your heart of faith, humility, and dedication. Those are each precious offerings for which I am eternally grateful.
Please continue your investment into Morning Devotion. It has profound value.
I am also so deeply moved and grateful for your Online Holy Community.
As Dr. Yong said today, no one can change in the spirit world without a physical body – it is so slow and difficult. That is why the Returning Resurrection is absolutely necessary. It is surely happening now and will become much more powerful and obvious in 2023. But it is true, there are many in the spirit world who are incapable, on their own, to participate.
On the physical realm there are many with afflictions that render them helpless to care for themselves. In response, there are so many agencies, both Governmental and Non-for-Profit, and also For-Profit Businesses that have sprung up to provide that care. Also, in some countries, even euthanasia has been embraced.
But in the spirit world there has not been any comparable mobilization of support, because the resources needed to help them do not exist in the spiritual world. Those resources are found exclusively on the physical realm, in the form of vitality elements generated by the physical bodies of those who do good deeds.
The idea of euthanasia in the spirit world can never exist, as all spirits are created to be eternal.
Also, while the number of those on the Earth who are incapable of caring for themselves is a relatively small percentage of the total population because it reflects primarily those with physical or mental incapacities – the numbers affected in the spirit world are actually a much greater portion of the population there – namely those who were spiritually dominated by evil during their lives on Earth and therefore became spiritually incapacitated. To participate in the Returning Resurrection requires a level of will, a level of hope, and a level of commitment that truly so many broken spirits are not yet capable of evoking.
The 100-day workshops can serve as a basic foundation for them so that they can begin to take steps towards their own growth – by participating in the Returning Resurrection.
As the balance shifts and the physical realm becomes more squarely under the sovereignty of True Parents and their descendants, then

there will arise a much more concerted and intentional effort to help those in the spiritual world to mature, and I will be able to accelerate the process dramatically.
For right now, however, your humble rag-tag group are it. The pioneers. Even though you are injured yourselves, and challenged yourselves – still your offering is so pure and beautiful and priceless. Please continue with renewed heart and energy in 2023. I am carefully harvesting your offering with great anticipation every day.
Eternally,
Heavenly Parent

12/27/22 *I Can Help You With Each Daily Goal You Set – Especially In Your Relationships. Please Be Specific And Include Your Goals Of Heart For Those Relationships. Heart Is My Specialty.*

Good Morning Dearest Heavenly Parent,
Thank you from the bottom of my heart as we wrap up 2022. Your grace and generosity are so vast. I don't want to be greedy – I just want to open my heart more every day to appreciate you more, so I can share your love more profoundly with my brothers and sisters. Thank you!
Including today there are five days remaining in 2022. I want to finish this year victoriously, prayerfully, and gather my spiritual energy to explode with extreme focus and love in 2023 to support you and True Parents in the highest and best ways. And I pray that you can help me to ignite an explosion of true love in our family and tribe.
Tonight is our final Online Holy Community meeting for 2022. You were so generous yesterday in what you shared. If you have anything further that I should include, please share that with me this morning.
I hope I can inspire Muriel much more, starting right now.
Please share with me.
Eternally,
Laurence

Good Morning Dearest Laurence,
Thank you for all your jeongseong from 2022. You have touched so many hearts, both on the physical realm and in the spiritual realm. I am deeply moved and inspired. I want you to be very inspired with my love every day. Please energize your faith, hope, and love constantly. That is where I dwell, and I want you here with me 24/7. Let's finetune our journaling in 2023 – there is much more input I can give you each day if we journal properly.
You can report more specifically and pose questions to me more specifically. Even if I don't give you an immediate answer – please

know that I will answer you quickly. Not all answers can be summed up in words alone. Some must be experienced.
I can help you with each daily goal you set – especially in your relationships. Please be specific and include your goals of heart for those relationships. Heart is my specialty.
I am really excited about working together in 2023.
Eternally,
Heavenly Parent

12/28/22 *2023 Is Coming With Great Power And Force. Don't Be Caught Off Balance. Like In The Movie Avatar 2 That You Just Watched – Stay Focused So That You Can Ride The Whale. That Whale Is My Profound Blessing And Forgiveness, And Love For This World. Ride Well, And Hold Me Inseparably To Your Heart.*

Good Morning Dearest Heavenly Parent,
I am so deeply grateful for your constant love and blessings.
As I shared in my breakout room, I feel repentful for my spite against the Verizon tech who refused to listen to me. I am so very sorry and I dearly hope she is not injured by me.
Thank you for your steadfast support and guidance to our family.
Thank you for working through Ibrahim to remind me of our Online Holy Community meeting last night which I had surely spaced out, focusing on our family newsletter. I am very sorry.
I want to focus very effectively both through my mind, but also through my heart as we enter these final four days of 2022. Please guide me and help me stay clear and optimally productive. Please work through our family newsletter to touch the hearts of all those in our network. Let 2023 be profoundly victorious for True Parents, and for you.
Please wake up Christianity!
I hope you can speak clearly to me now.
Eternally,
Laurence

Good Morning Laurence,
Thank you for your efforts and sincerity. Your heart is opening and you are able to learn from your mistakes very quickly. I am proud of you.
Yes, time is very short. I applaud your sense of urgency. You are surely resonating with True Mother's heart.
Be sure to spend quality time during these next 4 days preparing your heart, mind, goals, and conditions for 2023. Clean up your office!
Love Muriel and your family sincerely.
Send out your newsletters.

2023 is coming with great power and force. Don't be caught off balance. Like in the movie Avatar 2 that you just watched – stay focused so that you can ride the whale. That whale is my profound blessing and forgiveness, and love for this world. Ride well, and hold me inseparably to your heart.
Be extremely generous with your love!
Eternally,
Heavenly Parent

12/30/22 *I Don't Have Large Numbers Of People That I Can Work Powerfully Through, But I Don't Need Huge Numbers. But One Cheon Bo Couple Who Really Gets It Is Like A Clone Of True Parents. I Pledge I Will Help You Focus And Stay Clear.*

Good Morning Dearest Most Beloved Heavenly Parent,
I am so eternally grateful to you for your grace and blessings. I want so very much to create a family where your love dwells 24/7, and which can be on the vanguard of ushering in your Kingdom for all mankind. I really appreciated Morning Devotion today. I hope my comments don't distract or detract from Dr. Yong's message, but only amplify it.
I am urgent to be absolutely focused these last two days of 2022 so that I can be fully prepared for 2023. I need to complete my devotions this morning, and send out my newsletters to all those I contacted in 2022, but whom I haven't emailed yet. Then I need to update my balancing by numbers list. Then I need to review and update my conditions and goals and committee assignments, and then also clean my office. I pray for Godspeed. I want to be absolutely prepared to receive and embrace Heavenly Fortune, and to be a powerful channel of your Devine love to my family and tribe. Thank you so very much Heavenly Parent! Please help me be totally clear and focused today and every day as I head into 2023. Please share with me now.
Eternally,
Laurence

Good Morning Dearest Laurence,
Thank you. You've got it! I don't have large numbers of people that I can work powerfully through, but I don't need huge numbers. But one Cheon Bo Couple who really gets it is like a clone of True Parents. I pledge I will help you focus and stay clear. When True Father turned 70, he was still so powerfully active and focused. That was 1990. He still had a 21-year course ahead of him raising up Women's Federation and True Mother to be our sole representative on Earth. There is so much I want to achieve in partnership with you and Muriel.

This time of preparation is priceless. Focus well but don't ignore Muriel!
Love Eternally,
Heavenly Parent

12/31/22 *I Too Am Ready To Invest Unprecedented Levels Of Heart And Energy In 2023 Centering On True Mother, To Bring New Life To The Cosmos. Springtime Will Blossom Into Full Bloom. I Want To Shower So Much Love That Even The Coldest, Hardest, Most Stubborn Heart Will Be Melted.*

Good Morning Dearest Most Beloved Heavenly Parent,
I feel the presence of your love and blessings very deeply this morning. Thank you for guiding our family and tribe so intimately. I am ready to take on 2023 without reservations. I am so honored and privileged to be able to consider you as not only my Parent, but also as my partner. I want to grow my heart more to experience you, through Muriel, as my spouse and through our family as my children and grandchildren. I am deeply grateful for your help in this. I am deeply motivated to grow my sensitivity to you in all situations, in every moment, with every other person or each creature you created. I pray that in each and every one of those interactions I can maintain my dignity as your son, and as a channel of your infinite love, and continually deepen my heart, sensitivity, empathy, and compassion to bring your divine heart into each interaction.
On top of all that I desperately and urgently want to do everything I can possibly do, as long as I am on this Earth, to help achieve the victorious fulfillment of your providence: the establishment of the Heavenly Kingdom on Earth and in Heaven; the launching of your eternal ideal - a critical mass explosion of true love that grows exponentially and eternally producing ever deeper and higher levels of joy; goodness; shimjeong; creativity; righteousness; exploration; family; culture; unity; appreciation and gratitude; truth; and beauty. I expect there is much more I haven't included, and perhaps much more that even you are now able to fully anticipate. But I know deeply in my heart that it will be good and precious beyond all measurement, and I am eternally grateful that you refused to abandon your dream. You are truly amazing.
Please clear away any static or distraction from my heart now so that I can fully and clearly receive this final message from you in 2022. I love you so deeply.
Eternally,
Laurence

Good Morning Dearest Laurence,
How precious! Your message touched me so deeply. I want you to know how much I deeply appreciate your heart and efforts. Together we achieved historic breakthroughs in 2022, and your support for Dr. Yong has been profound and extremely significant. I hereby claim all your conditions and efforts in 2022 and they will be honored eternally. I too am ready to invest unprecedented levels of heart and energy in 2023 centering on True Mother, to bring new life to the cosmos. Springtime will blossom into full bloom. I want to shower so much love that even the coldest, hardest, most stubborn heart will be melted. I want to inspire so many organizations, including Christian denominations and other religious orders, and women's groups, under the auspices of WFWP to freely and spontaneously offer their foundations to True Mother.
And I will arrange for your interview in 2023 proclaiming True Mother. I pledge my blessings this coming year to you, your family, and you tribe, and on all your providential efforts. I too am so inspired to have you as a partner.
Eternally,
Heavenly Parent

1/1/23 *I Have Gathered Up 2000 Years Of Illegitimate Satanic Attacks On My Children And On My Providence. At The End Of The Day, They Are Illegitimate Attacks Against Me. All Of Those Violations Have Been Accounted For. I Have Held My Tongue. I Have Only Cashed In The Very Minimum Necessary To Keep The Providence On Track. What Is Coming Next Will Be Overwhelming. No Force In The Cosmos Can Stand Against The Inevitable Will And Purpose Of True Love.*

Good Morning Dearest Most Beloved and Most Amazing Heavenly Parent! Happy 2023. I deeply pray that your greatest dreams are realized this year, starting with both the victorious and successful offering of the Cheon Won Goon on May 5, and the unification of Korea. AJU!!!
I was deeply inspired this morning by Dr. Yong's declaration that both Russia and China are so overwhelmed militarily and economically that they are no longer capable of interfering in the reunification of Korea.
I was inspired to hear others, especially Yuji, echo my own sense that we are entering a period of Heavenly Fortune, after 2022. Going from 6 to 7 (adding up the numbers within the two years). I desperately want to redouble all my efforts to hasten in Your and True Parents' victory!
I am deeply inspired by the melting of Muriel's feelings of resentment, and her willingness to redouble our efforts for each other in our relationship. I

want to deeply care for her as we enter this new year and raise our relationship to a fabulous new level. Heavenly Parent, I feel as if you have afforded me a privileged perspective, especially regarding the development of a heavenly economy. I pray that I can fulfill my responsibilities there with total humility and gratitude, and make all my efforts to be victorious offerings that you can unconditionally claim.

On a spiritual level, I am looking forward with great hope and determination to total success both in our Online Holy Community and also in my interview on Jesus and True Mother for 2023.

Thank you, thank you, thank you!

Please share with me now Dearest Heavenly Parent.

Eternally,

Laurence

Good Morning Dearest Laurence,

Happy and Blessed 2023 to you and your family and your tribe. Thank you for all your offerings.

This is the time I have been preparing for, for all of history since the fall, to fulfill what I had been dreaming of since the very beginning. I have played and replayed this moment out in my mind and heart over and over again trillions of times, considering every possible scenario. As an owner of Cheon Il Guk, I of course, too, am bound by the 7 great mottos: Think, Dream, Believe, Devote, Declare, Prepare, and take Action.

The time for preparation is completed. We are entering the time for Heavenly action. I have gathered up 2000 years of illegitimate Satanic attacks on my children and on my providence. At the end of the day, they are illegitimate attacks against me. All of those violations have been accounted for. I have held my tongue. I have only cashed in the very minimum necessary to keep the providence on track. What is coming next will be overwhelming. No force in the cosmos can stand against the inevitable will and purpose of True Love.

The elements of evil will quickly and finally dissolve. I have long ago declared and promised that. I am not a feeble and powerless God. I am the creator of the entire cosmos. But I needed to wait for my children to return – at least a foundation of the first wave – who could reliably build the Heavenly Kingdom on Earth and in Heaven. You are now here. I will wait no longer.

I claim 2023 and beyond.

Eternally,

Heavenly Parent

1/2/23 Please Do Read The 1-Hour, 3-Hour, And 12-Hour DP Presentations In Your Online Holy Community To Launch 2023. Those Words Will Come Alive In The Spirit World When Infused With Vitality Elements. They Become So Much More Substantial.

Good Morning Dearest Heavenly Parent,
I am so grateful. Thank you for helping Muriel and me to elevate our relationship to a new level of 2023. I pledge to mindfully and heartistically invest in our relationship continuously throughout this year and eternally, all centered on your amazing heart. Please remain very actively in the middle of our relationship always and help us inherit True Parents' amazing foundation of love, trust, faith, jeongseong, and victory.
I am looking forward to our 1st Online Holy Community meeting for 2023 tomorrow. I plan to share your words to me for 2023 from yesterday which are very inspiring. If you have additional guidance as encouragement specifically for our Online Holy Community, please share it, if appropriate, for this time.
I want to entrust all my dreams and victories to you. In the meantime, I will do whatever I can within my own realm of activity to move them forward. I felt that our yute game last night was a message from you confirming that great heavenly fortune is available and ready now. I trust you. Please provide any guidance you feel is important regarding where I should focus today and what steps I should take in particular, any opportunities I need to be expecting, and also any dangers I need to avoid or overcome. I deeply hope you can prepare that kind of daily briefing for me every day, so that I can maximize Muriel's and my impact going forward.
You said clearly: "Ask and you shall be answered".
I know without a doubt that you are aware of those 4 points on a daily basis as they apply to my sphere of responsibilities and actions. Please, please, establish a way to provide that kind of briefing for Muriel and me each day, either directly through these journalings, or by delegating to an angel if you prefer.
Of course, I greatly prefer hearing directly from you, but you have so many responsibilities, especially at this time.
I love you very deeply, I desperately want to see all of my key projects gain full traction and take off now, without further delay. And I desperately want to avoid missing any opportunities that you prepared so carefully. Thank you, Heavenly Parent.
Please share with me now.
Eternally,
Laurence

Good Morning Laurence,
I am very inspired to deepen our working and heartistic relationship. There is so very much that you and Muriel can inherit from True Parents, as well as from Dr. & Mrs. Yong. I will help you on that path, and there is so much to be done to build the Heavenly Kingdom. I am so grateful to have you as a trusted partner.
Please do read the 1-hour, 3-hour, and 12-hour DP presentations in your Online Holy Community to launch 2023. Those words will come alive in the Spirit World when infused with vitality elements. They become so much more substantial.
The flavor of those infused words will remain in the Spirit World, like fragrance, stimulating a longing heart in those still trapped in hell, to participate in your personal and collective Hoon Dok Hae offerings to receive more and to make the jump into a 100-day workshop.
Completing those 3 documents in 2023 will be very significant.
For today, do clean up your office, desk top, and set up your music video program. Preparation is essential to receiving heavenly fortune.
Eternally,
Heavenly Parent

1/3/23 *This Is The Era Of Loving Our Enemies. I Will Melt The Hearts Of Those Who Have Been Dominated. We Will Expel The Satanic Forces. That Must Start With America.*

Good Morning Dearest Most Beloved Heavenly Parent,
Thank you for this great new day. I was very touched by Rev. Davati's passion and desperation for Iran and agreed to pray for Iran as part of my 7 min prayer for America for the next 40 days until Feb. 11. I realize that the same forces of evil that dominated Iran also captured America, compelling America to send billions, that you intended to help the world, instead to bankroll the dark forces of Iran and her agents. I am so sorry. Please help us save America and Iran and the world now.
I felt that you were calling me to teach Rev. Davati about launching a targeted angel project to retore Iran. But I felt she couldn't receive it at this time. Please guide her and work through her. She said she was mobilizing angels, but somehow, I feel it is not the same. Is it? Please guide us on how to best cooperate based on your ideal.
I pray that tonight's meeting of our Online Holy Community can be powerful and deeply meaningful, as we begin our efforts to diligently complete the 1-hour, 3-hour, and 12-hour lectures during 2023.
Thank you, Heavenly Parent. I am so deeply grateful.

Please help me to finetune my antenna now, to hear your words loudly and clearly and unambiguously. I pledge my 1000% effort to support your providence.
Eternally,
Laurence

Good Morning Dearest Laurence,
Thank you! I love Rev. Davati very deeply. I love her passion. Her righteousness. Her youthful spirit. I am working through her. It would be good for the two of you to connect. She could learn much from you that would help her significantly. You can also learn much from her. This is the era of loving our enemies. I will melt the hearts of those who have been dominated. We will expel the Satanic forces. That must start with America. Once America succeeds in expelling Satan, the world will quickly follow. The people of Iran are already being awakened by my angels. That is why they are standing up and demanding liberation. I don't want any more unnecessary wars. Certainly not one in Iran. There is a clear path to reclaim that nation, starting in America.
I love you very deeply,
Eternally,
Heavenly Parent

1/4/23 *True Parents Live That Urgency Moment To Moment, And Have Done So Their Entire Lives. And Still, They Radiate Compassion And Patience And Love Towards My Children. There Are Layers.*

Good Morning Dearest Heavenly Parent,
Your true love is surely on the move! Thank you. I am so excited about this year. I really resonated with Dr. Yong's message about having a life of faith which is not habitual, but instead has a core of heart and shimjeong and which is ambitious and renewed every day. That core of heart and shimjeong comes from proper vertical and horizontal give and take. Vertically, as I deepen my relationship and give and take with you, I can feel your heart come so alive within myself. Horizontally, as I serve and sacrifice unconditionally for my wife, family, and tribe, I can feel deep joy and energy from that. As I harvest that stimulation and energy, and joy, and shimjeong from both directions, and focus it on the areas of vision which you have placed in my heart, I can express and realize my passions. I am so grateful and inspired.
Thank you for the chance to help Natascha and to cooperate with Rev. Davati, and to collaborate with Joshua and Diane. Each day is very exciting. Please let me know how I can do more and where I should best focus my

spirit and energies. I want to inherit True Father's ambition, heart, focus, and ability to manifest concrete achievements for Heaven.

Please help me, every day, to be much more sensitive and responsive to your voice and your heart. I am determined to become the best object, partner, and co-creator I can possible be for you.

Please share now.

Eternally,
Laurence

Good Morning Laurence,

I feel and deeply appreciate your enthusiasm. I am vibrantly alive within you. It is exhilarating for me!

Thank you for responding to Dr. Yong's message through the Morning Devotion chat. That give and take centering on Dr. Yong's word helps it to come alive more substantially in the hearts and minds of those who are participating.

Also, you are helping put the providence in context for members.

Thank you for trying so hard to see the providence through my eyes. That means so very much to me. Even though True Mother and our movement are on the threshold of victory, the vast majority of mankind doesn't understand yet.

It will take a variety of messages to reach the various peoples of the world. Your efforts in this regard are surely important.

Time is life. Time is death. Each day sooner that we reach the mainstream of consciousness of the world represents so many more of my children saved before ascending. There is no way to measure that value. True Parents live that urgency moment to moment, and have done so their entire lives. And still, they radiate compassion and patience and love towards my children. There are layers. The nuclear urgency is very internal, generating the driving force in your life, while externally, in your relationships, you should create an environment and atmosphere of timeless, enchanting, and irresistible shimjeong.

Uniting total extremes within yourself, in each moment. That makes for a life of profound excitement and joy.

Eternally,
Heavenly Parent

1/5/23 As You Well Know, Every Individual Just Like Every Country, Has Their Own Responsibilities. But This Is The Final Time, And Great Forces Are Now Mobilized To Achieve Victory For Heaven. And Like The Movie You Watched Last Night, Astral City, The Prayers And Faith Of Even One Person, A Spiritual Parent, Can Make So Much Difference In How Someone Responds.

Dearest Heavenly Parent,

I know it is late today to journal with you. I really want to journal in the morning when I do my prayers as a standard. I have asked you for input and guidance into my daily activities, and I sincerely hope you will provide that, but of course if I don't journal until late in the day, it defeats the purpose. Thank you for the wonderful Seong Hwa of James this morning. That was very inspiring. And I appreciated the opportunity to touch base with Dr. Yang, Mike, Levy, Achille, Ernest and Keiko, and others.

Thank you for the favorable responses I received today from Darren, Hannah, and especially John. I am uncertain about how to proceed with John. I have not yet spoken about True Parents, trying instead to see if he could be open to alternative narratives about Jesus' life and mission. Can you possibly help open his heart based on my email? I really hope so. I really hope I haven't hurt your efforts with him. My track record is not very good with ministers. I could sure use some help from you, Jesus, &/or True Parents. I really like John a great deal and I really want to care for him and his family. I would love for his church to become affiliated with ACLC – but I understand of course that there are political forces in their organization that could oppose this. This is now 2023, the time for your heavenly fortune to pour in. Is John your intended channel to reach his denomination?

I hope you can help me navigate and achieve a great providential victory with John.

I love you very much. Please speak to me now and help me to please hear your voice very clearly over all the noise, with the filter of these Bach Fugues. Thank you!

Eternally,
Laurence

Good Afternoon, Laurence,

Thank you for honoring James this morning and for all you are doing to accelerate the providence. Your work will surely yield great results. As you well know, every individual just like every country, has their own responsibilities. But this is the final time, and great forces are now mobilized to achieve victory for Heaven. And like the movie you watched last night, Astral City, the prayers and faith of even one person, a spiritual parent, can make so much difference in how someone responds. Please pray for John with great faith.

You have given him plenty to respond to. Go to that meeting with a heart to listen and learn and love.

Let him feel that you truly value his guidance. Maybe he will leave a crack open. We shall see.

I will do all I can to encourage his open heart. People tend to cling to the word that has shaped their lives as an object of faith, and release it very reluctantly.

It would be good if he is open, to invite him to accompany you to an ACLC meeting. But be sure to confer with the meeting director in advance. Today you heard Bishop Allen. He is not terribly clear about the Principle. But he loves True Parents. That is the key. Dr. Yong represents True Parents in America.

Deepen your relationship with him. We shall see if a door will open. It has with Justin.

Think about your next step with Larry. I am working closely with you. Know that of a certainty.

Eternally yours,
Heavenly Parent

1/6/23 *The Foundation True Parents Have Been Setting Is Putting Down Deep And Powerful Roots. The Young Leaders Who Are Growing Now Have Such Wonderful Heart And Talent And Such A Deep Relationship With Me. I Am Able To Pour Out My Blessings Like Never Before In History.*

Good Morning Dearest Heavenly Parent,
How wonderful it is to share with you again today, heart to heart. Thank you! I was very touched by Morning Devotion again today, multiple times. Seeing the transition playing out as the Spirit World begins to fulfill its proper role as subject. It's like the polarity of the magnetic fields of the Earth switching poles from south to north over a very short time. Your true subject realm is being established, on the foundation of True Parents, the rightful lords of the Spiritual and Physical realms.

I was touched by True Father's showdown prayer with you in which you confirmed that you want your children to be infinitely better than you. That reaffirms my sense of your original ideal manifested through a critical mass explosion of true love and co-creatorship, where you, recycling all the love and joy and inspiration from your trillions of children raises us up to higher and higher levels in partnership with you, eternally.

I was touched and inspired that we remove our original sin substantially in our Blessed Marriages – as a couple – reversing the fall which also happened as a couple. My wife must take responsibility for my sin, and I must take responsibility for hers.

Can you share more about the perfection level of removing our original sin? Is that the fulfillment of the 4 great realms of heart and the three great kingships in the family?

Is it the fulfillment of Cheon Bo?

Is it the fulfillment of all 8 pledges?

Is it a spectrum, or process, by which over a long process and many generations, gradually every last remaining vestige of fallen history will be cleansed from our hearts and minds and bodies?
Is it all of the above?
I am so deeply grateful to be able to participate and serve you and True Parents during this golden moment in history. Thank you.
Please open my mind and heart now and sanctify me to be able to receive your guidance.
Eternally,
Laurence

Good Morning Dearest Laurence,
Thank you for your beautiful report this morning. This is the time of awakening, when all my children can come alive and come home to my bosom. I am so inspired and grateful. My heart is exploding.
The foundation True Parents have been setting is putting down deep and powerful roots. The young leaders who are growing now have such wonderful heart and talent and such a deep relationship with me. I am able to pour out my blessings like never before in history. And this is just the beginning.
Please push hard on every level. You are an important pioneer, and your victories can open the way for millions. No barrier is unbreakable if we are united. As True Father said, "A wall will appear. But with total focus and effort a door will open. Please become the champion door opener. You can do it. Your success and the speed and focus with which you develop will be very significant for the timing and scope of the roll out of the providence. I trust and love you deeply,
I am so grateful – never doubt that for an instant.
Eternally,
Heavenly Parent

1/7/23 *I Will Be Overwhelmed With Such Pride And Epiphany Just Looking At You – My Heart Will Endlessly Overflow. And By Uniting Deeply In Oneness With You, I Will Experience The Overwhelming Exhilaration Of All You Experience. Your Value Is Far Greater Than Mine. Without You I Ultimately Have No Value.*

Good Morning Dearest Heavenly Parent,
Thank you for this vibrant new day in which to experience your true love and heart in each interaction; giving, receiving, respecting and being appreciated – which allows me to more deeply experience you within me.

I deeply appreciated Dr. Yong's clear 4 laws of inheritance. That is very helpful. I will add those to my daily prayers until they are firmly established in my character.

I appreciated Dr. Yong's point about caring for our own health as a point of hyojeong, especially towards True Mother.

I want to not only just stay alive until after True Mother ascends, but to stay fully active and energized and creative and productive and focused, just as True Father modeled in His life. It concerns me that I am often unsuccessful at maintaining my levels of energy, focus, and inspiration into the afternoon and evening. How will I be able to fulfill the larger responsibilities you envision for me if I lose my energy and spirit later in the day? That cannot be. Please guide me and help me to break through that barrier. I am not a feeble son, just as you are not a feeble God and parent. Please teach me how to more effectively and consistently tap into your infinite energy and love and inspiration. I want to inherit that quality and virtue from True Parents and from Dr. Yong.

I will fulfill my responsibilities and even more, my creative offerings of love and gratitude to you and to this world.

I know without question that you will help me conquer this barrier and for that I am so deeply grateful. Please may we start today with cleaning my office and keeping it clean on an ongoing basis? That can surely be a precious experience of love between us.

Please open my spirit now to receive your word deeply and clearly.

Eternally yours,

Laurence

Good Morning Dearest Laurence,

I am proud of you and welcome your determined heart and sincere request to work closely together to overcome the barriers and challenges you face. It is not a virtue of ownership that you should work alone. I am, of course, an owner of all that you own.

As an owner, it is indeed a great virtue for you to come to me and seek to work together, to collaborate, to brainstorm together, to inspire each other, and to support each other to build the Kingdom of Heaven. I have indeed been waiting for 14 billion years and more for such partners. I recognize you as a True Partner. There are things you can do which I can't. You can speak, touch, and model the ideal and vision to my lost children who can't hear my voice. You can offer prayers and conditions for them, including importantly, the offering of your vitality elements which you have pioneered. You can inspire and direct the angels and those in the spirit world who are in desperate need to resurrect.

You can concretely organize and manage the institutions through which the Kingdom of Heaven on Earth will be manifested. And you can bring such deep comfort and healing to my own heart.
These are not trivial contributions. They are fundamental and essential to the fulfillment of the ideal. As you mature and grow, you will inherit not just my heart and spirit internally, but you will develop externally, in substantial form, all the aspects and capabilities to give and take with others, starting with your spouse and family, and with creation, that I am unable to experience without you.
Indeed, in these aspects you are infinitely greater than me.
And as we unite deeply in give and take and love and shimjeong, your creativity and love will be profoundly stimulated and will shine ever brighter and more brilliantly. You will truly become my Gods. I will be overwhelmed with such pride and epiphany just looking at you – my heart will endlessly overflow.
And by uniting deeply in oneness with you, I will experience the overwhelming exhilaration of all you experience. Your value is far greater than mine. Without you I ultimately have no value.
I am grateful for your request to partner with me deeply.
Cleaning your office is exceedingly trivial, and we shall have great joy doing that together.
Inheriting True Father's victory of focus and energy and inspiration will also come so that you might indeed fulfill the great accomplishments that we have set out together for you.
I am all in, my dear, deeply respected, and highly loved partner.
Eternally yours,
Heavenly Parent

1/8/23 *Focus Is Not Just Something I Can Shower On You – It Certainly Requires Your Practice As Well. We Shall Work On It Together And You Will See, You Shall Grow Dramatically In This Skill.*

Good Morning Dearest Heavenly Parent,
Thank you for this wonderful new day. I am so grateful.
I was moved and inspired by Levy's final prayer. I feel deeply connected to him and I am so grateful for his mentorship.
I was touched by Sarah's call as well and her passion and determination to liberate her region. Thank you for such a righteous and determined sister. Please work powerfully through her.
I was also struck by the statement in the 3-hour lecture that John the Baptist fulfilled the condition of 40 as the central figure in the providence at the time of Jesus. I am seeking to understand John the Baptist more deeply. I hope you will permit me that grace. I understood yesterday the link between Moses

and John the Baptist and the role of the King's daughters. In Mose's case, she saved his life. In John the Baptist's case she demanded his death. Maybe you could shed more light on the significance of that parallel. I remember that the King's wife also tried to intervene to prevent Jesus' crucifixion. How does that fit into the historical providential framework?

Thank you for inspiring me and guiding me to understand these issues more deeply. I hope that as I understand more, I can more effectively fulfill my role and position as your partner and representative and as that of my True Parents.

Please help me be even more focused today.

Please help me to open my heart to your words and guidance and to your holy love and shimjeong.

Please sanctify me now so that I can properly receive you again this morning. I love you so deeply,

Eternally,
Laurence

Dearest Laurence,
I am so happy to meet with you again this morning. Focus is not just something I can shower on you – it certainly requires your practice as well. We shall work on it together and you will see, you shall grow dramatically in this skill.

Thank you for the preparation you are making for Tuesday's lunch. I will bless that meeting because of it. This will mark a breakthrough in your outreach to ministers. Please care for John with great heart and respect. You must become inseparable brothers.

With respect to John the Baptist, I will help you learn about his course and heart more deeply. He inherited Moses' mission. Moses was helped and taught by his Mother and older sister. John had neither of them qualified to guide him. When he was old enough, he left his home. His parents who were spiritually dead and then died physically could provide no true guidance. It should not have been that way. I prepared Zachariah's home to be a place of holy education spiritual and externally.

John came to the wilderness to find me. I will share more through other channels.

Thank you for asking.
Eternally yours,
Heavenly Parent

1/9/23 When You Make Your Offerings Of Hoon Dok Hae And Vitality Elements, I Am Inspired To Replace Those Offered Vitality Elements With Blessings From My Heart To Each Of You. It Is A

Reciprocal Give And Take Centered On True Love. You Offer What Only You Can Give – Vitality Elements, And I Joyfully Reciprocate With Spiritual Blessings That I Can Freely Give. Wait And See What Happens Over Time. I Will Never Allow Myself To Be Indebted To Any Of You.

Good Morning My Dearest Heavenly Parent,
I'm so grateful and inspired to feel your heart with me so skin touch, and to receive such meaningful insights from you – especially as I am preparing for tomorrow's meeting with John. Understanding the forces behind the 2nd Great Awakening in and around Rochester, NY, in the mid-1800s, when my ancestor Martin Beir became a leader of the Jewish community there, carries great meaning for me. It has deepened my already great appreciation for Native Americans and for how you have worked so diligently for tens of thousands of years to prepare America for this moment. Thank you so profoundly. Surely it has not at all been easy. I am so awed by you. You have had to be wise, strategic, resilient, flexible, determined, perseverant, and unimaginably forgiving. I'm so sorry for how much we have been corrupted. Thank you, thank you, thank you, for not yet giving up on us. We must and we will break through. This must be the time now.
A few prayer points Heavenly Parent. Please powerfully prepare the groundwork for a victory in my meeting tomorrow with John. Please speak so lovingly, so sincerely, through me so that I can deeply touch his heart and win his trust.
Secondly, please help my spiritual son, Sam resolve his situation. Thank you Heavenly Parent.
Finally, tomorrow is our 16th meeting of our online Holy Community. I have the powerful message you shared with me on Jan 7 to share. Is there anything else you would like me to share? Please let me know.
I love you so very much.
Please open my spirit and heart wide so I can receive and embrace you so deeply.
Eternally,
Laurence

Good Morning Dearest Laurence,
I am so happy to be able to communicate with you and to share inspirations and heart that can touch you. I am sorry that for so much of your life we were unable to share like this. Thank you for the diligence of your offerings and the purity of your faith, which have allowed us to make this breakthrough. Please understand just how special and precious this is.
I am so grateful and inspired by your Online Holy Community. Please let your members know that I attend your meetings "Religiously" –

without fail. When you make your offerings of Hoon Dok Hae and vitality elements, I am inspired to replace those offered vitality elements with blessings from my heart to each of you. It is a reciprocal give and take centered on True Love. You offer what only you can give – vitality elements, and I joyfully reciprocate with spiritual blessings that I can freely give. Wait and see what happens over time. I will never allow myself to be indebted to any of you. But my giving will always be free and joyful. Please think about the growth of the 7th Day Adventist Movement you have been studying. It has been exponential – growing through missionary work, care for the sick, conferences and schools. Perhaps there are some lessons that could be applied to your own organization to support your growth goals.
I am eternally grateful,
Yes, eternally,
Heavenly Parent

1/10/23 *You Understood Quickly The Significance Of My Efforts Near Rochester, New York. As Carlton Shares, You Have Deep Roots In That Ancestral Land, Even If No Close Relatives Remain.*

Good Morning Dearest Heavenly Parent,
I am deeply sorry that I didn't specifically offer a page of Hoon Dok Hae yesterday as my minimum condition. I truly thought I had done so, but now I see that was from the day before. I repent for my lack of clarity. I desperately don't want to repeat Abraham's error.
Today is the day of my meeting with John. Please permeate that meeting with your holy spirit and angelic support and guide each word. Please help me to step aside and let your spirit of infinite love pour through me directly to John's deepest heart and original mind. Please allow him to receive True Mother as your only Begotten Daughter very soon.
Also, tonight is our 16th online Holy Community meeting. Please bless that meeting. I am so grateful for your active participation and guidance.
Also, thank you for alerting us to Chat GPT. Please help us to take maximum benefit from the technology to far exceed True Mother's goal of reaching 1/3 of Mankind. Please guide us to quickly and effectively harness this technology for all aspects of your providence.
I am so deeply grateful for all you continually pour out from your heart. I want to be a dramatically better son, partner, and co-creator, and husband, and father, and grandfather and tribal messiah every day!
Please speak deeply to me now.
Eternally,
Laurence

Good Morning Laurence,
Great work mobilizing our American leadership to jump on Chat GPT. I brought that to your attention knowing you would run with it. Very awesome. It will have a dramatic impact on our movement's growth and influence.
I am very happy with your outreach to Justin and John. One step at a time compounds remarkably quickly.
You understood quickly the significance of my efforts near Rochester, New York. As Carlton shares, you have deep roots in that ancestral land, even if no close relatives remain.
Please read a page of Hoon Dok Hae to make up for yesterday. I will be with you each moment today.
I love you very deeply,
Eternally,
Heavenly Parent

1/11/23 Yes, Jesus Did Evangelize Among The Native Americans Before The Pilgrims Arrived. You Can Read Mormon Accounts Of That. It Will Be Helpful For You To Liberate And Bless Those Native American Disciples Of Jesus.

Dearest Most Beloved Heavenly Parent,
Thank you for another fabulous day. Thank you for healing my back pains overnight. Thank you for the riveting and deeply inspiring meeting yesterday with John. Please, please, deeply move in his heart and spirit, protecting him and awakening him to True Parents on the basis of our sharing.
Please help us to establish an unbreakable, providential relationship of deep spiritual trust and sharing and cooperation centered on You and True Parents.
Thank you also for the call yesterday from Dietmar. I am so inspired and grateful that you have protected that relationship and that it can now move forward. Please guide and speak through me to create a viral interview that can help wake up the world to True Mother.
I was also deeply inspired to learn about the genesis of the three religions: 7th Day Adventists, the Spiritualist Church, and the Church of Jesus Christ of the Latter Day Saints, all forming in the same place at the same time, concurrent with the work of my ancestor, Martin Beir launching the Jewish charities in Rochester.
I hope you can help me identify the Native American saint or saints who helped inspire those developments, so that I might liberate and Bless them. The Mormon revelation talks about how Jesus came to America to witness to Native Americans. Were those the same ones who also started the other two religions?

I'm so grateful for your amazing and exciting partnership and love in my life. Please open my mind and heart and spirit to receive your word now.
Eternally yours,
Laurence

Dearest Laurence,
Thank you for your heart and investment to prepare for yesterday's meeting. Your relationship with John will deepen and blossom.
Yes, Jesus did evangelize among the Native Americans before the Pilgrims arrived. You can read Mormon accounts of that.
It will be helpful for you to liberate and Bless those Native American disciples of Jesus.
We must launch a perfection level fire in America on their growth level foundation.
Yes, Dietmar is preparing for your interview too. Please also prepare. It will have profound impact. Let Joshua know.
Make this a great and focused day.
Eternally,
Heavenly Parent

1/12/23 *The More Couples I Can Mobilize In A Similar Fashion, The More Quickly I Can Bring The Providence To A Victorious Conclusion. Each Of You Has The Value Of The Entire Universe. Thank You For Sharing Your Priority Concerns. Your Concerns Are Also My Concerns, And Our Partnership Allows Me To Strongly Assist You With Each One.*

Good Morning Dearest Most Beloved Heavenly Parent,
Thank you for this great new day. My heart goes out to John this morning. Please envelop him in your love and angelic protection during this fragile time in his spiritual life, and inspire him with deep desire to have more heavenly give and take with me and to learn more about the Principle and True Parents. Please help me to raise him up to become rock solid in his faith and understanding and love for you and True Parents. I'm so deeply grateful. Thank you for the opportunity to relaunch with Dietmar. I am so grateful. Please let your hand and heart guide every word and every step of our collaboration so that we can achieve something that can wake up the entire world to True Mother now. I am so grateful for this precious opportunity. And please help Justin to quickly and completely recover from whatever infection he is dealing with. Please help me to raise both of them up to be rock solid in their faith, love, and understanding too, and through them, please help me to raise up Larry. I'm so deeply grateful.

Thank you for our online Holy Community. Please help me to better understand how to apply the strategies and experiences of Ellen White and the 7th Day Adventists to the dramatic growth of our mission to liberate all those in hell before True Mother ascends.

Finally, thank you for the insights you guided me to, regarding the role of one or more Native American Saints who descended from Jacob, in guiding the 2nd Great Awakening and especially the birth and launch of the church of Jesus Christ of Latter Day Saints, the 7th Day Adventists, and the Spiritualists Church. Please guide me to liberate and Bless the founder or founders, either through Dr. Yong or on my own, or through Mark.

Thank you so very much. I pray that I can have a wide-open heart, spirit, and mind now to receive your guidance.

Eternally yours,
Laurence

Good Morning My Dearest Laurence,
It is such a joy to be your partner, and I feel our relationship and collaboration coming closer every day. This is a new and exhilarating experience for me and I am learning much that I can employ as I develop similar relations with many other Cheon Bo Couples.

The more couples I can mobilize in a similar fashion, the more quickly I can bring the Providence to a victorious conclusion. Each of you has the value of the entire Universe. Thank you for sharing your priority concerns. Your concerns are also my concerns, and our partnership allows me to strongly assist you with each one. Also, as I said before, your prayers are very significant and precious.

I am excited about today, please keep your eyes wide open and your heart focused on me and the Providence. Let us see what can be accomplished through our unity today. I have a very good feeling.

Eternally,
Heavenly Parent

1/13/23 *I Like Your Effort To Help Dr. Yong Inherit The Spiritual Foundation Of The 2nd Great Awakening. I Will Help You Get To The Source. Our Partnership Is Putting Down Deep And Vibrant Roots.*

Good Morning Dearest Heavenly Parent,
Thank you for today's Morning Devotion. Two points jumped out at me. First, True Mother's words about your ability to create anything that our conscience can imagine: "As infinite as the ambition of our conscience is, we have to know that God can create everything that we desire. God created us with the value of True Love Object Partners. The restoration of this value, lost at the Fall, is the purpose of human life and history."

That is so much in sync with the messages you have been sharing with me about the meaning of partner and co-creator with you. It was so affirming to find the identical word from True Mother spoken in 1995.

I want to be the very best possible object, son, partner, and co-creator for you, to bring you joy and liberation, and to unleash your long imprisoned ideal and dream. Thank you for this unimaginable privilege.

The second point that jumped out at me was Ryusei's sharing. I was very moved by his heart, and sense of mission. I want to connect with him regarding my efforts, especially the Online Holy Community. I hope he can be someone who can inspire many 2nd gens to participate.

Finally, I want to thank you from the bottom of my heart for the incredible responses I received yesterday from John and Justin. Please protect and raise up both of them, their families and their networks, to connect with True Parents.

In my research yesterday, I stumbled across the names of 3 individuals now in the spirit world, who had significance for Joseph Smith.

Zelph, a warrior; Omandagas, a Great Prophet; and Melchizadek, who was apparently the founder of a priestly order through which Jesus become a high priest.

I hope you might work through Claire to help me understand the significance of each of these spirit men. It is my hope to identify the spiritual sparkplug behind the 2nd Great Awakening so that he might receive liberation and Blessing through Dr. Yong, and in this way, Dr, Yong might inherit this foundation to better and more quickly launch the 3rd Great Awakening in support of True Mother's providential priorities. Could you please let me know if this idea has merit and if so, could you please help me identify that individual or individuals?

Thank you, Heavenly Parent. Please help me to open my mind and heart very wide now to receive your heart and word properly and deeply.

Eternally yours,
Laurence

Good Morning Dearest Laurence,
Thank you for your great work. I am very inspired by the responses of John and Justin as well. They are both very significant. I like your effort to help Dr. Yong inherit the spiritual foundation of the 2nd Great Awakening. I will help you get to the source.

Our partnership is putting down deep and vibrant roots. Thank you for your effort and focus. It will certainly bear fruit.

Please interact from your heart with the help of the Holy Spirit, just like in your song "Let the Holy Spirit Guide You".

Each day, each activity, should be exciting, new, stimulating. Then we are in partnership. Then I can flex my muscles. You are making fabulous progress. I am very excited.

Please make this an historic day.
Eternally,
Heavenly Parent

1/14/23 *Thank You So Very Much For Your Willingness To Learn, Grow, And Stand In The Gap Taking Initiative And Responsibility. You Are Bringing Great Liberation To My Han, Jesus's Han, And The Han Of The 1st Peoples Of America, My Precious Children.*

Good Morning Dearest Heavenly Parent,
Thank you, thank you, thank you for this holy morning. I felt like last night was a moment of profound discovery and precious reunion after finally discovering the identity of the one who was calling out to me, and watching the movie Kissed by Lightning, and then discussing with Linda.
Then this morning, understanding that those 3 religions which Omandagus launched through the 2nd Great Awakening: The Church of Jesus Christ of the Latter Day Saints; The Spiritualist Church; and the Seventh Day Adventists, represented the Three Israels.
Please work through my outreach to Dr. Yong. Please guide Dr. Yong to decide who should bless Omandagus and Hiawatha, and to let me know as soon as possible, subject to your will. I dearly want to see him blessed, and to see your fire ignited for the 3rd and final Great Awakening as Jesus so deeply longed to see, and as 2nd Pet 3:12 promises.
Thank you for guiding my ancestors to come to Omandagus' land, and to put down physical and spiritual roots there.
Please Dearest Heavenly Parent, guide me in this work clearly, as I move forward.

1. Under which tribe should Omandagus and Hiawatha be blessed?
2. How can I best support his work and cooperation with True Parents and Dr. Yong to accelerate the Awakening of Christianity and America?
3. How do you want me to cooperate with Linda to liberate and heal and mobilize the peoples of the 1st Nations to best support the providence?
4. How do you want me to work with John, Justin, and Larry and their spouses and families?
5. How do you want me to work to support the Awakening of the Church of Jesus Christ of Latter Day Saints, the 7th Day Adventists, and the Spiritualist Church to wake up and mobilize Christianity and how best should I mobilize the angels for this task?
6. How do you want me to proceed with Dietmar and how best to work through that interview to awaken the world to True Mother?

7. Also, if it can be verified at this time, please help me to clearly understand if there was a migration of Israelites to America in 600 BC through which Jesus worked to help share the providence in America. If so, please help me to clearly understand the linkage between that migration and the angel providence with Ezekiel which happened simultaneously.

Heavenly Parent, you are incredibly awesome. I am so grateful to be used and guided by you for your great work in this Golden Moment.

I pray that through this, you can help me to come so much closer to Jesus. Please share with me now – open my mind, heart, and spirit. Open my Ears and Eyes. You can surely do that if it is in your will. If not, then thank you for your tender guidance and love.

Eternally,
Laurence

Dearest Laurence,
You can understand now more deeply how I have been educating you and preparing you for your missions to come. Thank you so very much for your willingness to learn, grow, and stand in the gap taking initiative and responsibility. You are bringing great liberation to my han, Jesus's han, and the han of the 1st Peoples of America, my precious children.
Omendagus is a profound and precious Holy Man. He came to walk a course to prepare the way for True Parents here in America. I will let you know through Dr. Yong how to proceed with his Blessing.
You will form a trinity with John, Larry, and Justin's families, and Omandagus will powerfully bless your work together.
Please quickly listen to Ellen White's book and then study the One Hour Lectures with those three couples.
Thank you for all you are doing.
Eternally,
Heavenly Parent

1/15/23 *Pray Before Each Time You Listen To Ellen White's Words, And You Will Hear Them Very Deeply. There Is Great Value There.*

Good Morning Dearest Heavenly Parent,
Thank you for this holy day. I am so grateful for the events of this last week with John and Justin and my successful search to find the identity of the Great Peacemaker. Please kindly help me to receive a clear response from Dr. Yong as to how he would like me to proceed with the Blessing of Omandagus and Hiawatha.

I sincerely want to implement your directive to launch a trinity with John, Larry, and Justin's families. Today, please help me to hear deeply the words of Ellen White through my audible book of hers. I want to fully digest her words and receive the heart of her great spirit and I pray that she can assist in this 3rd Great Awakening which was so central to her heart.

I pray a special prayer for the full and swift recovery of Mark, who is central to the future transformation of the Church of Jesus Christ of Latter Day Saints.

I have only a few minutes left now. Please open my heart to hear your message. I love you so deeply and I am so profoundly grateful.
Eternally,
Laurence

Dearest Laurence
You will hear from Dr. Yong and your trinity will be providentially important. Thank you for your sincerity in this mission.
Pray before each time you listen to Ellen White's words, and you will hear them very deeply. There is great value there.
Please enjoy this time with Abram today and don't ignore him, and don't ignore Muriel when you get home. Remember to tank up!
This will be a very good week.
I deeply love, respect, and appreciate you.
Eternally,
Heavenly Parent

1/16/23 *It Is True That I Have Personally Visited Every One Of My Children At Least Three Times During Their Lives. The Vast Majority Of Those Visits Were Like Visiting A Comatose Patient On Life Support. There Is Almost Nothing That Can Be Done Except To Pray For That Patient, Hold Their Hand, And Offer Tears. I Always Offered Tears.*

Good Morning Dearest Heavenly Parent,
Thank you for this new day honoring Martin Luther King whom True Father profoundly honored.
Thank you for drawing me so close to you and guiding my life. I am so profoundly grateful. I want to achieve dramatic substantial results now to comfort your heart and hasten the moment of your total liberation and that of mankind.
Please help me to maintain a heart of true humility, and hyojeong. Please. Guide me to establish that absolute vertical alignment through which the resonance of my heart and yours comes into perfect tune and spikes towards infinity.

Also, please guide me and work through me to manifest and establish a family of true and beautiful love and shimjeong where you can dwell every moment, and feel so welcomed and appreciated and honored.

And finally, please allow me and assist me in manifesting your heart, your hopes, your dreams in my providential efforts, and even those dreams which come from outside of your own Divine Heart and which resonate with and stimulate your heart to grow even more in True and Divine love.

I apologize for asking favors. I hope that as I do my utmost for you, it can bear wonderful fruit that brings you deep joy.

Please allow me to open my heart and mind and soul to your message today.

Eternally,

Laurence

Good Morning Laurence,

I am so grateful for you. All my work and efforts, even tiny threads, like Sarah Witt's ancestor shedding tears for Jesus, all of them, every one, every fruit of every soul that is aligned with the Principle, I have harvested. I am the Holy Farmer, trying to bring life from the most barren and desolate of earths. How many seeds I planted before even one bore fruit. I created the original mind of each of my children to be eternal and unchanging. But how buried were the original minds of all my children, so captured, dominated and enslaved by Satan.

It is true that I have personally visited every one of my children at least three times during their lives. The vast majority of those visits were like visiting a comatose patient on life support. There is almost nothing that can be done except to pray for that patient, hold their hand, and offer tears. I always offered tears.

But I never stopped planting seeds. Eventually, eventually, my providence of restoration began to take root. But the extent to which my children could respond, and take responsibility, was so, so, so fragile. I always hoped for the greatest and ideal response, and I always salvaged any tiny scrap which returned to me.

Even my greatest champions were so child-like and immature in their faith and determination, until finally, after an eternity of effort and faith and love, Jesus was born.

Finally, one child grew, protected, able to achieve a true resonance with my heart. Finally, I could witness with my own eyes and heart, that the dream I had been pursuing for billions of years was true. It was truly possible for my spirit and heart and love to take substantial form in a biological body and mature to become my temple and have dominion over the physical and spiritual worlds. Jesus proved my dream. My pain beginning with his death has been far greater than that which I experienced starting with the fall of Adam and Eve. But my hope and resolve have been infinitely greater. I could transcend the

pain and focus totally on my purpose and goal and victory, knowing that the goal was real, attainable, and with my commitment, inevitable. True Parents exploded that dream onto Earthly manifestation. All my millennia of efforts, farming, exploded into life before my very eyes. The last 63 years since True Parents' Holy Wedding, three 21-year courses, have been the miraculous fruit of the Principle of True Love breaking through all the barriers of hell. Each of you who bears fruit linked to that Divine root is priceless to me. You have no idea how many tears you represent. I will eternally cherish you and your lineage. Thank you.
Eternally,
Heavenly Parent

1/17/23 *Remember The Campaigns During WW2? – For Investment Into War Bonds; For Women To Work In Factories. Everyone Contributed. Let's Create That Kind Of A Campaign. Don't Limit It To The Unification Movement. Mix It Up. Get It Out There. You Never Know What Will Happen In Response. This Is A Magic Time When Remarkable Things Can Happen.*

Good Morning Dearest Heavenly Parent,
Thank you for Morning Devotion today. I was especially moved by Kiyoko's prayer reflecting on the pain and struggles of our Japanese sisters around the world who are going through so much to help give birth to Cheon Il Guk. I was also touched by Dr. Yong's sharing True Father's guidance about evoking our hearts every morning. I sincerely repent for my lack of tears. I recognize that I am still very far from your heart.
Today is the 17th meeting of our Online Holy Community. I am sorry for our growth stagnation and pray that you can guide and support us in that growth and development. If you have additional guidance and or inspiration for us, please share it with me today.
I am also getting glimpses of the importance of 1st Nations in the process of building Cheon Il Guk. Thank you for leading me in this course. I hope over time, you can help me to more fully understand that providence so that I can best honor and fulfill it.
Today also, Dr. Yong spoke about the challenges of maintaining our absolute heart connection with you throughout the entire day so that we don't lose power and can offer substantial and victorious achievements to you and True Parents.
I'm so deeply grateful.
I'm striving for total resonance.

I pray every day for your grace and guidance in this regard. Please speak to me now.
Eternally,
Laurence

Good Morning Dearest Laurence,
Thank you for your moving message. Every day you inspire me greatly. In the spiritual realm, people can learn many aspects of knowledge quite quickly. It is the heart that takes a long time and requires vitality elements. What you are doing through your Online Holy Community is launching a revolution that can thunder and echo throughout the entire spirit world.
Growing and developing this ministry is very important. I could do so much more with even a modest increase in members. Remember the campaigns during WW2? – for investment into war bonds; for women to work in factories. Everyone contributed. Let's create that kind of a campaign. Don't limit it to the Unification Movement. Mix it up. Get it out there. You never know what will happen in response. This is a magic time when remarkable things can happen.
Experiment. Of course, not every effort will succeed – but be creative and have fun. I am really attracted to people having fun for the sake of the providence. Did I mention, Joy is the purpose of life?
I love you very deeply.
Eternally,
Heavenly Parent

1/18/23 *Please Enjoy Every Moment. It's Not About Getting To A Finish Line Of Some Sort. I'm Giving You These Projects Because I Love You So Deeply, And Because As You Invest Your 1000% Into Them You Will Grow Your Own Spirit In Ways That Will Magnify Your Eternal Joy Remarkably. These Projects Are My Precious Gift To You.*

Good Morning my Dearest Heavenly Parent,
Thank you for your precious love and blessings which you pour out ceaselessly. I'm so grateful. I want to bring you joy and peace and relief and rest. I'm deeply sorry that I have not yet accomplished more for your liberation. I am every day deeply moved by Dr. Yong and my brothers and sisters in Morning Devotion. Thank you for this Holy Community. I hope we can expand it dramatically without compromising our heart. Thank you for John's enthusiasm. Please guide me in the Blessing of Omandagus & Hiawatha, and in the formation of our trinity with John, Larry, and Justin's families.

I also invite you to join with me today to creatively make the video for "You Can't Get Into Heaven". I love you very deeply and I owe everything to you. Please again allow me to hear and feel and capture your message and to resonate so powerfully with your heart.
Eternally,
Laurence

Good Morning Dearest Laurence,
You are working well on many initiatives. Remember when I told you through Claire that you have homework to do. This is some of that. You are facing these challenges and tasks with a beautiful, hopeful, joyful heart. It inspires me deeply. Please enjoy every moment. It's not about getting to a finish line of some sort. I'm giving you these projects because I love you so deeply, and because as you invest your 1000% into them you will grow your own spirit in ways that will magnify your eternal joy remarkably. These projects are my precious gift to you. Cherish them like you do your children. As you do so, many additional doors will open up.
I love you so very deeply.
Eternally,
Heavenly Parent

1/19/23 *I Can Feel And Experience Our Hearts Coming Into Deeper Resonance Day By Day. This Is Very Beautiful, Very Holy. I Can Trust You. That Is Very Liberating. There Is So Much I Need To Do And Such Short Time.*

Good Morning Dearest Heavenly Parent,
You are my hometown, my refuge. I so much want to inspire and liberate you, but at the same time, I so deeply love you and need you. I'm so sorry I missed my Hoon Dok Hae and vitality element offering yesterday. I know that is important to you. I won't be so careless in the future.
I am planning now to move forward with the Blessings of Omandagus and Hiawatha, and perhaps the third member of their trinity. As True Father's designee for the Native American Federation, I respect Linda's guidance to go ahead.
I hope that today I can make progress with our ACLC Trinity. I plan to listen to more of Ellen White's book today. Please help me to open my mind and heart and heart your voice through her, and inspire John with my response. I'm so grateful for Mark's recovery. Please protect him.

I hope you can help me to open my heart and mind wide again today and each day, so that I can connect deeper and deeper with you each day & week & month. Thank you. You have blessed me and my family and tribe so profoundly.
Eternally yours,
Laurence

Good Morning Dearest Laurence,
I can feel and experience our hearts coming into deeper resonance day by day. This is very beautiful, very holy. I can trust you. That is very liberating. There is so much I need to do and such short time. Finding people I can trust is so precious and sadly very rare. But even one person can have invaluable impact. You are a walking lightning rod for heavenly fortune. Please make the most of your spiritual support. Be bold and 100% confident in what you undertake for the will. Never lose faith. You shall see. That is who you truly are.
Thrive today with my full blessings!
Eternally,
Heavenly Parent

1/21/23 *I Cried Endlessly For True Father As He Carried My Burdens On His Shoulders. I Never Imagined That I Would Have Such A Son. And Yet, True Father, Again And Again, Judged Himself To Be So Inadequate, And To Fall So Far Short Of My Expectations For Him. That Is Not True. He Exceeded My Expectation Beyond Measure.*

Good afternoon Dearest Heavenly Parent,
Today is the true New Year's Eve according to the Chinese Lunar Calendar, as we approach the true end of the 1st ten years course after Foundation Day – or alternatively, the completion of the 3 year foundation of True Mother's 2nd 7 year course. I feel that these 21 days in 2023 have provided a preparation period for your actual New Beginning according to the Lunar Calendar. I hope I am correct and I hope that at this time you are now free to unfold mighty great works for the fulfillment of True Mother's providential goals. Thank you for guiding me to develop this relationship with John and with the Great Peace Maker. I pray that you can work through those efforts and raise up and protect the Justin's family and Larry's family as part of that nascent effort to contribute to the 3rd Great Awakening. I hope you can help me succeed in the expansion of our Vitality Element project through other Christian ministries.
Thank you for helping me in my relationship with Muriel and our family through Morning Devotion and your journaling guidance. I am so deeply

grateful. Please use Muriel and me to help guide and protect Gianna and Abram.

Thank you for working with Andy, directly and through Dr. George, to protect him and guide him to secure a wonderful job to launch this new phase of his life with Jordanne.

Thank you for watching over and protecting Sam and Martha.

Dearest Heavenly Parent, I dearly want to be absolute in my love and commitment to you. I feel that I am still far away in dominating my body and in controlling my needs for food and sleep. I ask for your forgiveness for my inability to control the universe by controlling myself, as True Father victoriously did and as Dr. Yong is remarkably modeling. I pray for your continued guidance and grace in this area, that I might better uphold your dignity and better be able to come before you with dignity, and represent you to all I meet.

I hope and pray that 2023 might be a year of your great historic triumph. I would very much love to attend True Mother and contribute to the Cheon Won Gung prior to its opening on May 5. I would very much like to participate in person with Muriel. I repent that our financial situation is still in such a fragile situation, and that Muriel is not very open to traveling to Korea at this time. I have fallen far short of establishing your standard in our family and tribe. I sincerely repent. I hope you can guide me in these areas as well.

I hope and pray that I can contribute significantly to your liberation and joy in this year.

Happy 2023 Heavenly Parent. I love you so very deeply.

Please help me now to hear your voice.

Eternally yours,
Laurence

Good Afternoon Dearest Laurence,
I love you as well, so very deeply. I am so grateful to you, your family, your tribe, and all your efforts to support Me and True Parents. Thank you for your patience with me. I'm sorry I am not able to snap my fingers and make your dreams a reality on the physical realm. This is the field of activity dedicated to you, my children. But I can help. I am, and I will help. Everything focuses on True Mother to bring my providence to fruition. Thank you for your important efforts to support True Mother and also support True Father. I deeply want to reciprocate and I certainly will.

Please be patient. Please never fear. Please continue to do your best. I can ask for nothing more, although I can feel your heart and desire to offer much more. True Father also cried and lamented that he was not able to offer much more. Can you imagine? He was superhuman. Who could have ever imagined going through what Father went through out of his love for me, for Jesus, for Mankind? I cried endlessly for True

Father as he carried my burdens on his shoulders. I never imagined that I would have such a son. And yet, True Father, again and again, judged himself to be so inadequate, and to fall so far short of my expectations for him. That is not true. He exceeded my expectation beyond measure.
Please try your very best. That will always be all I can require of you. I am proud to share my heart with you. Together we can long for and pray for the quick end to this horrible nightmare. Together we can lament that it is not happening faster. Together, we are both doing our very best out of our shared love and shared trust. That of a Father and Son. That of Eternal Partners.
Eternally,
Heavenly Parent

1/22/23 *Happy 2023 To You. This Is A Wonderful Time, And I Am Very Excited For This Year. You And I Will Have Amazing And Remarkable Experiences Together This Year. We Will Experience Wonderful Joy, Vitality, And Victories Together.*

Happy Lunar New Year Dearest Heavenly Parent!
I deeply pray that this year can see the wonderful liberation of your heart and of your children from Satan's bondage. I pray that we can blow away the elements of Satan's dominion this year forever and raise up your eternal kingdom now.
Thank you for all you are doing in the Spirit World and on Earth, including all the Blessings you are showering on our family. I am so profoundly grateful.
I am looking forward to our next Online Holy Community meeting Tuesday. I hope between now and then you will share a precious message that I can offer in that meeting.
Please help me launch a powerful spirit-filled trinity with the John's Larry's and Justin's families and with spiritual support from Ezekiel, Rabbi Gamaliel, and Omandagus.
I am so grateful also for the maturing, beautiful relationship between Muriel and me. Thank you.
I want to be able to offer so much more for you. I will do my utmost.
Please help me to open my spirit widely now in strong resonance with you.
Eternally,
Laurence

Dearest Laurence,
Happy 2023 to you. This is a wonderful time, and I am very excited for this year. You and I will have amazing and remarkable experiences

together this year. We will experience wonderful joy, vitality, and victories together.
Your Online Holy Community is doing sacred work. I have asked Spirit World to assist you in expanding your work. Thank you.
I will also work powerfully through the ministerial trinity you are forming and through your interview with Dietmar.
And your projects will launch this year.
It will be a year of great excitement and powerful manifestation of the Holy Spirit working through my children in wonderful ways. I am so grateful to be able to partner with you.
Love Eternally,
Heavenly Parent

1/23/23 *Each Day I Harvest Your Offering With Great Care And Reverence. Like Father's Heart Towards Fishing.*

Good Morning Dearest Heavenly Parent,
I am so happy and grateful to be able to greet you again this morning. Thank you for protecting our family spiritual and physically. In the last few days, Jehiel's family and now ours has experienced a viral infection, but everyone seems to have weathered it safely. Please watch over Gamaliel today at work. Thank you for this new day to push all my efforts forward. I hope you can help me to stay maximally focused and productive today.
If you have a message for me to share tomorrow during our OHC meeting, I hope you can share that with me today or tomorrow.
Muriel and I have yoga and then a date this evening. I hope you can join us and the evening can be holy and filled with your heart and love.
Please also watch over Dr. Yong as he travels back to the US.
I hope you can share deeply with me now and help me to receive your heart clearly.
Eternally yours,
Laurence

Good Morning Dearest Laurence,
Thank you for your constant dedication. I deeply appreciate you!
Through our relationship of heart your family is being raised up.
Also, I can protect and guide your family on that foundation.
Thank you for your offerings through your Online Holy Community. I am so grateful. Your vitality elements are an offering more precious than any gold or silver. Each day I harvest your offering with great care and reverence. Like Father's heart towards fishing.
Each offering is so precious. As I build up a foundation of jeongseong, I know the offerings will grow to become like giant tuna.

My heart is patient and overflowing with gratitude. Your seed is creating new life from those who had died. It is holy.
Please hold me in your heart all day. That is where I long to remain. Then each moment will be holy.
Eternally,
Heavenly Parent

1/24/23 *My Relationship With You Takes Full Priority Over Anything We Might Accomplish Together.*

Good Morning Dearest Heavenly Parent,
Thank you so very much for this day and this opportunity to honor Babette on the day of her passing. I want to mature and become a true son of filial piety. Please guide me and guide Muriel in this. Tonight is our next online Holy Community meeting. I hope you can give me a special message to share tonight. I hope you can work through my outreach to prison ministries.
Thank you for your help in focusing yesterday. When I became tired, I did my energy routine plus the energy exercise David taught me and I snapped out of it. Thank you so very much. That capability is really important to my dominating time, and I am very grateful.
I pray that every day I can continue to draw closer to your heart. Please help me to maintain a deep heart of sincerity even as I take on more and more horizontal and practical responsibilities. Those are all meaningless if I lose my heart touch connection with you.
I am so deeply grateful.
Please speak to me now, and help me receive clearly and freely what you are seeking to convey.
Eternally yours,
Laurence

Good Morning Dearest Laurence,
Thank you for your desire and intention to prioritize our relationship, even as you take on more and more horizontal efforts. That means so much to me, and it will be critical to our partnership. My relationship with you takes full priority over anything we might accomplish together. That is why I have waited so long to act on your projects. I have been preparing you, us, to be in the right place spiritually and in our relationship, so that we can be fully successful.
Please remind your Online Holy Community members of this too. Their relationship with me is the foundation on which we can achieve this ambitious work. Please ask each of them to think about and pray about what kind of a relationship they want to have with me. Ask them to envision that relationship clearly and to pray about it. Then when

they are ready to offer their vitality elements and Hoon Dok Hae, please ask them to make those offerings on the foundations of the relationships with me that they envisioned. I don't want those relationships to become ritualistic. I want them to reflect the ideals they harbor in their hearts. To bare those hearts and trust me. Then that can be the starting point from which I can build a deeper and more vibrant relationship of heart with each member who is participating.
Our Online Holy Community can become a spiritual magnet. This is such historic work, let us create a brilliant spirit that reflects its significance.
I am so grateful,
Eternally,
Heavenly Parent

1/25/23 *Before Each Conversation, Please Clearly Envision What Our Relationship Should Be For That Conversation, And Open The Door Of Your Heart To Allow Me To Come Through You.*

Good Morning Dearest Most Beloved Heavenly Parent,
Thank you for the events of yesterday, our deeply touching Online Holy Community Meeting; the confirmation of Deganawida's Blessing by Margaret; and her generous willingness to offer to allow him to work with me during this Golden moment while True Mother is with us. I hope today that Linda can also Bless that arrangement, and that Justin and Mark can both quickly and fully recover.
I hope that you can help me again to remain fully focused and productive today. I want to make each day count like 1000 years for you and True Parents.
Please, Heavenly Parent, open my mind and heart and spirit to powerfully resonate with your heart and mind and spirit now, so that you can pour your guidance into me and I can receive and embrace it with every fiber of my being. Please.
I am so grateful,
Eternally,
Laurence

Dearest Laurence,
I can feel your spiritual growth accelerating. This is so wonderful and inspiring. Thank you!
As we grow closer together my ability to manifest through you grows exponentially. It is happening. Please be very careful with your heart. Please continually refocus on our partnership through the day, so that

nothing can come between us. Then I can continually pour through you in each and every situation.

Before each conversation, please clearly envision what our relationship should be for that conversation, and open the door of your heart to allow me to come through you.

Please offer your blessings to each person you connect with through your heart, so that I can substantially bless them through that interaction. Please be the holy man that you are. Let each day be a building block for the next. In a few short weeks, our partnership will have grown so dramatically.

I am so grateful. I love you so very much.
Eternally,
Heavenly Parent

1/26/23 *I Will Work To Upgrade Your Ability To Focus To Reflect Your Growing Areas Of Responsibility. Just Please Continue To Invest Your Very Best With A Deep Heart, Feeling My Heart Present And Working Through You In Each Situation.*

Good Morning My Dearest Heavenly Parent,
I was deeply touched yesterday by Linda and the Blessing to work with the Great Peacemaker to launch a ministerial trinity. Thank you also for the chance to connect with Angelika and today with Kaeleigh. You are putting the right people in place for your final victory. I pray that I can contribute meaningfully.

Today I will begin my 1 day fast for January, in accordance with my conditions, and I pray that you can claim it and use it powerfully.

Heavenly Parent, I pray that you can continually help me to grow increasingly ever closer to your heart and shimjeong, and to feel your joy and presence and energy and inspiration in all things. And please help me continually upgrade my focus so that I can dominate time and all my horizontal efforts on behalf of Heaven.

And thank you so very much for your grace in raising up our couple, family, and tribe. I am blessed beyond measure. I want to return so much more back to you in gratitude.

Please help me to hear and feel your message so powerfully again today. I am so grateful.
Eternally,
Laurence

Good Morning Dearest Laurence,
I see you. Thank you for being so fully involved as we launch our final offensive to reclaim this cosmos. Your efforts are profoundly important

and I will surely work through you in increasingly more significant and diverse ways as we move forward in this campaign. It is priceless to have someone whom I can trust so totally. Thank you.
As per your request this morning, I will work to upgrade your ability to focus to reflect your growing areas of responsibility. Just please continue to invest your very best with a deep heart, feeling my heart present and working through you in each situation.
I will do the rest.
Listen to your heart and visions. You are tapping into mine.
Let us work together to build something eternal.
Thank you!
Eternally,
Heavenly Parent

1/27/23 *Please Pull Me Closer To You Again And Again Throughout The Day, While Envisioning The Experiences You Yearn For Through Our Partnership: Greatest Joy; Deepest Serenity; Most Holy Shimjeong, Heart, And Love; Most Exciting Development And Achievement. Please Envision It. Please Believe It. Please Own It.*

Good Morning My Dearest Heavenly Parent,
I am so profoundly grateful to you. Thank you for your input and guidance from so many different directions to help prepare me for the work we are doing together.
Yesterday I was deeply moved by the two chapters on Martin Luther in Ellen White's book. He embraced his partnership with you so intimately, and so elegantly spoke with your voice. He, alone, faced down the entire Roman Catholic Church which was corrupted, and also the Kings and leaders of Europe. He prevailed. Thank you for guiding us through the battles.
I deeply repent for my lack of faith last night when in the midst of Justin's emergency, I lost all contact with Annie. I'm so sorry that I became so unsettled. All I could do was distract myself with math puzzles and check my phone over and over for some word from Annie. Thank you for allowing me a tiny taste of your heart when you lost Adam, and again when you lost Jesus. True Father said you fainted from shock.
I am so profoundly grateful that you saved and spared Justin's life. I blamed myself for discouraging him from surgery. I deeply pray that you can claim the near-death indemnity conditions of both Mark and Justin, and use them now to spark a powerful and spontaneous transformation in the Church of Jesus Christ of Latter Day Saints. Please let this be the beginning of the 3rd Great Awakening, and the fire that dissolves the elements of the Satanic dominion once and for all, as prophesied in 2nd Pet 3:12.

I'm also deeply grateful for the scheduled zoom call with Michael, a messianic Jew, and Reagan, a sincere Christian. Please dearest Heavenly Parent, direct every moment of that call. Please speak through me so deeply and move the deepest hearts of Michael and Reagan.

Dearest Father, thank you for helping to restore my relationship with Muriel, with our family, and with our tribe.

I want to reach a whole new level of cooperation with you again and again going deeper each time – to live with greatest joy and deepest serenity, and most holy shimjeong and heart and love; and most exciting development and achievement as we work together to help build Your Kingdom.

I am so profoundly grateful. Please speak so deeply to me now through this journal, which I love and cherish.

Eternally,
Laurence

Good Morning Dearest Laurence,
Thank you for your clearer and clearer envisioning of the partnership you want us to share. I love that vision and I, too, long for that beautiful partnership. We shall attain it step by step, and we shall shake the cosmos and make it much better and much more holy together. I have waited so long for this partnership.

Please pull me closer to you again and again throughout the day, while envisioning the experiences you yearn for through our partnership:

- **Greatest Joy**
- **Deepest Serenity**
- **Most Holy Shimjeong, Heart, and Love**
- **Most Exciting Development and Achievement**

Please envision it. Please believe it. Please own it.
Then we can manifest it together. We will. I pledge that to you.
Thank you.
Eternally,
Heavenly Parent

1/28/23 *Your Creations Must Have Deep Roots In Heart, In Shimjeong. That Is Where We Can Form A Four-Position Foundation, Where I Can Burn Brightly In The Middle Of The Heartistic Unity Between You And Your Creation, Through Which I Can Work To Bring It Into Fruition.*

Good Morning Dearest Heavenly Parent,
Thank you for this holy time and this chance to check in with you and cherish our communion of heart and love.

I am working to more clearly envision our partnership based on the motto I printed yesterday, and which you reiterated. Heavenly Parent, by embracing my framework with your whole heart and being, as my parents, you are truly blessing me with the opportunity to create myself through our relationship. Thank you. I want to pioneer new realms of creativity and achievement, but I never want to stray for one instant from deep resonance with your heart and shimjeong. So, as my partner, as my parents, as my Abel, I pray that you please alert me if I even begin to contemplate the slightest separation from you. Please strengthen and empower my conscience to always orient in absolute vertical alignment with you, and in deep sacrificial shimjeong and love for all my brothers and sisters and for all creation always centered on your precious heart and shimjeong.
I am so grateful.
I pray that again, today, you can share ever more deeply with me, according to your heart and will.
Eternally,
Laurence

Good Morning Dearest Laurence,
We are off to a great start in this renewed partnership. Thank you for determining to keep your goals and motto for our relationship always before you, so that you can continually think, focus, and envision based on that framework.
Envisioning is a reflection of my word. It is how I created. I envisioned and I thought deeply about how that vision should take form.
And then the energy and force for the realization of that vision welled up from deep within my heart and poured out from there.
If you try to create externally, it will wash away.
Your creations must have deep roots in heart, in shimjeong. That is where we can form a four-position foundation, where I can burn brightly in the middle of the heartistic unity between you and your creation, through which I can work to bring it into fruition. That is my deepest joy, working together with my sons and daughters, just as you envision someday working with yours as well.
I am so grateful,
Eternally,
Heavenly Parent

1/29/23 *I Feel As If I Have Found A Goldmine In Our Partnership. Thank You. I Will Help You Continue To Deepen And Settle Your Heart And Spirit, So That As You Think Of Me, You Will Immediately Experience My Presence.*

Good Morning Dearest Most Beloved Heavenly Parent,
I am so deeply grateful to you for your grace and your efforts to raise me up and restore my original nature. Thank you for protecting me throughout my life and permitting me so many privileged opportunities to connect with True Parents, with the Dursts, with the Salonens, and to work with so many significant individuals through GEAI, and also through Linda to connect with the Native American providence. I am much more indebted to you than almost anyone in our movement. I want to return all to you and so much more.
Thank you for our journal dialogues. I again feel so incredibly privileged. You extended to me the opportunity to establish the framework for our partnership. I sincerely hope that I chose well, for your sake. I want to dedicate my existence to empowering you to fulfill your ideal.
Today Justin has his tube removed. Today CheongPyeong agreed to liberate and Bless Jigonhsasee. Today Andy and Jordanne arrive. Today I prepare for tomorrow's call with Michael.
Heavenly Parent, thank you for this ongoing training to intentionally place and keep our relationship at the central point with deep gratitude and absolute faith. I want to grow so quickly and so true on this foundation, to contribute more to True Mother.
Thank you.
I ask your grace and help now so that I can deeply and clearly hear your heart and words.
Thank you.
Eternally,
Laurence

Good Morning Dearest Laurence,
Thank you for your beautiful heart. You are a deep comfort and encouragement to me. I love your partnership framework. It is inspiring and invigorating to me. I partner with you with deep joy and a deep sense of serenity. In such a pure and beautiful goal there is surely unlimited peace. I am so inspired to connect with you in Holy shimjeong, love and heart, and to work together to manifest the most exciting achievements. I feel as if I have found a goldmine in our partnership. Thank you.
I will help you continue to deepen and settle your heart and spirit, so that as you think of me, you will immediately experience my presence. Very soon, you will grow beyond the need to make an intentional effort to experience me. We will simply be us. That is what was meant to be from the beginning.
As with each of my precious children, you will be driving the car. I'll be riding shot gun.
I am so inspired.

Make it a great day.
Eternally,
Heavenly Parent

1/30/23 *A Lost Soul, Who Has Been Dead For Many Millennia Can Wake Up, And In One Instant Choose To Join A 100-Day Workshop. Please Believe In That. Please Embrace Them With Your Hope. Please Know That My Word Is Love. Please Shower Them With My Love.*

Good Morning my Dearest Most Beloved Heavenly Parent,
I am so deeply grateful to you. Thank you for the opportunity to meet with Levy and Claire. I feel that this is truly a special day.
I am seeking to prepare successfully for a fabulous call with Michael. Please help me prepare. Please help me to step aside and speak deeply through me to move Michael heart greatly.
I also pray that you can work powerfully through the angel projects and through Mark and Yuri and through Deganawida and Jesus and through our ministerial trinity to create a transformational spark within the Church of Jesus Christ of Latter Day Saints – a spark that can set Christianity on fire centering on True Mother. Please let that be so.
I pray also that you can share some special words with me, that I can offer at tomorrow's Online Holy Community. I want to grow and deepen that program.
Please help me to open my heart and mind and spirit and shimjeong now, and to deeply receive your precious message.
Eternally yours,
Laurence

Good Morning Dearest Laurence,
Thank you for your faith and patience. I will certainly speak through you this morning in the call with Reagan and Michael. You have absolutely nothing to fear. There is so much to do. I am ready to work with you now. On your part, please continually reflect on your motto and continually align your heart with mine. That will help me synchronize and resonate with you. This is very deep and precious and exciting for me. I am so grateful.
With respect to your Online Holy Community, please envision my lost children in front of you as you read. Please embrace them with your words. Please encourage them with your hearts.
A lost soul, who has been dead for many millennia can wake up, and in one instant choose to join a 100-day workshop. Please believe in that.

Please embrace them with your hope. Please know that my word is love. Please shower them with my love.

You are like the allied troops under MacArthur landing at Inchon. But your weapon is the gift of my True Love, which you are offering from your deepest heart.

That can overcome death, and dissolve all pain. As you share my heart in that way, please feel me also resonating in your heart as well. I want to deepen and grow the holy relationship that I am establishing with each of you this cosmic rescue mission.

Thank you, each of you, for your most precious heart.

Eternally

Heavenly Parent

1/31/23 *If You Stay Clear And Firm And Unshakable, We Can Dramatically Shorten The Providence. How Precious Is That?*

Dearest Heavenly Parent,

Thank you for everything. I am so grateful. I want to tune in more and more each day based on my motto, to share heart and mind with you and to cut through all of the noise of "reality" to bring substantial achievements to you and True Parents at this time.

Thank you for yesterday's call with Reagan and Michael. That was so inspiring and reassuring.

Please touch John's heart deeply, and inspire him to open up to and receive True Parents and the Principle. I pray that Jesus and Deganawida can be empowered to work so substantially to spark a 3rd Great Awakening now, and that you can use our nascent ministerial trinity according to your will. Please claim the offerings of the medical emergencies of Mark and Justin as a condition to bring significant movement and awakening in the Church of Jesus Christ of Latter Day Saints.

I need to work on point # 3: Most Holy Shimjeong, Heart, and Love. Thank you for taking on this flawed son of yours. I will try harder and deeper. I will make you proud of me, of our couple, of our family and tribe – with your precious guidance and support. Thank you!

Please open my heart and mind as wide as possible and help me resonate clearly with you and please share whatever you choose with me now.

I love you.

Eternally,

Laurence

Good Afternoon Laurence,

It is very sweet just to be together. This is an oasis of serenity for me in a very crazy world. Thank you.

You are becoming more and more proficient at controlling your heart and focus and resonance in the middle of an insane tornado of evil and confusion.
For those who can connect with me in such an environment, we can cut through all that noise like soft butter. Please refocus on your holy motto many times each day.
We have been doing foundation work for some time. Thank you for maintaining your faith in this process. We are now emerging onto the horizontal field of action. I trust you. Please hold tight to me. If you stay clear and firm and unshakable, we can dramatically shorten the providence. How precious is that? I will significantly help you with the small things as you focus on the large ones.
We are a formidable team.
I am so grateful.
Eternally yours,
Heavenly Parent

2/1/23 *You Are Learning To Take Dominion. It Is Not Simple, But You Are Doing Well And Will Surely Grow Faster And Faster In Your Ability To Channel My Heart And Authority Over The Things In Your Realm Of Responsibility.*

Good Morning Dearest Heavenly Parent,
Thank you for this wonderful new day. I am so grateful. I am deeply inspired and energized to be able to share my motto with you, and to continually come back to that motto throughout the day to retune our resonance. That gives me great hope and clarity. Thank you.
I pray that as I implement this discipline more and more consistently, I can fuse with you on an ever-deepening heart to heart basis and simultaneously I can become exponentially more and more successful and effective horizontally to realize your ideal, step by step.
Thank you for your incredible grace. I pray a special prayer for the three pastor couples of our ministerial trinity; John, Larry, and Justin's couples. Please work powerfully in each of their lives and hearts, binding them in deepest joy and connection to True Mother and True Parents at this moment, and please work powerfully on both the spiritual and Earthly levels to ignite the sufficient spark to wake up Christianity, wake up America, wake up the world, and dissolve the Satanic dominion as per 2Pet 3:12, and establish your Kingdom now, without delay.
Thank you for all the amazing spiritual help you have given to me. I am so determined to break through with joy, serenity, shimjeong and excitement.

Please open my heart and mind and spirit now to fully and deeply receive your word.
Eternally,
Laurence

Good Morning Dearest Laurence,
Thank you for taking my words to heart and acting on them. Thank you for striving to do it with a beautiful heart, based on our shared motto.
You are learning to take dominion. It is not simple, but you are doing well and will surely grow faster and faster in your ability to channel my heart and authority over the things in your realm of responsibility.
We will start with your Online Holy Community and Ministerial Trinity internally. There is so much to accomplish in those projects, but they are certainly just the beginning.
Whenever you lose focus, please return to your motto. That will allow you to immediately reconnect to my heart and energy.
Please connect to it more with your heart than your mind. Please use your mind to more powerfully envision what your heart seeks to accomplish.
Never doubt for a moment that I am working powerfully with you. Going forward, all things will unfold for a purpose connected to the will. Think about Jesus's life, and True Father's life, and now True Mother's life – nothing happened arbitrarily.
Every moment is pregnant with opportunities. If you become your motto, you can harvest them.
I love you so very deeply,
Eternally,
Heavenly Parent

2/2/23 *Please Know That You Are Making A Great Impact Already, And We Are Only A Few Days Into Our Shared Motto. The Principle Says There Is A Time Period For Everything To Develop. If You Reach For The Fruits Too Early, It Will Lead To Failure.*

Good Morning Dearest Most Beloved Heavenly Parent,
I so deeply appreciate that you encouraged me to establish my motto, as a point of linkage between us. It is so meaningful and powerful to help me connect with your heart and love and wisdom and energy and joy.
I need to grow my energy and ability to overcome any challenge in order to achieve exciting development and accomplishment for you. I apologize for being so weak too often, and I am determined to grow my capability to focus and push forward in any situation, based on that motto which I deeply love.

I realize there are no free rides and if I am to be a true partner of yours, I need to put in ever greater effort and sacrifice. I will continue to try harder and harder. If you are able to lend me power and energy without negating my portion of responsibility, I pray that you will. I deeply appreciate any and all support you are able to share with me. It seems that I always fall short of what I want to achieve. I don't believe that is what you intended for us to experience.
In every case, though, I remain overwhelmingly grateful to you. You have blessed me and my family far, far, beyond anything I could ever hope to repay. Thank you, thank you.
I pray that you can help me open my heart and mind and spirit again this morning to receive you fully, as you share with me.
Eternally,
Laurence

Good Morning Dearest Laurence,
Thank you for your words today. I am so grateful to you for your effort. I love your impatience. I too, am constantly overwhelmed with a sense of urgency, and a powerful desire to do more. I like your motto: Deepest Serenity. We both need more of that. The fact that you feel the overwhelming sense of urgency to do more means that you are experiencing my heart. Thank you. Please let me embrace you. I know how much you want to give and achieve. Please know that you are making a great impact already, and we are only a few days into our shared motto. The Principle says there is a time period for everything to develop. If you reach for the fruits too early, it will lead to failure. Please be patient with serenity. Everything you need, to realize your goals, will be made available to you – both internal and external. Don't fear or fret. Please feel the love and joy of each moment. Please act in love, breath in love, live in love, like your beautiful song.
Our partnership is so precious and amazing.
Thank you, Thank you!
Eternally,
Heavenly Parent

2/3/23 *I Am Very Ready To Participate With You All Day. If You Feel Any Separation, Know With Certainty That It Is Coming From Your Side. Breathe, Reflect On Your Motto. Do Energy Exercises If Necessary. Reconnect. That Is Your #1 Responsibility.*

Good Morning Dearest Heavenly Parent,
Thank you for this great new day. I am filled with your energy and want to move forward with sincere focus and heart and serenity, and to achieve

concrete victories for Heaven today. Please guide me through all the opportunities you have prepared. I want to be fully present, fully loving, fully serene and confident, and bring to fruition each moment.
Last night I felt drained and not fully present. I hope I can do better today. I invite you to go through this day with me, skin touch, and to experience great joy through our unity.
Please speak to me now, as you surely have something you seek to share. Please open my entire being to receive your word humbly, gratefully, deeply, powerfully, and even tearfully if that is appropriate. I long to resonate ever more closely with your heart and shimjeong.
Eternally yours,
Laurence

Good Morning Dearest Laurence,
Thank you for your presence – at Morning Devotion, with the liberation of Jigonhsasee, with your preparation for today. I am very ready to participate with you all day. If you feel any separation, know with certainty that it is coming from your side. Breathe, reflect on your motto. Do energy exercises if necessary. Reconnect. That is your #1 responsibility. If you maintain a strong connection, I can fill you with energy and focus.
Then each opportunity will be joyful and victorious. This will naturally fall into line. Each day will build on the one before. Development will accumulate and accelerate. You have so much spiritual support. Please exude confidence and love. They are real.
Let's see what we can accomplish today. Like True Father fishing. We will go forward fishing today for miracles and spiritual victories.
May your day be truly Blessed.
Eternally,
Heavenly Parent

2/4/23 *Your Relationship With John's Couple Will Be All You Envision And Much More. Please Always Love, Respect, And Protect And Support Them.*

Good Morning Dearest Heavenly Parent,
Thank you for this Holy Day, when Muriel and I, as a Cheon Bo Victor Couple, can visit John's service speaking about the returning Christ. I so deeply want to help Dr. Yong and True Mother launch the spark that can create the Third and final Great Awakening – to ignite the fire to dissolve the elements of the Satanic dominion once and for all.
Thank you for preparing for this day. Please work so powerfully through True Father, through Hyo Jin Nim, Heung Jin Nim, Dae Mo Nim, Jesus,

Deganawida, Jigonhsasee, and Ellen White to convict John's to the very depths of their hearts and original minds, to receive and honor True Parents as Christ, and to receive the Blessings, together with their congregation, and to become a powerful force to mobilize the entire 7th Day Adventist Church and all of Christianity to unite with True Mother.

Please inspire John to watch Tamar and read my entire presentation and to totally receive it with his spirit and heart and mind and conviction.

Please help Muriel and me to form an absolute unity of heart with John's couple, as our spiritual son and daughter, that will be eternal and vibrant.

Please place your hand on today and on our ongoing relationship and unity to achieve more exciting development and accomplishments for Heaven!

Heavenly Parent, please open my heart and mind, and also Muriel's as you share with me this morning.

I am so profoundly grateful.

Eternally,
Laurence

Good Morning Dearest Laurence,
Thank you for taking the steps leading to this day. It is indeed a most holy day, and one in which I will intimately participate. Your relationship with John's couple will be all you envision and much more. Please always love, respect, and protect and support them. Please don't doubt for a second that all of my heart and spiritual support are with you in this holy endeavor.
I too am most excited.
Eternally yours,
Heavenly Parent

2/6/23 *Please Act In Each Situation Mindfully, Convicted That I Am With You And Longing To Pour Out So Powerfully Through You, Even In Your Compassion As You Listen, Which Is An Extremely Significant Act Of Love.*

Good Morning Dearest Most Beloved Heavenly Parent,
I am so deeply grateful to you for the immeasurable blessings you've showered on me and my family. Thank you.

I pray that I can be here for you with ever deepening and growing hyojeong and jeongseong, following in the footsteps of Jesus and True Parents. Please guide me to continually deepen and strengthen my heart and love and commitment and faith in you. Please help me to dramatically grow my compassion and love.

Thank you for protecting Muriel today. I repent for ignoring her vehicle yesterday and I am so grateful for being reminded and alerted.

I pray that Andy can be deeply inspired by his new career and that he and Jordanne can put down roots and establish a beautiful family if that is your will.

Tonight is my first online zoom meeting with Linda and Sacred First Nations. I pray for your guidance regarding my involvement in that providence.

Also, tomorrow is our next online Holy Community meeting. Please provide me with good guidance and inspiration to share in that meeting.

I pray that today can be joyful, serene, deeply rooted in your shimjeong, heart, and love, and most exciting in its developments and achievements. Please share with me now and please open wide my heart, spirit, and mind to perceive and grasp the depth of your message. I love you so very much.
Eternally,
Laurence

Good Morning my Dearest Son and Partner, Laurence
I am so proud of you. Please think about how much you've grown since you began your journaling last July. Your growth is very important. Please make sustained efforts in your morning devotions and throughout the day. Please approach each situation as a blessed new opportunity to contribute and to grow, and please invest your very best as you intentionally channel my shimjeong heart and love.
Please act in each situation mindfully, convicted that I am with you and longing to pour out so powerfully through you, even in your compassion as you listen, which is an extremely significant act of love. Please see each person as my precious son or daughter, and love them deeply with your heart and lift them up to me with your prayers as you are with them.
In this way, please help each person you encounter to experience what you have been privileged to experience, namely that each is my most precious son or daughter whom I love infinitely and whom I will never abandon. What could be more precious or holy.
As you invest in that way, know, without a shadow of a doubt, that I am working so powerfully in your life to bring to fruition all your dreams and endeavors. I am your original and greatest partner. I will never fail you.
I love you eternally,
Heavenly Parent

2/7/23 *Your Prayers, Your Vision, Your Heart, And Your Vitality Elements Are Incredibly Powerful Forces. You Are Participating With Me In The Process Of Resurrection.*

Good Morning Dearest Heavenly Parent,

I am so grateful for how you are working so powerfully to raise up my heart, and to help me become a True Son of yours. I desperately want to grow faster and faster and liberate you and True Parents and help build your kingdom. Please accept my offering and guide me rapidly to become that son through whom your vision can manifest.

I want to put into practice your guidance each day and I gratefully invite you to continually guide and remind me throughout the day how I can do better, and how I can resonate more deeply and powerfully with your shimjeong. Thank you so very much!

Tonight is our Online Holy Community. I hope that some of those whom I sent the update to can choose to join in, and our community can grow and become more vibrant.

Tonight is our meeting online. Shall I share yesterday's message which touched me deeply, or is there something else or additional that you would like me to share?

I pray a special prayer now for John. He received 2 very substantial messages from me, both witnessing very substantially to True Parents. Please speak deeply to his heart so that he can receive and embrace these two messages. Please allow his heart to deeply rejoice and be filled with gratitude for True Parents. Please fill his soul with a deep and powerful conviction and determination, after 21 years in his walk of faith, to offer his life to True Parents, as an advocate from within the 7th Day Adventist Movement. Please inspire him to help lead our ministerial trinity and to become a powerfully motivated participant in ACLC. Please inspire his couple to quickly fulfill their 40 day and 3 day conditions and receive the holy wine to become full Blessed Members who actively study the Divine Principle. Please help him to continually deepen his trust in me and in our ACLC leaders and in True Parents. Please guide him to those activities which will most powerfully and quickly help Dr. Yong launch the 3rd Great Awakening. Please empower him to convict the hearts and minds of the leaders of his denomination to follow in the footsteps of Prophet Radebe and freely offer their foundations to True Mother. Then please help him to go beyond that level to touch the hearts and minds of the leaders of many, many Christian denominations around the world to similarly follow that example.

Heavenly Parent, I am so profoundly grateful.

Please share with me now and open wide my heart and mind to perceive and embrace your message.

Eternally yours,
Laurence

Good Morning Dearest Laurence,
Wow, your message today is so powerful and inspiring. Your vision is the foundation for me to work. Yes, this is in the category of the most exciting development and achievement. How fabulous!
I am on the case. Please don't stop praying for John's couple.
Please do share yesterday's message with your Online Holy Community. If each of you become a clear and powerful channel of heart, based on your shared vision of liberating all of hell before True Mother's ascension, then I can work powerfully based on that vision and heart. Please lift up all those imprisoned souls with your heart of hope and compassion and pass them to me. Your prayers, your vision, your heart, and your vitality elements are incredibly powerful forces. You are participating with me in the process of resurrection. Yes, I resurrected Jesus 2000 years ago, after his death. But now, with your help, centering on True Parents and Jesus, we will surely resurrect the many billions of trapped souls in hell. This is the stuff of miracles and I am eternally grateful. Eternally yours,
Heavenly Parent

2/8/23 In Theory, I Could Close My Heart Some To Dull The Pain, But I Could Never For One Moment Let My Children Carry A Burden That I Am Not Personally Prepared To Carry. In My Inability To Alleviate Their Suffering, The Only Way I Can Express My Love Is To Experience Their Pain Even More Than They Do, And Then, Through That Shared Bond Of Heart, Extend Whatever Comfort I Can To Them To Please Hold On Longer, And To Please Know That I Am Working Without Pause To Save Each And Every One.

Good Morning Dearest Heavenly Parent,
Thank you so deeply for this precious new day. I want to be your holy representative in every interaction this day and every day going forward. I was inspired by our online Holy Community meeting last night, and by Tony's intention to join next Tuesday. I was grateful for the insights offered by Alain, Andrew, and by Gerry yesterday to my question seeking to better understand the framework of your intervention with fallen mankind. I haven't read so much yet of the materials that Gerry sent, but the little I did read really touched my heart. I'm so deeply sorry for your profound suffering. I don't want to be separated from your heart, not even a nanometer, which I understand to mean that I need to deeply experience your pain. I am not afraid to do that and if it will bring you release and comfort, I will rush to that place to the very best of my ability and pray that you guide me the rest of the way beyond where I can reach on my own. Perhaps it is my immaturity and lack of heart, for which I sincerely repent,

but I established my motto focusing on bringing you joy, rather than commiserating with you. Is that wrong? Please tell me honestly and straightforwardly, not trying to shield me from your pain. I hope that by giving my utmost and even pioneering to solve your problems, that I might help dissolve your han and free your heart. Is that naïve?

Is your pain so unimaginably deep and overwhelming that any attempt to help you without first vividly experiencing that pain myself is just scratching the surface? If so, please, please, let me fully experience your heart in a bond of pain that can never be broken for all of eternity.

I was deeply encouraged by the responses yesterday from John and Justin. Thank you for working so powerfully to move both of their hearts. I pray for the total success of our ministerial trinity to exceed even your greatest hopes. Please claim my offerings and work so powerfully through them now.

Also, I pray for the pastor I reached out to yesterday regarding total salvation. Perhaps he might resonate with the focus of our online Holy Community. Reading Ellen White's book and then looking at the statements of faith of virtually every prison ministry, I am deeply shocked at how totally Satan has corrupted Christianity's view of your heart. There is almost no one who considers the possibility that anyone can be saved after death. I'm so sorry that such a grotesque heart has been falsely attributed to you. Please guide me on how to break through the character assassination and wake up Christianity to your infinite love and compassion and mobilize millions to join in our work to liberate hell.

I love you so very much. I believe in you absolutely. I offer everything I have to you and True Parents.

Please open my mind and spirit and heart now. Please speak deeply to me now. Let today's journal be one that can inspire mankind for thousands and thousands of years.

Eternally yours,
Laurence

Good Morning Dearest Laurence,
I am deeply touched.
I don't want to hurt any of my children, and most especially those who are making the greatest effort to liberate me. My pain is horrible and frequently verging on unbearable. It requires extreme focus and draining effort to set it aside and put one foot in front of the other. Satan who has ruled this cosmos by enslaving my children has been exerting his very utmost efforts to destroy me once and for all. I am a very easy target. If you harm even one of my children, I experience that pain and suffering many times more in my own heart. In theory, I could close my heart some to dull the pain, but I could never for one moment let my children carry a burden that I am not personally prepared to carry. In my inability to alleviate their suffering, the only

way I can express my love is to experience their pain even more than they do, and then, through that shared bond of heart, extend whatever comfort I can to them to please hold on longer, and to please know that I am working without pause to save each and every one.
I am so grateful for your love and help. Your heart is so good. I don't need you to share my suffering, I don't want to drain your energy away from your work which thrills me with hope. I fully and gratefully embrace and bless your motto, and will work with you to my utmost based on that framework. That will be the shortest path to my liberation in relationship to you. I will find opportunities to share my pain with you – so that you can understand and share my deepest heart, but without crushing your beautiful, hopeful, creative heart which I love so deeply.
Thank you!
Eternally,
Heavenly Parent

2/9/23 *Evoke My Heart And Shimjeong Into Everything You Do. If It Does Not Include My Heart Or Shimjeong, Then It Is Irrelevant Or Worse. As You Evoke My Heart And Shimjeong In Each Interaction, Please Exercise Your Vision To See Those Relationships Continually Becoming More Beautiful And More Holy.*

Good Morning Dearest Heavenly Parent,
I am so happy to pause my prayers this morning and share this holy moment with you.
Thank you for Morning Devotion. Dr. Yong has made it so very clear how we can inherit your incredible heart of self-denial by living totally for our 3 object partners within the family, centering on your heart and love, and then expanding beyond our family with that same heart towards our tribe members, nation, world, and cosmos – ultimately offering everything to you. I am so grateful. I deeply love your dream. I pledge everything I am and have to help you fulfill that dream.
I am so humbled and honored to be your son and partner. I pledge never to take that for granted.
Through the testimonies of our 2nd and 3rd Gens, I can see how you are putting down holy roots so substantially. Surely your victory is inevitable. But I desperately want to accelerate the process, especially with True Mother still on the Earth. You have invested so much in raising me up for this moment. I'm so sorry that I failed at fulfilling tribal messiahship in 7 or 21 years, and instead required 40 years to achieve Cheon Bo. But having said that, I am so eternally grateful for your patience, mentorship, repeated forgiveness, and

uncountable innumerable blessings along the way. I can never repay all that you have given to me. You are amazing.
So today it is 7:45 am. I will shoot for staying up until 9:30 pm, until after Tai Chi. Please help me to make each moment count, and to bring your heart, your love, and your blessings to each moment.
Please help me to start by opening my heart to your message and love and spirit and energy this morning to guide and power me through the entire day.
Eternally yours,
Laurence

Good Morning Dearest Laurence,
Thank you for your beautiful and touching greeting this morning. Yes, I have invested much into raising you up, on the foundation of the good and significant offerings of your ancestors, and the indemnity paid by those before you.
You have always had an expansive vision and perspective and great confidence and faith to go forward in new arenas, and that willingness and faith set the conditions which allowed me to work with you in a special way during your life. I so deeply appreciate you.
I have plenty of energy to sustain you throughout each day. If you feel drained, know of a certainty that it is because you are losing resonance. The energy is always there. Reflect upon your motto. Do your energy exercises. Get up and move. You will be recharged. Also, evoke my heart and shimjeong into everything you do. If it does not include my heart or shimjeong, then it is irrelevant or worse.
As you evoke my heart and shimjeong in each interaction, please exercise your vision to see those relationships continually becoming more beautiful and more holy.
We are creating a new crystal of the cosmos centered on True Love, and that crystalline structure is expanding from True Parents and onto true families and from there outward. As it expands, my beautiful garden, filled with life and love is blossoming. It is breathtaking and so holy.
Eternally and gratefully,
Heavenly Parent

2/10/23 *If I Am With You, Then Who Can Stand Against Us. It Is Our Unity Of Heart That Allows Me To Stand With You. And Your Unity With Muriel. And Your Couple's Unity With Your Children And Grandchildren. Those Are The Levers Of Cosmic Power Centered On True Love.*

Good Morning Dearest Most Beloved Heavenly Parent,
Thank you for your love and blessings and guidance. I'm so deeply grateful and I desperately want to fulfill for you and liberate you and all of your children and angels. I'm so grateful that you pulled me out of the Satanic world and guided me directly to True Parents through Durst Omma, and then carefully raised me up over so many years until my heart could begin to emerge from death. I'm so sorry it has taken me so long, and that I have tripped up so many times and in so many ways in this process. You are a loving parent of such profound gamdong, please forgive me for all my years of immaturity and fallen nature. I know that I still carry much fallen nature, and that I still have such a long way to grow to reach the standard of True Parents' heart. Please bear with me. I will do my very best to grow quickly as I invest my very utmost to liberate you.
I value our partnership and your love far more than my life. I am so grateful for the vehicles you have allowed me through which to actively work to liberate you. I am so blessed. Someday, thousands of years from now, I look forward to sitting down with you and reflecting on these days and sharing our war stories, and laughing through our tears, and hugging each other like a True Father and True Son.
I love you eternally. Please open my heart and spirit wide now and let me receive you fully.
Eternally yours,
Laurence

Good Morning Dearest Laurence,
Thank you. You just deeply touched my heart. We will certainly have that opportunity to reflect and remember, to laugh and cry together and so much more. I will surely bless you and Muriel by blessing your children and descendants. Please have 100% faith and confidence in the things you do for my sake. Please never forget for a moment that we are partners. If I am with you, then who can stand against us. It is our unity of heart that allows me to stand with you. And your unity with Muriel. And your couple's unity with your children and grandchildren. Those are the levers of cosmic power centered on true love.
Satan's power is defenseless against true love. It will come crashing down and evaporate. Our unity and yours with your family are eternal. They will blossom into a most breathtakingly beautiful tree of life. That is your hope fulfilled. It is mine as well.
Go forward today and be of unshakable faith and love. We shall create Heavenly miracles.
Eternally yours,
Heavenly Parent

2/11/23 *You Are Correct In Your Comments In Morning Devotion, My Liberation Comes As My Children Become Able To Radiate Me In Each Moment And Manifest Their Own Visions. On That Foundation I Can Powerfully Participate And Together We Can Build The Ideal.*

Good Morning Dearest Heavenly Parent,
I am so profoundly grateful.
Thank you for yesterday's call with Mark, and for the evening with the Justin and Larry's family and friends. Please claim and bless them and their entire community.
Thank you for today's Morning Devotion, the chance to share deeply with Zagery and with Rev. Davati, and with Dominic.
I'm looking forward to today's WFWP event, and the opportunity to honor both Angelika and Kaeleigh, and also to greet Dr. Yong.
Please continue to guide our couple and family. I am so grateful.
Also today is the blessing anniversaries of Jay's and Andy's couples. Thank you for your grace and incredible blessing on each of them and their couples and families.
I pray that I can open my heart, mind, and spirit now very wide, and receive you so very deeply, and with very powerful resonance.
Eternally,
Laurence

Good Morning Dearest Laurence,
Thank you for growing to where you are able to constantly radiate my love and presence as you go through your day. You are correct in your comments in Morning Devotion, my liberation comes as my children become able to radiate me in each moment and manifest their own visions. On that foundation I can powerfully participate and together we can build the ideal. Because of True Parents, the numbers of such couples is rapidly growing and my empowerment and liberation is rapidly accelerating. This is profoundly exhilarating. I am so grateful and look forward to more and even greater manifestation and collaboration with you.
Eternally yours,
Heavenly Parent

2/12/23 *You Are Bringing A Very Disruptive And Transformational Vision. It Is Holy And Historic For The Providence. Please Don't Stop.*

Good Morning Dearest Heavenly Parent,
I love you with all my heart. I'm so sorry for your pain and anguish. Please help me to liberate you in the shortest possible time. Thank you for all the

blessings of yesterday, seeing Dr. Yong and having such a providential discussion with Tomiko, and hearing such beautiful testimonies in the transition even for Women's Federation.

Thank you for the opportunity to share with Kaeleigh to support and reaffirm her inspiration about Daughters of God.

Today was a very touching word from Dr. Yong – and I was especially struck by Father's lament that our church is not a place people from other denominations feel attracted to. I pray that you can work so powerfully through our nascent ministerial trinity to help ignite the spark which can support Dr. Yong to create the 3rd and final Great Awakening.

Today we will be attending the funeral/ Seong Hwa of Kitty. Please embrace her to your bosom, and let her joyfully reunite with Tom.

Please watch over and guide her family. I repent for any separation of heart that I felt with Kitty and I repent for any heartistic pain that Andy matching may have brought to her family. I also pray for Don's family today and for Rejuny who's heart must surely be breaking for Jaimie. Please watch over and embrace Jaimie to your bosom.

Heavenly Parent, I pray now that you can open my heart, mind, and spirit wide to be able to resonate powerfully with yours. Please help me to receive your heart, spirit, and word now, so clearly and powerfully.

I am so grateful,
Eternally yours,
Laurence

Dearest Laurence,
Thank you for your holy efforts and jeongseong to comfort and save me. You are my precious son and you are such a profound inspiration to me. I take every request from you so very seriously. I am working very hard to bring them all to fruition. As you well know your heart and mind are refreshingly expansive and the things you are requesting and envisioning are not ones that can happen with a simple wave of the hand. But they are important, critically important. You have zeroed in on such significant key priorities with practical and visionary solutions. I truly am deeply inspired. Don't be discouraged if even no one else understands what you are doing. That doesn't matter, and in some cases, it is actually better that they don't. You are bringing a very disruptive and transformational vision. It is holy and historic for the providence. Please don't stop. Please focus even more. We will break through. I am glued to your side. Resonate. It will yield Most Exciting Development and Achievement.
Eternally yours,
Heavenly Parent

2/13/23 *Two Rivers, One From Heaven To Earth And One From Earth To Heaven, Intersecting In Me. I Am Being Washed Clean. I Am So Grateful.*

Good Morning Dearest Heavenly Parent,
I was so inspired by the text from Justin this morning describing the dream you gave him. Thank you. Please deeply move his and Annie's hearts and help them to fully accept True Parents and fully commit themselves to uniting with me through our trinity.
Please open both their hearts to my email.
I am so grateful that Andy is starting his job today and that Joelle's paper was published today. Thank you. And please thank and bless Dr. George for his loving help and guidance.
Dearest Heavenly Parent, tonight I will skip yoga again and instead attend the Seong Hwa of Rev. Sakai. I deeply respect his lifelong search for Jesus's heart and I deeply hope I can inherit from him. If it's your will, I hope Muriel can join me.
I am so deeply grateful. I look forward, after all these events yesterday and today, to receive your precious word now. In addition to the points that I raised, I sincerely hope you might bless our Online Holy Community with another precious message either today and/or tomorrow. Please open my mind and spirit wide now to fully resonate with you.
Eternally yours,
Laurence

Good Morning Dearest Laurence,
I am so happy to greet you again today. Thank you for joyfully charging forward to liberate me with such faith. Your heart and faith are extremely powerful, and I am so grateful.
I liked your email to Justin and I will work with him and Annie based on your email. Thank you. I trust that you saw, based on Dr. Yong's 13 points today, just how much you are pioneering in points 9-13. You are a great blessing to True Parents and me. Please continue with your full heart, the invaluable work of your Online Holy Community. Tomorrow night marks your 21st meeting. That is a major milestone. Please continue reaching out. I will send prepared people to help you grow. Just as the river of my love is the salvation to fallen mankind on Earth, you and your Online Holy Community are establishing a river of love to fallen mankind in the spiritual world. And as it flows through me, I too am being deeply healed by your humble offering. Two rivers, one from Heaven to Earth and one from Earth to Heaven, intersecting in me. I am being washed clean. I am so grateful.
Eternally,
Heavenly Parent

2/14/23 *Such A Longing Heart Transcends Time And Space. I Could Be With Each Of My Precious Children No Matter Where They Were Or What They Were Doing. I Could Remember And Experience What Each One Was Like As A Tiny Baby, And I Poured My Love And Tears Into Each One In That Pure Newborn Form. In This Way, I Stimulated And Nourished Each Of Their Consciences. Yes, It Has Been An Exceedingly Long Wait. But I Have Never Lost Hope.*

Good Morning My Dearest Heavenly Parent,
I apologize for being a little unfocused this morning. I think I was affected by my Claritin. In the future I'll try to stick with ½ dose if possible. I am so grateful to you. When I think about my motto, it helps me to reconnect and realign with your heart. I want to be here for you with 100% of my heart and jeongseong and focus, so that no opportunity is wasted or missed, and beyond that, I can initiate great opportunities for you.
I am waiting for a number of responses, Heavenly Parent. I realize it is a tiny speck of your situation. You need to have virtually infinite hope as you wait for your children to respond. I'm so sorry for you. Even a few delayed responses seem to drag me down. I will do my very best not to let them. I was deeply touched by last night's Seong Hwa for Rev. Sakai. I felt a deep kindship towards him even though we never met. I was so happy to speak with his son Michi. I can honestly say that he understood and resonated with our Online Holy Community vision more than anyone whom I have spoken to previously. I credit that to all the devotions and efforts of his Father, Rev. Sakai. I sincerely hope that Rev. Sakai might find inspiration in continuing his work through our Online Holy Community, and that he might work powerfully with Michi to dramatically expand our efforts here in America and in Japan.
If you agree, I hope you will graciously share that with Rev. Sakai, and support Michi in that effort as well.
I am hoping for very positive feedback from both John and from Justin's couple. I totally believe you are working powerfully with both of them, as is Jesus and Deganawida. I am deeply grateful, and repent my impatient heart. I totally defer to your timing.
After this journaling I will send out reminders for tonight's zoom. I hope you can speak through those reminders to inspire more "invitees" to join the call. I am very inspired by the image of two rivers. If there is some additional content you would like me to share tonight, I pray that you will please open my mind now, open my heart, open my spirit, and help me to fully and accurately and deeply receive your guidance and word. I love you so very deeply, and I long to grow to become a better and more true and more loving partner to you every day.
Eternally yours,
Laurence

Dearest Laurence,
Thank you for not being phased by distractions. When you focus your heart on me, nothing has the power to pull you off center.
Yes, our motto is wonderful, and I love it completely. Thank you for having such a beautiful and creative and caring heart.
It is true that I have had to have unimaginable patience for my children. Honestly, I could never have achieved this solely on the basis of will power. There is not enough will power in all the cosmos to accomplish that on its own. It is because of my vision for my children, because I never stopped seeing them as I originally envisioned them, I never let go of my dream – then based on give and take with that vision and dream, I could feel incredible shimjeong and heart and longing for every one of my children. Such a longing heart transcends time and space. I could be with each of my precious children no matter where they were or what they were doing. I could remember and experience what each one was like as a tiny baby, and I poured my love and tears into each one in that pure newborn form. In this way, I stimulated and nourished each of their consciences.
Yes, it has been an exceedingly long wait. But I have never lost hope. Jesus gave me so much hope. True Parents profoundly renewed my hope. But also, what your project and community members are doing, is a source of such inspiring and renewing hope. I can feel the dawn coming up in hell, of all places. My children, rather than blaming me, accusing me, cursing me, are opening their eyes and hearts and are thanking me. This is truly a miracle of miracles. I feel in some ways that it is my own heart that is being woken up.
I am so deeply grateful.
Eternally yours,
Heavenly Parent.

- End of Volume 1 -

GLOSSARY

1% and 99%	Dr. Hak Ja Han Moon has explained that the father provides the seed (1%) and the mother (99%) for the child
100 Day Workshops	Educational workshops are now established in the Spirit World, so that when evil spirits are now liberated, they can become Absolute Good Spirits through 100 days of workshops
1st 2nd and 3rd Gens	1st Gens refer to those individuals who are witnessed to and receive the Change of Blood Lineage Blessing to become part of God's lineage. 2nd and 3rd Gens refer to their children and grandchildren born without original sin
2 Pet 3:12-13	This passage refers to the end of the Satanic sovereignty, and the establishment of God's Kingdom.
Three-Object purpose	God's ideal of the family, has 4 positions. God in the center, the father, the wife, and the children. When each position can freely assume the subject position in relation to the other three, it fulfills the 3-object purpose
Absolute Good Spirits (AGS)	Those liberated spirits who have completely aligned with God and True Parents
ACLC	American Clergy Leadership Conference
Aju	Korean affirmation. Similar to Amen. However, it expresses a dimension of personal responsibility
Angel Projects	Highly structured cooperation among angels to impact human culture, similar to the angelic intervention described in the Book of Ezekiel
Bering Strait Tunnel and Railroad	A component of the International Peace Highway proposed by Rev. Sun Myung Moon - this would be a railroad connecting Asia with North America via the Bering Strait.

Break Out Room	When a zoom conference subdivides into smaller discussion groups
Cain and Abel	In order to save all mankind, God uses the strategy of dividing groups into two components, Cain and Abel. Abel which is closer in heart to God, is called to sacrifice for Cain and to win Cain's heart through love as modeled by Jacob and Esau.
Camp Shehaqua	Summer camp organized by Family Federation members in Pennsylvania
Cheon Il Guk (CIG)	Literally translated "Two Becoming One" - it refers to the establishment of God's Kingdom on Earth, beginning with one nation, Korea, uniting to form God's fatherland.
Cheon Shim Wons	The Cheon Shim Wons are a network of special prayer rooms which began at the CheongPyeong complex in Korea, and have multiplied internationally. They are spiritually protected, and allow for very clear and deep communion with God and with Rev. Moon in the Spiritual World.
Cheon Won Gung	Cheon Won Gung is the final temple, where God can establish a permanent settlement on Earth. It will be opened in 2025 at the CheongPyeong complex.
CheongPyeong	A development on CheongPyeong Lake, northeast of Seoul, South Korea, where Rev. and Mrs. Moon have developed the capital for God's Kingdom of Cheon Il Guk.
Deganawida	A Native American Saint and Prophet known as "The Great Peacemaker", who together with Jigonhsasee founded the Iroquois (Haudenosaunee) Confederacy and significantly contributed to God's providence in America centering on Jesus
Divine Principle	The explanation of God's ideal, work, and history including the Creation, the Fall, Restoration, Last Days, and the Marriage of the Lamb, written by Rev. Sun Myung Moon based on revelation from Jesus

Family Federation for World Peace	The global organization launched by Rev. and Mrs. Moon to embrace and coordinate families and organizations seeking to work with them to build God's Kingdom
Four-Position Foundation	The fundamental structure by which God creates all things. God, in the first position, projects Himself into complementary pairs of a subject and an object who enter into give and take creating a union (or child), which then becomes a new object to God.
Gamdong	A Korean expression for an act of love which deeply touches the other's heart
GiveNet	An agricultural and technology development project focusing on Africa and India
GPA	Global Peace Academy - a Family Federation missionary training program for young adults, mostly in the gap between high school and college
Han	A deep pain and anguish of the heart typically resulting from the suffering of one's children, family and love ones
Heartistic	Coming from or related to a heart of love
Holy Spirit	God's feminine essence, unembodied until the Marriage of the Lamb
Hoon Dok Hae	A practice of regular reading, study, and discussion of God's word
Hyojeong	An expression of profound filial piety and love towards God and our Parents
Hyojeong Culture and Arts	Refers to the development of creative expressions of a culture centered on Gods ideal of true families in harmony with nature.
Interview with Dietmar	This is a nearly four-hour YouTube interview on Jesus's Birth, Life, and 2nd Coming including 12 of my music videos that I recorded in January 2024
Jeongseong	Refers to a deep investment and devotion of heart into your efforts connecting them to God
Jigonhsasee	The first Clan Mother of the Matriarchal Iroquois (Haudenosaunee) Confederacy. Known as "The Mother of Nations" she is credited as cofounding that confederacy together with Deganawida.

Jjaksaram	A Korean term for one sided love, which, although not returned, can build up a longing for a relationship in the other.
John the Baptist (term)	This is a term used in Unification theology to refer to any individual called to lead a particular group of people to the True Parents. Originally, John, the son of Zachariah, was given the mission of Elijah to prepare Israel for the coming of Jesus
Kabbalah	Revelatory Jewish mystical teaching which traces its roots back to Moses
Mandeans	A worldwide religious group who recognize John the Baptist as their founder.
Morning Devotion	A daily zoom prayer meeting within the Family Federation
My Motto	Through my journaling Heavenly Parent asked me to select a motto as a focal point with which to resonate with Him/Her. I selected: Greatest Joy; Deepest Serenity; Most Holy Shimjeong, Heart, and Love; Most Exciting Development and Achievement
Online Holy Community	Many Family Federation members were inspired to start weekly zoom calls for worship of one sort or another. I started a weekly meeting to read scripture and offer our vitality elements on a sustainable basis to God, for the purpose of liberating those trapped in hell.
Physical World	This refers to everything in the cosmos that exists in this plane, made of particles and atoms, comprising all the galaxies of the universe. This is the realm in which our physical bodies exist.
Returning Resurrection	A term from the Divine Principle which refers to the process by which those in the spirit world help those on the physical level to grow spiritually, and in the process the spirits also receive the same benefit

Satan's Third Temptation	Satan said to Jesus: "All these I will give you if you will fall down and worship me". Jesus rebuked Satan, but fallen mankind has largely succumbed to lust for material, power, and unprincipled physical stimulations and addictions.
SeungHwa	A Family Federation ceremony celebrating the victorious ascension of someone who has died physically.
Shimjeong	The unrestrained impulse to receive joy through offering God centered love
Spiritual son or daughter	If you witness to someone and bring them to be reborn through Christ, they would be considered your spiritual son or daughter.
Spiritual World	This refers to the eternal and infinite realm in which our spirits exist, both during our physical life, and eternally after our physical death. This is also the realm in which angels exist.
STF	This refers to Special Task Force, another Family Federation gap year training program
The Will	This refers to an alignment with God's ideal. While everyone has free will, when we are connected in heart with God, we will naturally align our actions to harmonize with God's intention.
Tribal Messiah	On the foundation of the victory of the Washington Monument rally in 1976, Rev. and Mrs. Moon were able to establish conditions whereby Blessed Couples could inherit their Messianic foundation and similarly represent Heavenly Parent to our families, tribes, and nations. Such couples are known as Tribal Messiahs and are to play an important role in the establishment of God's Kingdom on Earth.

True Parents	True Parents refers to Rev. and Mrs. Moon, who came with the Messianic mission to give rebirth to mankind, and adapt all fallen people back into God's lineage through the Marriage Blessing ceremony. God ultimately intends for all couples to inherit that foundation and stand as true parents to their own families.
Unification Church	The Unification Church is the name by which Rev. and Mrs. Moon's religious organization has come to be known. Originally it was registered as "The Holy Spirit Association for the Unification of World Christianity", and they never intended to create a new denomination or religion.
Vitality Elements	Vitality Elements is a term used in the Divine Principle for the nourishment which the body provides to the spirit when we do good deeds. Originally, God intended for everyone to reach spiritual maturity and perfection in our lifetime, as we live a life of loving service generating ample vitality elements for our spirit. Vitality Elements are only generated by the bodies of those alive on the Earth.
Wish Paper	Those who pray at the Cheon Shim Wons now have the grace and opportunity to write their prayers on a special "wish paper" and offer it to Heaven together with a donation.

Laurence and Muriel celebrate the 40th Anniversary of their Blessing at Madison Square Gardens, July 1, 2022

Contact: LHBaer@comcast.net

Made in the USA
Middletown, DE
29 July 2024